W9-APL-967

اللـؤلـؤ المنـثور

Gems
&
Jewels

© **Maktaba Dar-us-Salam, 2003**

King Fahd National Library Cataloging-in-Publication Data
Mujahid, Abdul Malik
Gems and Jewels: true events, stories and sayings from history of Islam. / Abdul Malik Mujahid. - Riyadh, 2003
341 p.; 14x21 cm
ISBN: 9960-897-59-1
1 - Islam - History I - Title
210 dc 1424/5531

Legal Deposit no. 1424/5531
ISBN: 9960-897-59-1

Gems & Jewels

Wise Sayings, Interesting Events and
Moral Lessons from the Islamic History

(1)

Compiled by:

Abdul-Malik Mujahid

DARUSSALAM

GLOBAL LEADER IN ISLAMIC BOOKS

Riyadh, Jeddah, Sharjah, Lahore
London, Houston, New York

ALL RIGHTS RESERVED © جميع حقوق الطبع محفوظة

No part of this book may be reproduced or utilized in any form or by any means, electronic or mechanical, including photocopying and recording or by information storage and retrieval system, without the permission of the publisher.

First Edition: October 2003

Head Office:

P.O. Box: 22743, Riyadh 11416, K.S.A. Tel: 00966-01-4033962/4043432 Fax: 4021659
E-mail: darussalam@awalnet.net.sa Website: http// www.dar-us-salam.com

K.S.A. Darussalam Showrooms:
Riyadh
Olaya branch: Tel 00966-1-4614483 Fax: 4644945
Malaz branch: Tel 4735220 Fax: 4735221

- **Jeddah**
  Tel: 00966-2-6879254 Fax: 6336270
- **Al-Khobar**
  Tel: 00966-3-8692900 Fax: 00966-3-8691551

U.A.E
- Darussalam, Sharjah U.A.E
  Tel: 00971-6-5632623 Fax: 5632624

PAKISTAN
- Darussalam, 36 B Lower Mall, Lahore
  Tel: 0092-42-724 0024 Fax: 7354072
- Rahman Market, Ghazni Street
  Urdu Bazar Lahore
  Tel: 0092-42-7120054 Fax: 7320703

U.S.A
- Darussalam, Houston
  P.O Box: 79194 Tx 772779
  Tel: 001-713-722 0419 Fax: 001-713-722 0431
  E-mail: sales@dar-us-salam.com
- Darussalam, New York
  572 Atlantic Ave, Brooklyn
  New York-11217, Tel: 001-718-625 5925

U.K
- Darussalam International Publications Ltd.
  226 High Street, Walthamstow,
  London E17 7JH, Tel: 0044-208 520 2666
  Mobile: 0044-794 730 6706 Fax: 0044-208 521 7645
- Darussalam International Publications Limited
  Regent Park Mosque, 146 Park Road,
  London NW8 7RG Tel: 0044-207 724 3363
- Darussalam
  398-400 Coventry Road, Small Heath
  Birmingham, B10 0UF
  Tel: 0121 77204792 Fax: 0121 772 4345
  E-mail: info@darussalamuk.com
  Web: www.darussalamuk.com

FRANCE
- Editions & Librairie Essalam
  135, Bd de Ménilmontant- 75011 Paris
  Tél: 0033-01- 43 38 19 56/ 44 83
  Fax: 0033-01- 43 57 44 31
  E-mail: essalam@essalam.com

AUSTRALIA
- ICIS: Ground Floor 165-171, Haldon St.
  Lakemba NSW 2195, Australia
  Tel: 00612 9758 4040 Fax: 9758 4030

MALAYSIA
- E&D Books SDN. BHD.-321 B 3rd Floor,
  Suria Klcc
  Kuala Lumpur City Center 50088
  Tel: 00603-21663433 Fax: 459 72032

SINGAPORE
- Muslim Converts Association of Singapore
  32 Onan Road The Galaxy Singapore- 424484
  Tel: 0065-440 6924, 348 8344 Fax: 440 6724

SRI LANKA
- Darul Kitab 6, Nimal Road, Colombo-4
  Tel: 0094-1-589 038 Fax: 0094-74 722433

KUWAIT
- Islam Presentation Committee
  Enlightenment Book Shop
  P.O. Box: 1613, Safat 13017, Kuwait
  Tel: 00965-244 7526, Fax: 240 0057

INDIA
- Islamic Dimensions
  56/58 Tandel Street (North)
  Dongri, Mumbai 4000 009, India
  Tel: 0091-22-3736875, Fax: 3730689
  E-mail:sales@IRF.net

SOUTH AFRICA
- Islamic Da`wah Movement (IDM)
  48009 Qualbert 4078 Durban,South Africa
  Tel: 0027-31-304-6883
  Fax: 0027-31-305-1292
  E-mail: idm@ion.co.za

Contents

Publisher's Note

Darussalam is presenting *Gems & Jewels* for the readers. This book is based on excerpts and passages collected from many books written by the scholars of Islam. The wise sayings, interesting events, logical deductions, intelligent approaches, admonitions, moral lessons and teachings etc., have been compiled to give the readers the opportunity of knowing what the great personalities of Islam have been doing in their life and how their character has been an example for us to follow.

We hope that the presentation of *Gems & Jewels* will be a continuing process, and we will be compiling and publishing one volume after the other providing the readers gems and jewels from our glorious history.

The writings in this series will be of equal interest to all Muslims whether they are children or adults, and similarly they will gain a lot of virtues, develop good character patterns, and adopt intellectual behavior in their lives. Because of the usefulness of the series, we are planning to produce it in other languages also so that a majority of the Muslims may be able to benefit from it.

We pray to Allâh for the success.

Abdul-Malik Mujahid
General Manager Darussalam

Publisher's Note

The Story Of Ibn Jud'an

When one thinks about pre-Islamic times in Makkah, certain names come to mind - such as 'Abdul-Muttalib, the Prophet's grandfather, or Waraqah bin Naufal. But there is another important person who is little remembered today: 'Abdullah bin Jud'an, the first cousin of Abu Bakr As-Siddeeq's father. In the early years of his life, 'Abdullah bin Jud'an was neither successful nor happy. In fact, growing up hungry and poor, he soon became embittered by life. For solace or perhaps out of spite, he turned to evil and committed many crimes. He was caught so often for his evil acts that he was considered by most to be an incorrigible criminal. People thought that he was evil incarnate and that there was no way that he could ever improve. Everyone hated him, including his fellow clansmen, his family, and even his own father; and he reciprocated that hatred with equal or greater vehemence.

One day, as he was walking in the valleys of Makkah, ruefully thinking about his bitter existence, he noticed a small opening in a mountain, perhaps an entrance to a cave. He thought that there might be something harmful inside, perhaps a venomous snake. That foreboding did not stop him from approaching; instead, it encouraged him to go to it, for his situation was so hopeless, that he actually wanted to be killed by some venomous lizard or snake, so that he could part from his miserable existence.

When he came near to the mouth of the cave, he saw a lean shape inside, and through the darkness, he perceived it to be a snake in an erect position, the position most favored by a venomous snake when it is ready to strike. Overcome by madness, 'Abdullah bin Jud'an was terrified, and suddenly realized that he did not really want to die. He imagined that the snake was coming at him, and so he jumped wildly, trying to fend off a lethal bite. After a short while, he calmed down, realizing that it was only him that was moving and that the snake was actually in a still position. And when he came nearer, he realized that it was only a statue of a snake, which was made of gold and had two eyes made of precious emeralds. He broke the emeralds off and took them. He then entered deeper into the cave, and from the writings he saw around him, he realized that the cave was a graveyard for the kings of the Jurhum tribe. At the head of each grave was a gravestone made of gold; on it was written a short history of the king who was buried underneath. Surrounding the graves were treasures of gold, silver, pearls, precious stones, and much else.

'Abdullah bin Jud'an picked up a few small treasures, made a sign outside the cave so that he could find it again, and then returned to his people. He was generous with his newfound wealth, giving to family, friends, and to the needy. He was especially generous in gathering people together and serving them food. As time went on, he gained status in society until he became one of the leaders of the Quraish. Whenever he ran out of funds, he would return to the cave and take some more. His generosity extended even beyond the boundaries of Makkah. Once when the people of Ash-Sham were suffering hard times, 'Abdullah bin Jud'an sent 2000 camels to them, loading each one with wheat, oils, and other provisions. And every night, someone stood on the roof of the Ka'bah and called out: "Come to the bowls (filled with food) of 'Abdullah bin Jud'an."

Yet in spite of all of that, the following is related about him in *Sahih Muslim*. 'Aisha ﵂ said to the Prophet ﷺ, "Indeed, Ibn Jud'an used to provide food (for the people) and he would be hospitable to his guest[s]. Will any of that benefit him on the Day of Resurrection?" The Prophet ﷺ answered, "No. Indeed, on no day did he ever say: O my lord, forgive me my sin on the Day of Recompense."

Sustenance

Among the signs of Faith is that one does not look to please others and incur Allâh's anger in that process. One avoids praising others for the sustenance that they have received from Allâh (the Exalted), and also refrains from blaming others for sustenance that he has not received from Allâh (the Exalted). Allâh's distribution of provision is not increased for a recipient by the amount of greed or ambition that he shows, nor is it blocked by his hate or envy. Allâh in His infinite justice grants provision and contentment for those with strength of Faith and satisfaction with what is divinely ordained. Likewise, misery and discontent are for those that live with doubt and anger. Let us be satisfied with His Will.

"They have brought My Evil Deeds only."

A Bedouin was accused of speaking too freely about the governor, and he was being led to him for judgment. The Bedouin knew that the followers of the governor were going to level at him many other accusations that he was not guilty of, so that they could be free of him and have him in prison. And so he prepared a letter, in which he attempted to appease the governor and drive away from himself those accusations that were leveled at him. When he entered the gathering of the governor, he read many plots that were written on the faces of those who were present, and so he took the letter from his pocket and gave it to the governor. He said, "Here take it and read my book," but the governor did not read the letter and instead merely said, "This is only said on the Day of Judgment, and not to us." The man quickly responded, "This day is worse than the Day of Judgment, for there both my good and evil deeds will be brought; as for your men, they have brought my evil deeds only, and have left off my good deeds." The governor was impressed by his words and freed him.

"And He died!"

Ash'ab was about to relate a story to a ruler, and he began: "There was a man..." But at that point he noticed a tray of food being brought to them. He paused as he was staring at the tasty food. The ruler said, "Yes...and then?" Ash'ab said, "And he died!"

He made the Ruler laugh...

Asma'i relates from his father that a prisoner was brought before 'Abdul-Malik and was accused of having rebelled against the ruler. 'Abdul-Malik said, "Strike his neck." The prisoner said, "O Leader of the Believers, this should not be the reward that I receive from you. By Allâh, I did not join the ranks of such and such person except because I cared about you and was looking out for your best interests. I am an unlucky man, and I have never fought side by side with a man, except that we were defeated. Throughout the years, I have been better for you than 1000 people on your side who cared about you. I was with such and such person and we were defeated, and then I was with such and such person and we were defeated..." He went on mentioning the people that were defeated by 'Abdul-Malik. 'Abdul-Malik laughed upon hearing this and freed the man.

Fiqh

A man looked at his wife as she was climbing stairs and he said, "You are divorced if you climb a single step, divorced if you descend a single step, and divorced if you stand still!" She threw herself down over the railing and remained his wife.

The Forbearance of 'Ali bin Husain ﷺ

'Abdur-Razzaq related that a slave girl who belonged to 'Ali bin Husain ﷺ was pouring water over him so that he could make ablution, but the jug fell from her hand, landed on his face, and fractured his bone. He raised his head to her and she recited a part of Verse:

"...who repress anger..." (Qur'ân 3:134)

He said, "I have indeed controlled my anger." She then recited:

"...who pardon men..." (Qur'ân 3:134)

He said, "May Allâh forgive you." She then recited the end of the Verse:

"...verily, Allâh loves Al-Muhsinun (the good doers)." (Qur'ân 3:134)

He said, "You are free for the Countenance of Allâh."

A Bedouin's Saying

A Bedouin once said that if authority is given to people who are not accepted, and weapons are given into the hands of those who do not use them, and wealth is in the hands of those who do not spend it – then, surely, the affairs of society will be at a loss.

A Dialogue between a Scholar and an Alcoholic

Alcoholic: Do you think I am doing wrong by eating a date?

Scholar: No.

Alcoholic: And if I ate with it some grass?

Scholar: There is nothing wrong with that.

Alcoholic: And if I were to wash them down with water?

Scholar: Drink and enjoy.

Alcoholic: Since all of that is permissible, then why do you forbid us from alcohol, which consists of the above-mentioned ingredients?

Scholar: If I poured water on top of you, would that hurt you?

Alcoholic: No it would not.

Scholar: And if I were to sprinkle some dirt in that, would you be hurt?

Alcoholic: That would not harm me.

Scholar: But if I were to mix water and dirt together and through a process make a large brick from those two elements, and then were I to throw that large brick at you, would you be hurt?

Alcoholic: That would kill me!

Scholar: The same goes for alcohol.

Love of Allâh

Ibn Qayyim ﷺ said that there are ten things that bring about the love of Allâh:

1) Recitation of the Qur'ân with reflection and with understanding of its meanings.
2) Seeking closeness to Allâh by performing voluntary deeds after having performed obligatory ones, for that leads one to the highest levels of love.
3) Remembering Allâh during every situation - with one's time, heart and deeds ... one's share of that love is to the degree of one's share in that remembrance.
4) Preferring what He loves to what you love when your desires are strong.
5) Allowing your heart to reflect on His Names and Attributes.
6) Reflecting on His many favors and blessings, both the apparent ones and hidden ones, for that leads to His love.
7) Having your heart softened as it is worshiping Allâh.
8) Being alone with Him in worship when He descends during the last third of the night. And this means to invoke Him, to recite His Speech, to stand with all sincerity and with good manners and with good submission, and then to end that with repentance and with seeking His forgiveness.
9) Sitting with those who are truthful in their love of Allâh.
10) Staying away from all that creates barriers between the heart and Allâh.

The Worshiper Who invokes against the Oppressor

Ziyad (Ibn Sumaiyyah) wrote to Mu'awiyah stating, "Indeed I have taken Iraq from my right hand yet my left hand remains empty." He said this implying a desire to have the Hijaz added to his governorship. News of this reached the god-fearing, pious Companion, 'Abdullah bin Umar bin Khattab ﷺ who knew of Ziyad's tyranny and oppression. He raised his hands towards the sky and supplicated: "O Allâh, keep us safe from the harm of Ziyad's left hand." A cancerous ulcer began to grow on Ziyad's left hand that ultimately caused his death.

Who should be followed?

A judge from Khurasan wanted to marry off his son, so he sought counsel with a man who was a follower of the Majus religion. The man said, "People come to you seeking judgment, and here you are coming to seek counsel from me!" The judge said, "You must advise me." He said, "Our leader, Khosrau (Kisra), would choose wealth (when seeking a wife); the leader of the Christians, Caesar (Qaiser), would choose beauty; and the pre-Islamic Arabs would choose based on ancestry and status; and your Prophet would choose based on religion – so choose which among them you will follow."

Humility before Three

Al-Kisai was the tutor of Ameen and Mamun, the two sons of Harun Rasheed (the ruler of the time). One day, the tutor got up to leave and both boys ran to their esteemed teacher in order to hand him his shoes. After much argumentation, they both agreed that each would give one shoe so both could share in the display of reverence. Upon hearing this act, Harun Rasheed went to Kisai and asked, "Who is the most honorable of people?" The teacher replied, "I do not know anyone more honorable than the Leader of the Believers." Harun Rasheed quickly replied, "No, most honorable among people is he for whom two fight to present him with his shoes, and to please both he instructs them to each give him one."

Kisai became somewhat anxious and began to justify what he had done. Harun explained, "If you had prevented them from giving you your shoes, indeed I would have unquestionably blamed you. Certainly, their deed did not compromise their honor; rather their status, inner merit and worth have increased. One can never be dishonored if he displays humility before these three: a leader, a teacher and parents."

The Prodigious Understanding of 'Ali

A woman gave birth to a child only six months after she got married; obviously, however, most women only give birth after nine months, or if the case is really premature, after seven months. People began to become suspicious, thinking that the child was not that of her husband, but of a man with whom she had relations prior to her marriage.

They took her to the caliph, so that she could receive her punishment. The caliph at the time was 'Uthman bin 'Affan ﷺ. When they went to him, they found 'Ali ﷺ to be in his company, and he was 'Uthman's judge. 'Ali said, "You have no right to punish her for this reason."

They were surprised and asked, "And how is that?" He recited to them two Verses:

> "And the bearing of him, and the weaning of him is thirty (30) months." (Qur'ân 46:15)

(this means that the period of pregnancy as well as the period of breast-feeding is a total of 30 months.)

> "The mothers shall give suck to their children for two whole years." (Qur'ân 2:233)

(this means that the period of breast-feeding is two years – in other words, 24 months.)

Then 'Ali said, "It is possible, therefore, for the period of pregnancy to be six months only." And thus was the woman saved from stoning.

The Strange Inheritance Case

A woman once went to an Islamic scholar, and asked, "My brother died, and he left behind 600 dirhams. When they distributed that wealth, they gave me only one dirham!" The scholar thought for a while and then said, "Perhaps it is because your brother left behind a wife, a mother, two daughters, and 12 brothers (other than you)." The woman was stunned and confirmed that what he said was true.

He said, "This dirham is your share, and they have not wronged you in the least. The wife's share is 1/8th, and that is equal to 75 dirhams; the share of the two daughters is two thirds, and that is equal to 400 dirhams; the mother's share is 1/6th, and that is equal to 100 dirhams; only 25 dirhams remain, and that is distributed among his 12 brothers and one sister, and in such situations, the male receives twice as much as does the female. So each brother receives two dirhams, and all that remains for the sister - i.e., you - is a single dirham." Thus was the sister made to comprehend that her brothers did not wrong her.

Leave Him in the Fire

A man who was an adherent of the Majus religion died and left behind a huge debt. Some of his creditors said to his son, "Sell the house and pay off your father's debt." The son said, "If I sell the house and pay off my father's debt, will he enter Paradise?" They said, "No." He said, "Then leave him in the Hellfire and leave me in the house."

Iyas and His Quick Decisions

Iyas bin Mu'awiyah was a famous judge known for his intelligence and insight; some people, however, were jealous both of his status and of his ability, so they tried to raise doubts about him. They said, "He has in him a fault that no judge should have: when people come to him seeking judgment, he is quick in issuing his ruling."

When Iyas became aware of what they said about him, he called them to him, and bestowed upon them wonderful hospitality. He extended forth one of his two hands, and asked them, "How many fingers do you see?" They immediately said, "Five." He said, "How come you were so quick to answer? Why did you not first count them – one, two, three ... and become from those who do not hasten in their judgment?" They said, "We are not slow in counting that which we already know." He said, "Likewise with me; I do not delay in a matter regarding which I already know the ruling." And in this way, the distinguished judge showed them that he did not issue rulings in a quick or hasty manner.

In Short...

Luqman said to his son: "My son, if you have doubts about death, then do not sleep, for as you sleep so too will you die. And if you have doubts in the resurrection, then do not wake up from your sleep, for as you wake up from your sleep, so too will you be resurrected after you die."

The Intelligence and Insight of a Judge

'Umar bin 'Abdul-'Aziz wrote the following to 'Adi bin Artah: "Meet with Iyas bin Mu'awiyah and Qasim bin Rabi'ah Al-Jawshani, and appoint the more skilled of the two as a judge."

When 'Adi gathered the two together, Iyas said to him, "Ask the two jurists of Basrah about me and about Qasim: Hasan Basri and Ibn Sirin." Qasim knew that whereas he would go to Hasan and Ibn Sirin, Iyas wouldn't, and so he knew that if the two of them were asked, they would advise that he should be made judge. And so he quickly said, "Ask not about me nor about him. By Allâh, and none has the right to be worshiped except Him, indeed Iyas bin Mu'awiyah has a better understanding and is more knowledgeable than me in issuing rulings. If I just lied, you should not appoint me, and if I was truthful in what I said, you should accept from me."

Iyas said, "You have come to a man, making him stand at the edge of the Hellfire, and so he saved himself with a false oath, for which he will ask Allâh for forgiveness, and thus save himself from that which he fears." 'Adi said, "Based on your understanding of what he said, it is you who must be appointed." Then he appointed Iyas as a judge.

The Good and the Bad Deed

Imam Ibn Qayyim Al-Jawziyyah ﷺ, in his book *Ad-Da' Wad-Dawa'*, said that surely sins are like the seeds of fruits that always bear like fruits. Some of our pious predecessors have said that indeed the punishment for committing a sin is that one is compelled to commit sin again, and the reward for committing a good deed is the guidance to follow that up with yet another good deed. This singular action of doing a good deed bears a series of good deeds and in turn one's profits multiply. Similarly bad deeds beget more bad deeds and begin to take shape and permanence in one's character.

If a righteous person were to leave a good deed, he would feel confined and constricted, though he lives in a world of vast magnitude. Much like a fish out of water, the soul finds rest only in the tides of moral decency. So it is the same for the sinner, who finds comfort only in the familiarity and repetition of an old sin. He, too, feels the same sense of longing as the righteous person does. He sins not for the pleasure that is derived from it, but to pacify the pain that being away from it brings.

He left without Anything

Hasan, the son of Abul-Hasan, entered upon Abdullah bin Ahtam, visiting him during his illness. He saw Ibn Ahtam point his finger toward a box in his house. He went to the box and asked Hasan, "O Abu Sa'eed, what would you say about one hundred thousand in this box, of which I have never paid *Zakat* and from which I have never joined ties of relations." Hasan replied, "May your mother lose you. For whom were you gathering this wealth?" Ibn Ahtam explained, "I gathered it for difficult times, or the harshness of a cruel ruler, or for an increase in wives and children."

Shortly after this meeting, Ibn Ahtam died and as he was being buried, Hasan said to those present, "Look at this pitiable person. Satan came to him, making him fear poverty and kept him from spending of that which Allâh (the Exalted) gave to him. And now he has departed from this world, empty-handed and miserable." Hasan then turned to the inheritors of the deceased and said, "Let not this wealth deceive you as it deceived this companion of yours. This wealth has come to you in a *Halal* manner, so do not let it be your destruction. For indeed the greatest sorrow on the Day of Judgment will be to see your wealth, for which you toiled to gather (from both *Halal* and *Haram*), in the scales of your inheritors – if they do good with the money (charity, etc.), the good deed is with them, and the sin of that wealth is upon you."

Preserving the Honor of the Muslim

One day, 'Umar ﷺ left his home with Abdullah bin Mas'ud ﷺ and during the late hours of the night, they saw the glow of a fire burning from a distance. He followed the light until it led them to a home with a burning lamp. Upon seeing the lamp, 'Umar entered the house and saw an old man sitting with alcohol in front of him and a female singer entertaining him. The old man was caught off-guard by 'Umar's sudden attack when he said to him, "I have not seen a sight more shameful than what I have witnessed tonight from an old man who should be awaiting death."

The old man responded, "Indeed, O Leader of the Believers, what you have done is more shameful. You have entered my house without my permission and spied on me - and is not spying forbidden in Islam?" 'Umar admitted to the truth of his statement and left the old man's house, biting his garment and crying as he said, "May the mother of 'Umar lose him if Allâh does not forgive me." Thereafter, the old man stopped attending the gatherings of 'Umar. After some time passed, 'Umar saw the old man in one of the last rows of his gathering and wished to speak with him. Fearing harshness from 'Umar, the old man approached him cautiously, being asked to come closer and closer until he was finally seated near the Leader of the Believers. 'Umar asked to have his ear next to his mouth and said, "By the One Who has sent Prophet Muhammad with the truth, I have not informed anyone of what I saw of you that night, nor have I informed 'Abdullah bin Mas'ud, for indeed he was with me." The old man replied, "O Leader of the Believers! By the One Who has sent Prophet Muhammad with the truth, I too have not returned to those evil actions since the night you entered upon me." Umar uttered out loud, "*Allâhu Akbar*!" yet no one from the gathering knew what had occurred between the two men.

As Time passes

'Abdullah bin Mas'ud ﷺ said: "Indeed I hate to see a man idle, neither working for this world nor for the Hereafter."

Hasan Basri ﷺ said: "O son of Adam, indeed you are only but a number of days. Whenever a day passes, a part of you leaves with it."

Hassan said: "I have met (pious) people who are more miserly with their time than they are with their wealth."

Hassan also said in a sermon, "Do not let the temporary and little charms of this world distract you and entice you...and do not say tomorrow and tomorrow, for indeed you do not know when you will be heading to Allâh."

Knowledge must be followed up by Action

Ibn Qayyim ﷺ said, "Whoever has profound knowledge of what Allâh revealed to the Prophet ﷺ, will notice that most of the people that are reputed to be religious are often the least religious. What kind of religion or goodness is in a person who sees evil being committed, Allâh's boundaries being transgressed, religion being lost, the *Sunnah* of the Prophet ﷺ being abandoned and warned against - and yet remains cold in his heart? His tongue is quiet; he is a mute devil just as the one who speaks against religion is an articulate devil. Is not affliction in religion the situation of those who, when they attain leadership and sustenance from religion, care not about what happens regarding the religion? Certainly, the best of them are those that are at the very least saddened by the evil state of affairs. If one were to attack such a person in his honor, wealth, or status, he would surely take all necessary steps to prevent himself from that attack. Such people have been tested, have failed, and have fallen from Allâh's eyes, yet they do not perceive it. The trial they have been afflicted with is the death of their hearts. When the heart is alive and functioning at its peak, it rises to anger for the cause of Allâh and His Prophet ﷺ and will seek to promote His religion.

The Scholar and the Laborer

A scholar of Islamic jurisprudence, Bakr Al-Muzani, saw a laborer carrying goods with him while constantly uttering, *'Alhumdulillah* (all praise is for Allâh),' and *'Astaghfirullah* (I seek forgiveness from Allâh).' The scholar said that he waited for the laborer to rest from his load before he spoke to him. When he did, Al-Muzani asked him, "Do you not know anything other than this (*Alhumdulillah* and *Astaghfirullah*)?" The laborer responded, "Indeed I know much else and I do read the Book of Allâh, except that a slave of Allâh is constantly shifting between a state of blessing (from Allâh) and sin. This being the condition of man, I praise and thank Allâh for the blessings He has given me and seek His forgiveness for my sins." The scholar said, "Certainly this laborer has a deeper understanding of the religion than Bakr (himself)."

Respect for the Scholars

Muhammad bin 'Amr related from Abi Salamah that Ibn 'Abbas ﷺ stood to hold the saddle of Zaid bin Thabbit ﷺ (his teacher). Ibn Thabit said, "O cousin of the Messenger of Allâh, move away." Ibn 'Abbas replied, "This is how we treat our scholars and noble ones."

Ibn Qayyim

Ibn Qayyim ﵀ related the saying of the Prophet Muhammad ﷺ: "Whoever lives after me, shall see much conflict and trouble...then upon you is my *Sunnah.*" Ibn Qayyim said that this saying is judgmental in tone to those who dispute and it is a warning against following their way. For indeed great disagreement and conflict results from blind-following, giving way to self-interest, which causes disagreement and division and ultimately changes the message. This happens despite the fact that we have one Prophet, one Qur'ân and one Lord. Therefore, it is incumbent upon us all to be led by the words of Revelation that are common to all of us and to follow only the message of the Prophet ﷺ. We must not equate anyone's sayings or deeds to that of the Messenger ﷺ, nor should we take any as a Lord other than Allâh (the Exalted). If we were to agree upon that, if we were led by Allâh's Message through the Prophet ﷺ, and if we sought judgment through his *Sunnah* and the sayings of the Companions, then certainly discord would diminish, if not disappear altogether. That is why you will find that those that disagree the least among themselves are the people of the *Sunnah* and *Hadith,* since they build their actions upon that foundation. The further a party or sect is from *Hadith,* the higher the level of disagreement will be among that group. For whoever leaves the truth finds that he is in a state of confusion, unsure of what the truth is or where to find it.

> "Nay, but they have denied the truth (this Qur'ân) when it has come to them, so they are in a confused state (cannot differentiate between right and wrong)." (Qur'ân 50:5)

The Beard

Shaikh 'Abdur-Rahman As-Sa'idi stated that the Prophet Muhammad ﷺ ordered us to trim our moustaches and grow our beards. He also informed us that to trim it (facial hair) is from the Majus and the polytheists. He warned his nation from following that misguided custom. So, truly it is strange that we see someone who believes in Allâh and His Messenger, yet is stingy in following the example of the Prophet ﷺ, the Companions, and the *Tabi'een* (successors of the Companions). Allâh has honored men with beards and has made their beauty and character apparent in it, so woe to the one who shaves it, for he has disobeyed his Lord openly. Do all of those that shave their beards think that they have achieved a handsome appearance? Surely, they have not, since it shames the face of a man and takes away from its nobility. Following the misguided example of others often makes evil things seem comely. Did the people of knowledge not say that if anyone attacked another by shaving his beard and that if it did not ever grow again, then upon the attacker is the responsibility of paying full blood money? This illustrates the honor and good that Allâh (the Exalted) has placed in men who keep beards. In parallel to the previous example, then imagine the state of one who assaults his own honor and dignity by removing his own beard.

The Completeness of Religion and the Superior Mind

The noble Islamic jurist Sahnun bin Sa'eed taught others knowledge in religion. Malik, 'Abdul-'Aziz bin Salamah, Muhammad bin Ibrahim bin Dinar, and others would go to him seeking Islamic rulings. However, when Ibn Dinar and his relations would ask questions, they would not receive any answers. Ibn Dinar questioned Sahnun bin Sa'eed by inquiring why he would withhold knowledge when that is not lawful. He replied, "And what is it that I do, my brother?" Ibn Dinar continued to explain, "Malik and 'Abdul-Aziz ask you and you answer them while my people and I ask you and you do not respond." The scholar inquired, "O son of my brother, has this affected your heart toward me?" Ibn Dinar stated definitely that it had changed his heart. The scholar explained, "Indeed, I have become old of age and my bones have become brittle and I fear that that which has affected my body has also affected my mind. Malik and 'Abdul-'Aziz are scholars, so when they hear a truth from me, they accept it. And when they hear an error, they abandon it. Yet, you and your people accept everything from me without question."

Of this response, Ibn Harith has stated that this is what completeness of religion and a superior mind represent - as opposed to those that seek out status for their words in the minds of people - such a status that should only be occupied by the Qur'ân.

He had to choose between Money and His Beliefs

Ibn Hanbal said that he took Abu 'Abdullah and Ibn Ma'een with him to see 'Affan after Ishaq bin Ibrahim invited him to accept false beliefs against the Qur'ân. After 'Affan was tested, Ibn Hanbal and the others went to him and asked to know what Ishaq had said to him. He responded, "O Abu Zakariyya, I will not blacken your face or the faces of your companions; indeed I did not answer his request (referring to Ishaq's request coming from the ruler to accept false beliefs)." One of them asked what exactly had took place between the two. 'Affan replied, "Ishaq invited me, reciting the letter that Mamun, the ruler, had sent to me, and it was said in the letter that I was to be tested with falsehood about the Qur'ân. And if I accept it, all is well. If I do not, then my stipend will be taken away."

'Affan continued to say, "After Ishaq read the letter to me, he asked me my response. I recited: 'Say, indeed, Allâh is One...' until I finished that chapter of the Qur'ân. I then responded to Ishaq asking if this (the Qur'ân) was created (i.e., a rhetorical question, meaning, of course it is not)?" Ishaq said, "The Leader of the Believers said that if you do not answer, then your stipend will be taken away." 'Affan responded to this with:

> "And in the heaven is your provision, and that which you are promised." (Qur'ân 51:22)

From this we can see how faith in the true Words of Allâh had more bearing than any monetary reward offered to those persons of guidance.

Good Advice

Shu'bah and Qatadah related from Yunus bin Jubair, who said that he accompanied Jundub and he and his companions said to him, "Give us some advice." He replied, "I advise you to fear Allâh. I advise you to adhere to the Qur'ân - for it is light in the darkest of nights and it is guidance during the day. Apply it...but if a trial, such as poverty, comes to you, give precedence to your religion over wealth. If that trial worsens, continue to put your religion before your wealth and your soul, for indeed the only one who is destroyed is the one whose religion is destroyed; the one who is poor is the one who has lost his religion. Know that there is no poverty after Paradise and there is no richness after the Hellfire."

Who is more Honored?

Ash'ath bin Shu'bah Al-Missisiy related that Harun Rasheed, the ruler of the time, came to Ar-Raqqa, where the people did not gather around him, but rather around Ibn Mubarak. The enormous crowds caused dust to rise and people would lose their sandals in the rush to gather around him. The wife of the ruler asked, "Who is that?" The people responded that he was a scholar from the people of Khurasan. She replied, "By Allâh, that is a kingdom, unlike Harun's, where people do not gather except with the force of the security and police." One can conclude that the honor bestowed upon a learned man far surpasses that of a ruler in the hearts of the masses.

A Simple Approach to complete the Qur'ân once a Month

Allâh's Messenger ﷺ said: "The most blessed of deeds is that which is done consistently, even if it is a minute one." (*Sahih Bukhari*)

Brother Muslim, the Qur'ân is made up of thirty parts, like the month. One should read one part of the Qur'ân every day so that it can be completed in its entirety in one month. Furthermore, each part consists of twenty pages. If one were to read four pages during the daily obligatory prayers, it would facilitate the completion of one part every day. See, brother Muslim, how much good escapes us because we do not know how to organize our lives? When you practice this habit with regularity, you will not only be one of the guided ones, but also you will find profound pleasure and fulfillment in a consistent act of worship. You will also see the benefit and reward in a small act done continuously, as opposed to much done at irregular intervals.

The Idol whose Counsel is sought

'Amr had an idol called Manat, made of the most expensive wood, that he visited and anointed daily. He became fascinated with it, spending money to maintain it and attending to it morning and night. One day, 'Amr stood in front of Manat in a very humble manner praising it and said, "O Manat, you know of what has occurred in our city because of this caller (referring to the Prophet), who wishes to take us away from your worship. Indeed, I detest taking any decision without your counsel, so please counsel me in this matter." Yet Manat did not answer him. 'Amr said, "Perhaps, Manat, you are angry at me for some reason that I am unaware of, so I will leave you for a few days until your anger subsides."

'Amr's children wanted to take advantage of this opportunity, so they plotted among themselves along with a friend, Mu'adh bin Jabal ﷺ. They came at night, after their father had fallen asleep, and took Manat tossing it onto its head into a garbage pit that belonged to Bani Salimah. 'Amr, upon waking up, went to seek blessings from Manat and when he did not find it, he called out in a loud voice, "Woe unto you, who has transgressed against our gods on this night." The children did not answer him, pretending to be asleep. 'Amr was outraged and began to search for his beloved idol, voicing threats at whoever was responsible. He finally discovered it in the filthy pit, washed it immediately and anointed it with perfume, and then he put it back in its place. The next night, the children repeated their actions. 'Amr, again upon waking did not find his idol in its proper place, but rather in the garbage pit. However, this time the idol had been covered by the filth from the tip of its head to its toes. Again, he repeated the ritual of washing and anointing it, only this time he placed it with a sword around its neck, saying to it, "O Manat, if anyone comes near you, then deal with that person with that sword." The third night, the children, tossing away the sword, decided to tie the idol to a dead dog and then throw it into the pit once again. 'Amr, upon waking, once again went to his deity and searched madly, only this time to find it not only in a heap of filth, but also tied to a dead dog. 'Amr finally came to his senses, leaving the worship of false gods and idols, and announcing his acceptance of Islam. He crushed his idols, feeling regret for his idolatrous past and accepted Faith with his heart and soul. He offered his wealth and children and soul for the sacrifice of Islam, hoping to wipe away past evil.

The Benefits of the *Siwak*

Research has shown that *Siwak*, a tooth stick from a tree that is used to clean the teeth and whose use is highly recommended in Islam, consists of many beneficial elements from nature - minerals like chloride, sodium, potassium and other elements that contain a pleasant odor. It also contains certain elements that strengthen the gums, as well as purifying agents that prevent ulcers in them. This is taken from a study from Rostock University in Germany.

The Responsibility of a Ruler

Sa'eed bin Sulaiman said that he was once in Makkah and beside him was Abdullah bin 'Abdul-'Aziz Al-'Amri. At that time, Caliph Harun Rasheed was performing *Hajj*. A man said to Al-'Amri, "O Abu Abdur-Rahman, there is the Caliph, making circuits between Safa and Marwah and that area has been emptied out for him." Al-'Amri said to the man, "May Allâh not reward you well, for you have placed upon me a burden that I was happy to be free of (referring to the burden of advising the caliph)." Al-'Amri then took his shoes, stood, and walked over to where Harun Rasheed was performing his circuits, heading towards Safa. Al-'Amri called out to the caliph, asked him to climb Safa to look out at the House of Allâh - the Ka'bah. Al-'Amri asked Harun as to how many people he saw, would anyone be able to count them, and how many like them are spread throughout the Muslim nations that are not even present. Harun responded, "Indeed, an amount that none could count, except Allâh." Al-'Amri advised, "Know, O man, that each one of them will be asked about his own deeds and you alone will be asked about each one of them. So, imagine the burden on you on the Last Day." Harun began to cry and passed to him handkerchief after handkerchief for his tears.

Al-'Amri continued, "Another word, I would like to pass onto you." Harun said, "Speak, O uncle." He explained that a man who wastes his wealth deserves to have the

Hajar (a restriction placed by a judge upon a wastrel or spendthrift) imposed upon him, so again imagine what would happen to the one who is extravagant and wasteful with the wealth of the Muslims." Upon hearing this, Harun continued to weep.

"If You see it befitting, free Her Prisoner..."

When the Prophet Muhammad ﷺ migrated to Al-Madinah, he couldn't take his daughter Zainab رضي الله عنها with him. She remained behind with her husband, Abul-'Aas, who at that time was not a Muslim. After the Prophet's migration, during the Battle of Badr against the Quraish, Abul-'Aas bin Rabi'ah bin Abd Shams became a prisoner of the Muslims in Al-Madinah with the Messenger ﷺ. The people of Makkah began to send wealth to ransom the relatives that were taken for prisoners. Zainab, too, sent wealth along with a necklace that her mother Khadijah رضي الله عنها had given her upon her marriage to Abul-'Aas. When the Prophet ﷺ saw that necklace he became very emotional and told the Companions, "If you see it befitting, free her prisoner and return to her the wealth she has sent." They agreed to do so and this resulted in Abul-'Aas' acceptance of Islam.

The Brave Judge

Fadl bin Rabi', the minister of Harun Rasheed, went to the renowned judge, Abu Yusuf to give testimony in a case. However the judge rejected his testimony. Harun Rasheed reproached the judge about this and Abu Yusuf explained, "Indeed, I heard the minister say to you that certainly, he was your slave. If he was truthful in what he said, then the testimony of a slave is not accepted. Similarly, if he was lying, then the testimony of a liar is not accepted. Furthermore, if he does not care for lying in your gathering, then he will not care for lying in my gathering."

'Umar bin 'Abdul-'Aziz

Fatimah, the wife of 'Umar bin 'Abdul-'Aziz, once entered his prayer room and found him with his hands on his cheeks, as tears poured from his eyes. She asked, "O Leader of the Believers, what has occurred to cause you to cry?" He responded, "O Fatimah, indeed, I have taken the responsibility for the nation of Prophet Muhammad ﷺ and as I think about the state of the hungry, the poor, the lost, the sick, the oppressed, the imprisoned, and the burdened, I fear that on the Last Day, with the Prophet representing them as my opponent, no proof will be established on my behalf as their guardian. I think about my fate with pity and cry."

Inscribed in Gold

Asma'i said that Abdul-Malik once delivered a very profound sermon, during which he began to weep while begging Allâh: "O Lord, my sins are great, but a small amount of Your forgiveness is greater than them. O Allâh, forgive the greatness of my sins with a little of Your mercy." Asma'i said that when these words reached the ears of Hasan Basri, he too began to cry, stating that if ever words were uttered that should be inscribed in gold - these would be those words.

Our Pious Predecessors and Their Fear of Allâh

Ibn Mas'ud ﷺ used to say: "Indeed, with the passing of nights and days, your stay on this earth is decreasing, yet your deeds will remain preserved and death will come suddenly. Whoever sows seeds of goodness will reap a harvest of hope. Whoever sows evil will reap the harvest of misfortune and regret. Indeed, each shall reap of that which he sows. The one who works slowly shall not be prevented from his share, and the one who works eagerly will not get more than is decreed for him (referring to worldly pursuits). Any blessing that is received is from Allâh and any protection from evil is also from Allâh. The ones who fear Allâh are the leaders, as are the scholars, and joining their company can only lead to personal benefit."

The Honest Muslim Merchant

Nadr bin Shumail said that in a certain place the price of silk had increased and that if it increased there, it should also increase in Basrah. Yunus bin 'Ubaid was a silk manufacturer and when he learned of this fact, he bought from a man a quantity of goods for thirty thousand. Yet, afterwards, he asked the seller if he was aware of the price increase. The seller replied that he was not and that had he been, he would not have made the sale at such a price. Yunus insisted that his money be returned for the goods that were sold to him. This illustrates the piety of our predecessors, for even in their business transactions they attempted to maintain the highest level of honesty and clarity in all matters, pertaining to both the buyer and seller.

Our Pious Predecessors

'Abdullah bin Mubarak related that it was said to Hamdun bin Ahmad, "Why is the speech of our pious predecessors more beneficial than our speech?" He replied, "Because they spoke for the honor of Islam, for the salvation of the soul, and for the pleasure of the Most Merciful. However, we speak to honor ourselves, to seek out the world, and to please creation."

Constant Strife of the Soul

Ja'far bin Barqan said that the news of Yunus bin 'Ubaid's piety reached him and he wrote to him: "O my brother, I have learned that you are a righteous man and I wanted to write to you. Please write to me and tell me what state you are in." So, he wrote back to him saying, "I have received your letter, and I will inform you that I presented to my soul that it should love for others what it loves for itself, and that it should hate for others what it hates for itself; and I discovered my soul to be far from that state. Then on another occasion, I presented to my soul that it should refrain from the mention of others except for the sake of good. I learned that it would be easier for my soul to fast on a hot, difficult day in the middle of the desert than it would be easier for it to refrain from the mention of others in an evil way. O my brother, this is my state. Peace be with you."

Moderation in Worship

Anas ﷺ related that the Messenger ﷺ entered the mosque and noticed a rope stretched out between two columns. He asked what it was there for and was told that it belonged to Zainab ﷺ and when she became tired from continuous worship, she leans on it for support. The Prophet ﷺ said: "Unfasten that rope. Let one of you pray when he is active and when he is tired, let him rest." (*Sahih Bukhari* and *Sahih Muslim*)

A Manifestation of Justice

It has been related that one of the sons of 'Amr bin Al-'Aas ﷺ, the governor of Egypt, struck a young Christian Egyptian with his whip. This young Egyptian complained to the Leader of the Believers, Umar Faruq ﷺ, who in turn wrote to the governor and asked his immediate presence along with his son. 'Umar also invited the young man who had been stricken. When they all gathered in Umar's chamber where he issued rulings, Amr's son admitted that he had wronged the young man. The Leader of the Believers handed his whip to the Christian boy and said to him, "Strike this son of the most noble!" The boy raised his whip and struck the son of the governor. 'Umar said, "Put the whip on Amr's forehead as well." The boy responded, "O Leader of the Believers, I have stricken the one that struck me." 'Umar said, "By Allâh, had you stricken him, I would not have prevented you, for this son of 'Amr only hit you under the authority of his father." Turning to 'Amr, Umar related a renowned saying to him: "When have you taken people for slaves, when their mothers have bore them as ones that are free."

The Question

Hasan bin Sahl asked Dinar bin 'Abdullah, "What is your religion?" He said, "I never thought that anyone alive would ask this question, for it is the question of Munkar and Nakir to the dead."

A Mother Who spent Wisely on Her Son

A man came back to his home in Al-Madinah after many years of journey. He asked his wife about his son and an amount of thirty thousand dinars which he had entrusted her before starting his journey. His wife said to him, "First go and pray in the mosque of the Messenger of Allâh ﷺ, then I will tell you about them." He went to the Prophet's Mosque and saw a gathering of many eminent attendees and as soon as the crowd gave him space, he saw Rabbiyyah, his son there. Rabiyyah had become a famous scholar and was heading a study circle at the Mosque which included the likes of Malik, Hassan, Zaid, Ibn 'Ali Al-Lahbi, As-Musami'i, and other figures of repute and intellect from Al-Madinah. The father confirmed the scholar's identity with a man from the gathering and then left the crowd to return to his home. He said to his wife, "Indeed, Allâh has elevated your son to an unparalleled level." His wife responded, "What is more beloved to you, thirty thousand dinars or the status that your son has achieved?" He replied, "Certainly the ranking that my son has attained." His wife continued to explain, "I have spent all of that wealth upon him." The father replied in a satisfied tone, "Indeed, you have not wasted it on him."

The Many Guises of Backbiting

Shaikhul-Islam, Ibn Taimiyyah ﵀, said that there are those from the people that backbite or listen to backbiting, and they do so to please the company they keep, with the awareness that the victim is likely to be innocent of some of the things that are uttered about him. Often such offenders feel that if they were to attempt to end such conversation in a gathering, their presence might become unwelcome or burdensome. There are many methods and guises that are employed when one mentions another in a negative way. Under the pretense of being informative, one could say that it is not one's habit to mention others, except for the sake of relating another's condition to someone. Or one could state that by Allâh, indeed so-and-so is one to be pitied, thereby showing superiority over one who is to be rejected. Another method might be to say that so-and-so is a good person; however, he has such and such qualities. Again, one is justified in revealing another's faults. One could also simply state that we should forget so-and-so, and make supplication for their forgiveness as well as our own, intending only to belittle the one that was mentioned. In reality, all these tactics are designed to try to deceive Allâh (the Exalted) and to please the creation; and in reality, the many that follow these methods only serve to deceive themselves.

Then there are those that backbite to raise their own status. When they hear of someone's error, they employ words like, "Had I prayed for so-and-so last night in my prayer, the news of their sin would not have reached my ears." Again, when a person states of another that he lacks understanding in a matter, the implication is personal superiority for the one that mentions the other's shortcoming.

There are also those that couple jealousy with backbiting – the act of being critical or belittling to those that are praised in the company of others. Some people also backbite for the sake of humor, playfulness and lightheartedness. A person finds a certain amount of satisfaction from being appreciated for his story-telling abilities; speaking ill of someone in a humorous fashion adds flavor to a tale. Others engage in backbiting by showing surprise and amazement at another's actions: "How is it that someone could do such a thing?" Yet others mention people and their actions with the pretense of sympathy for their actions or misfortunes. In reality, the one who backbites actually finds contentment and satisfaction at the mention of others and their misdeeds. Another form of backbiting is relating someone's misfortune to their enemies, so that they, too, may find pleasure in putting them down. From these examples, one can surmise that backbiting pertains to a disease of the heart... May Allâh save us from this most evil of actions and protect us from its temptations.

Tremendous Rewards for Simple Deeds

Bukhari and Muslim related from Abu Hurairah ﷺ that Allâh's Messenger ﷺ said: "As a man was walking on a pathway, he found a thorny branch. He removed it from the trail and Allâh (the Exalted) was pleased with his deed, accepted it, rewarded him, and forgave him."

In some narrations related by Muslim from Abu Hurairah, Allâh's Messenger ﷺ said, "A man passed by a branch of a tree in the middle of a road and he removed it so it would not hurt or harm Muslims. Allâh so loved the act that he was made to enter Paradise."

In another narration related from Abu Hurairah, the Prophet ﷺ said: "Indeed, I saw a man living comfortably in Paradise because of a tree he cut down from the middle of a pathway which was the cause of harm to many."

O Cousin, You spend extravagantly!

Hasan and Husain one day went to their cousin, 'Abdullah bin Ja'far ﷺ, and said to him, "Indeed you spend in an extravagant manner!" He said, "...Indeed Allâh has made me become accustomed to having His favors, and I have made it a habit to do favors for His slaves. I fear that if I break off this habit, provision will be cut off from me."

The Believer is not stung from the same Hole twice

After the Battle of Badr, Abu 'Azzah Al-Jumahi, a poet, was a prisoner in the hands of the Muslims. He was from the Quraish and through his poetry he would incite battle against the Muslims. After his capture, he said to Prophet Muhammad ﷺ, "Indeed, I am poor and I have many dependents that are needy and you know of this, so please have mercy upon me and may Allâh have mercy upon you." The Prophet ﷺ did so and released him. Before the Battle of Uhud, Safwan bin Umaiyyah, one of the leaders of the Quraish, said to the poet before they were to fight the Muslims, "O Abu 'Azzah, indeed you are a poet, so help us with your words to incite the men to battle." Abu 'Azzah replied that the Prophet ﷺ had bestowed a favor upon him by giving him his freedom and he did not wish to go against that kindness. Safwan said, "Help us and if you return alive from this battle, I will make you rich and if you are struck down, I will make your daughters partners with my daughters in my wealth." So, Abu 'Azzah went forth with them and again was taken as prisoner by the Muslims for a second time. Again he pleaded with the Prophet asking to be pardoned. The Prophet ﷺ said to him, "By Allâh, your cheeks will not touch Makkah and you will not be able to say that indeed, you have deceived Muhammad twice. Indeed, the believer is not stung from the same hole twice. O Zubair, strike his neck!" Zubair struck his neck and he was killed.

Do not Judge by One's Clothes

On the day of Qadisiyyah, during the caliphate of 'Umar ﷺ, the famous Companion, Sa'd bin Abi Waqqas ﷺ sent Rib'i bin 'Aamir ﷺ to Rustum, the leader of Faris (Persia). Ibn 'Aamir entered upon Rustum's gathering place that had been beautified with gold, silk, pearls, and gems and upon Rustum's head was a crown. Ibn 'Aamir continued to ride on his mount until he reached the edge of the extravagant carpet, where he descended. He wore a simple, tattered garment along with his armor and helmet. The guards asked him to remove his armor and he replied, "Indeed I have not come to you, except after you had invited me. If you leave me as I am, I will see your king. If not, then I will return from whence I came." Rustum advised his guards to let him proceed. Ibn 'Aamir went forward, leaning on his spear, which tore the carpet. The king's advisors asked him what had brought him to them. He responded, "Allâh has sent us to take whom He pleases from the worship of slaves to the worship of Allâh and from the narrowness of the world to its vastness and from the oppression of religions to the justice of Islam. He has sent us with His religion to the creation so that we may invite them to it, and whoever accepts it, we leave alone. However, whoever refuses, we fight continually until we reach Allâh's Promise." They asked what Allâh's Promise was and Ibn 'Aamir replied, "Paradise for he who dies while fighting those who refuse and victory for those who remain." Rustum said, "I have heard your speech and will you grant us reflection on this matter for us and yourself." Ibn 'Aamir agreed and asked if he should return in a day or two. Rustum replied that they would require time to take counsel to which Ibn 'Aamir replied that the Prophet ﷺ had not set a precedence for them to delay the enemies while they are about to meet with them for more than three days. Rustum asked if Ibn 'Aamir was the leader and he replied to this inquiry that no, he wasn't, but the Muslims act as one body and that the least of them in status may take one into their protection without the permission of those with higher status. Rustum gathered with the leaders of his people, and at first he was inclined to Ibn 'Aamir's words. He said, "Have you ever seen anything more honorable, upright, and superior than the speech of this man." They replied, "We seek refuge in God that you lean toward anything that he said, leaving your religion for this dog. Did you not see his garments?" Rustum answered, "Woe unto you. Do not look at one's garments, but rather at his words, opinion, speech, and character..."

The First University

The first university in the world was the University of Qarwiyin in the city of Fas, in Morocco, which was ordered to be built by Muhammad bin 'Abdullah Al-Fihri Al-Qirwani.

Fatimah and Maryam, his two daughters made sure it was built as per their father's request.

It was completed in 859H and was originally a mosque for prayer as well as an institution for knowledge and Islamic jurisprudence.

The Sagacity of Suhail bin 'Amr

Suhail bin 'Amr, Harith bin Hisham, Abu Sufyan bin Harb and other leaders and chiefs of the Quraish were waiting at the door of 'Umar bin Khattab ﷺ. Also waiting there were Suhaib, Bilal and other freed slaves who participated with the Muslims in the Battle of Badr. The permission was given to the freed slaves to enter and not to Suhail and his companions. Abu Sufyan said, "I have never seen a day where slaves such as these have been allowed to enter while we have been left at the door, and 'Umar has not even turned to see us." Suhail bin 'Amr, a profound and poignant speaker, said, "O people, by Allâh, I see by your faces that you are very angry, but be angry at yourselves. They were invited to Islam and you were invited to Islam. They hastened to accept and you tarried."...Hasan replied, "By Allâh, Suhail has spoken the truth. Allâh (the Exalted) does not equate the slave who hastens to Him with the slave who tarries."

'Aishah bint Talhah

Hasan bin 'Ali bin Husain said to his wife, 'Aishah bint Talhah, "Your affair is in your hand (i.e., if you want divorce, then I grant it)!" She said, "For 20 years it has been in your hand, and you have done well to preserve it. I will not let it be wasted in my hand for even a single hour, and so I have returned the matter to you!" He was so impressed by her words that he decided to keep her as his wife, and not divorce her.

The Flock is the Responsibility of the Shepherd

Sa'eed bin 'Aamir ﷺ said to 'Umar bin Khattab ﷺ, "Indeed, I advise you with words that are taken from the comprehensive precepts of Islam. Fear Allâh in how you deal with people and do not fear people with how you are with Allâh and let not your speech be contrary to your actions, for indeed, the best of speech is that which is in accordance with action. Love for those Muslims that are near to you and those that are far that which you love for yourself and for your family. Do not fear blame or hardship in your quest for what you know to be true."

Patience

'Ali bin Abi Talib ﷺ went to Ash'ath to console him upon the death of one of his sons. He said, "If you are sad, then you are deserving of mercy, but if you are patient, then Allâh gives you something in place of what was lost or destroyed. And know that if you are patient, everything that was destined for you and preordained for you will occur and you are rewarded. If you complain and are hopeless, then likewise all that was destined for you will occur, except that you will be blamed for your impatience at Allâh's Will."

Allâh's Angels

The famous and eminent Companion, Abdullah bin Salam ﷺ, was a righteous Jew before the coming of Islam and in fact was a known scholar for his religion. He accepted Islam with great sincerity. The Prophet ﷺ said to him, "You have two rewards - one for your previous religion and the second for this time after your acceptance of Islam." Many years later, those who were rebellious during the caliphate of Uthman ﷺ, wanted to kill him, 'Abdullah bin Salam said to them, "O people, do not unsheathe your swords against him, for if you do, you will not put them back in their sheaths. Your leader today stands with a shield, but if you kill him, he will stand with a sword. Woe unto you. Indeed, Al-Madinah is surrounded by angels and if you kill him, those angels will leave us." They said, "O son of the Jew, what is it to you this affair?" So, he left them. The fighting ensued and all that he warned against did occur. Indeed our return is to Allâh and to Him we belong.

The Slow One

Muhammad Ad-Dari related the following: "Among us there was a rather slow and heedless man. He left the city of Dar, taking with him ten donkeys. He mounted one of them and then counted 9 donkeys in his flock; he descended and then counted 10. He did this a number of times and then said, 'For me to walk and gain a profit of one donkey is better than for me to ride and lose one donkey.' He continued to walk, and almost died from weakness, until finally, he reached his village."

Mother of the Martyrs

When Muthanna bin Harithah Ash-Shaibani went to Qadisiyyah, during the caliphate of 'Umar bin Khattab ﷺ, Khansa' was with her four children that were accompanying the army on the day of battle and the night before it. Khansa' gathered her children to guide and incite them to fight with bravery. She warned them from wanting to flee from battle while reminding them of the merits and rewards of martyrdom in the way of Allâh (the Exalted). She said to them: "O my children, you have accepted Islam in obedience and you have migrated by your own choice...and you know of the plentiful reward that Allâh has prepared for the believers for fighting those that do not believe. Know that the final abode is better than this transient one." Allâh (the Exalted) says:

> *"O you who believe! Endure and be more patient (than your enemy), and guard your territory by stationing army units permanently at the places from where the enemy can attack you, and fear Allâh, so that you may be successful."* (Qur'ân 3:200)

Khansa's children went forth to fight with determination and firmness in Faith. They were all martyred, by Allâh's Will. Upon hearing this news, she uttered: "All praise is for Allâh, Who has honored me with their martyrdom and I hope from my Lord that He unites me with them in the final destination, under His mercy." May Allâh bless all mothers with Khansa's sacrificing and patient heart.

A Glimpse of the Prophet's Forgiveness

Abu Hurairah ﷺ related the story of a man from Banu Hanifah named Thumamah bin Uthal who was taken prisoner by the Muslims. After the Muslims captured him, this leader of Yamamah was tied up to a column in the mosque. The Prophet ﷺ would come out to him and say, "What is with you, O Thumamah?" He would reply, "O Muhammad, I have much with me that is good, and if you kill me then you are killing one that has many relatives. If you show favor to me, then you are showing favor to one that is thankful. If you wish for wealth, then ask and you shall be given wealth." The Prophet ﷺ left him and then returned the next day to ask again, "What is with you, O Thumamah?" He replied, "It is as I have told you." The Prophet ﷺ left him only to return the following day to ask again, "What is with you, O Thumamah?" He said, "With me is what I have said to you. If you show kindness, then you are showing kindness to one who is grateful. If you kill, you are killing one who has a large clan. And if it is wealth you desire, I can provide you with wealth." The Prophet ﷺ said to his Companions, "Free Thumamah." Thumamah then went to a date-palm tree near the mosque, washed himself, entered the mosque and declared: "I bear witness that none has the right to be worshiped but Allâh and I bear witness that Muhammad is His Messenger and slave." He said, "O Muhammad, by Allâh, there was no face that was more hated to me than your face and now it has become the most beloved face to me. By Allâh, there was no religion that was more hated to me than your religion and now it is the most beloved to me. By Allâh, there was no land that was more hated to me than your land and now your land has become the most beloved to me...I wish to perform *'Umrah...*" The Prophet ﷺ, upon hearing this wish, gave him glad tidings and told him to act upon his noble intentions. When he went to Makkah, someone said to him, "Indeed you have apostatized." He replied, "No, indeed I have accepted Islam with the Prophet and by Allâh, you will not receive even a grain of wheat from Yamamah, unless the Prophet allows it."

Patience and Lawful Sustenance

'Ali bin Abi Talib ﷺ entered the mosque of Kufah one day, where he saw a man standing at the door of the mosque. He asked that man to hold his mount for him so he could enter. Upon his exit, 'Ali had two Dirhams in his hand that he had intended to give to the man in return for his services. However, he found that the mule was still there, without its reigns. So he gave the two Dirhams to his servant Qanbar to purchase new reigns for his mule. At the marketplace, Ali's servant found the exact reigns that the thief had sold for two Dirhams. So Ali said to him, "Indeed, the slave forbids himself from lawful sustenance by abstaining from patience."

The Supplication of Those Who are Wronged

Ibn 'Umar ﷺ reported that Marwan sent a group to Sa'eed bin Zaid ﷺ to speak to him about an issue concerning a woman named 'Urwah bint Aws. She was a plaintiff to the ruler Marwan, complaining that Sa'eed bin Zaid took some of her land and in it there was her well also. When that group from Marwan approached Sa'eed bin Zaid about this issue, he replied, "They think that I have wronged her, and indeed, I have heard the Prophet ﷺ say that whoever wrongs someone of their land to the degree of a span of a hand, he will be clasped on the Day of Judgment from seven earths." He continued, "O Allâh, if she was lying, then do not let her die until she loses her sight and make her grave her well." 'Umar relates that indeed she did not die until she lost her sight. She met her death by falling into her well.

The eminent Companion, Sa'd bin Waqqas ﷺ, was one whose supplications were answered. The Messenger ﷺ supplicated for him and said, "Make your food pure and lawful and your supplication will be answered."

It is reported from Jabir bin Samurah in *Sahih Bukhari* and *Sahih Muslim* that the people of Kufah complained to Caliph 'Umar about their governor Sa'd concerning all matters. They even said of Sa'd that he did not pray properly. Sa'd explained that he prayed with them the prayer of the Messenger ﷺ. 'Umar ﷺ said that this is what he would expect from him. 'Umar sent people to Kufah to inquire about the governor, Sa'd. In all the mosques, people praised him well, but in the Mosque of Bani 'Abs, a man named Usamah bin Qatadah who was generally called Abu Sa'da, stood up and said, "Indeed Sa'd does not distribute the wealth of the Muslims equally among the people and he is not just in his rulings." News of this statement reached Sa'd and he said, "O Allâh, if this slave of Yours has stood up to show off or to gain a reputation (by uttering falsehoods), then prolong his life, prolong his state of poverty, take away his sight, and afflict him with trials." The narrator continues to report that after that he saw him as an old man, whose eyebrows fell over his eyes, standing in the road, winking at young girls. He even said about himself that he was an old man put to trial through the supplication of Sa'd.

They were trying to make Him Angry

Ahnaf bin Qais was famous for his forbearance and patience and for not becoming angry. Some of his companions gathered together and decided that they would try to do something to arouse his anger. One of them went to him, proposing to him to marry his mother! Ahnaf said, "We are not rejecting you because we think your status is too low, nor because we lack the desire to be related to you through marriage; rather, it is because my mother is old in age - she is almost 70. And you are a young man, in the prime of your youth. You need an affectionate and fertile woman, who will take from your manners and learn from your character." He then said to the young man, "Return to your people and inform them that you were not able to make me angry!"

A Beautiful Approach to exhorting to Islam

Abu Hurairah ﷺ related that one day he passed by the marketplace of Al-Madinah, and stood there and said to the owners of the shops, "O people of the marketplace, what has rendered you incapable?" They replied, "What are you referring to, O Abu Hurairah?" He said, "There is the inheritance of the Prophet being distributed and you are here? Will you not go there and take your share of the inheritance?" They said, "Where is it?" He replied, "In the mosque." So they raced out all together from the marketplace to the mosque to receive their share and Abu Hurairah remained there waiting for their return. They came back looking disappointed. Abu Hurairah asked them what they found at the mosque. They replied, "O Abu Hurairah, when we went to the mosque, we did not find any inheritance or estate that was being distributed." Abu Hurairah asked them what they saw in the mosque. They recounted that they saw a group engaged in prayer and another busy in the recitation of the Qur'ân and another studying what is lawful and not lawful." Then Abu Hurairah said to them, "Woe unto you, for that is the inheritance of Prophet Muhammad."

Knowledge

Those who are most comprehensive in their knowledge are those who know Allâh (the Exalted) through His Speech, i.e., the Qur'ân. For such a person knows his Lord in Whom the qualities of perfection and the highest possible attributes are present, Who is free from all defects and Who has no partner. All His Names express perfection and beauty. He presides above all things and does as He pleases. Allâh (the Exalted), Sustainer of the universe, orders and forbids and is greater than all things, more Beautiful than the beautiful, the most Merciful of the merciful, and the most Able of the able. Hence the Qur'ân was revealed to acquaint Allâh's slaves with Him and with the path that leads to Him.

The Bests

The Messenger of Allâh ﷺ said, "From my nation, the most merciful to the believers is Abu Bakr, the strongest of them upon Allâh's religion is 'Umar, truly the most modest of them is 'Uthman, the best judge among them is Ali bin Abi Talib, the one possessing the best recitation of Qur'ân is Ubai bin Ka'b, the best concerning inheritance law is Zaid bin Thabit, the most knowledgeable of them concerning forbidden matters and lawful matters is Mu'adh bin Jabal. Greenery has not given shade, nor has the earth carried one with a more truthful speech than Abu Dharr Al-Ghifari. Every nation has a trustworthy one and that one for this nation is Abu 'Ubaidah bin Al-Jarrah."

Allâh will make a Way

Malik Al-Ashja'i went to the Messenger ﷺ and said to him that his son 'Awf had been taken prisoner. The Messenger ﷺ said, "Ask him to repeat frequently: 'There is neither might nor power except with Allâh'." They tied 'Awf with a cord or with a strap and it fell from him. He went out quickly to escape and found a camel, which he began to ride on. The other camels of those that had taken him prisoner began to follow him back to his land. When 'Awf's parents heard a disturbance outside their house, they were shocked to see their son and a garden full of camels. The father went to the Prophet ﷺ to ask him what they should do with all the camels, which during those times signified great wealth. Allâh's Messenger ﷺ said to them that they should do with them (camels) what they would do with their wealth. And the Verse from the Qur'ân was revealed:

> "And whoever fears Allâh and keeps his duty to Him, He will make a way for him to get out (from every difficulty)." (Qur'ân 65:4)

In another narration, which differs slightly, Malik Al-Ashja'i went to the Prophet ﷺ to relate the situation of his son who had been imprisoned by the disbelievers. The Prophet ﷺ ordered him to be patient and that Allâh (the Exalted) would provide a way out for him. And indeed only a short while passed before Malik's son escaped to his freedom.

Allâh's complete Justice and Mercy

It is related that a woman went to the Prophet Dawud عليه السلام and said, "O Prophet of Allâh, is your Lord an oppressor or is He just?" The Prophet replied, "Woe unto you, O woman, He is the All-Just, Who never oppresses. What is your story?" She explained that she was a widow, with three daughters and that she provided for them by what she would spin with her hands. She explained, "Yesterday, I tied what I had spun into a red cloth to sell in the marketplace so as to provide for my children. As I was walking, a bird came and snatched the cloth from me and flew away, leaving me with nothing to sell for the provision of my children." As the woman was speaking to Dawud, someone came knocking on his door. He gave permission for them to enter and learned that they were ten businessmen bringing with them one hundred dinars each. They said, "O Prophet of Allâh, give this wealth to the one that is deserving." Dawud asked them what had brought them to him with their wealth. They explained, "O Prophet of Allâh, we were on a boat, the wind was very violent, and we were about to drown when a bird came and dropped a red cloth upon us. In this cloth was some yarn and with this we were able to block the hole in the ship until the winds subsided and we vowed that each one of us would give one hundred dinars in charity. So give that amount to whomever you please." Dawud turned to the woman and said, "Your Lord does business for you in the land and in the sea, yet you ask whether He oppresses!" He gave her the 1000 dinars and said, "Spend this on your children."

The Declining and the Waning

In his book, *Tammulat Fid-Deen Wal-Hayat* (Reflections on Religion and Life), Imam Ghazali ﷺ mentioned a story that he found to be wholly expressing the state of Muslims. There was a rich man who had a son who was practically blind. Despite all the efforts of many doctors, his son was only able to perceive some shapes and colors. The father sat down one day with his friends and said that he had decided to give his son for the cause of Allâh and he will enter Al-Azhar, a renowned Islamic university, as soon as he memorizes the Qur'ân. Soon, thereafter, his son started memorizing the Qur'ân, entered Al-Azhar under the guidance of a blind scholar, known for his skill in recitation. Indeed, as fate would have it, as each day passed, the boy's sight improved incredibly. The father was amazed and began to doubt his decision of sacrificing his son in the way of Allâh - a decision he had taken based on the fact that his son was nearly blind! This story illustrates the idea that we want what is best for us in this world:

> "They assign to Allâh that which they dislike (for themselves." (Qur'ân 16:62)

Faced with the sudden change of events, the father drove the blind scholar from his home and decided to send his son to a technical school. One can gather the lack of importance that Muslims give to the quality of the individual who studies in the path of Allâh. Muslims donate the blind, the sick, the declining, or waning. Those that are blessed with beautiful faces, sharp minds, and healthy bodies are not sent to join Allâh's ranks. I fear that the level of health amongst our nation will improve to such an extent that we will not find anyone who will study Islam.

The Story of a Woman and Her Children

'Aishah ﵂ said: A woman came to me with her two children, asking for help. All that I could find with me was a single date. I gave it to her and she divided it into two, giving half of the date to each of her two daughters, herself abstaining from eating anything from it. I left her, and when Allâh's Messenger ﷺ came to me, I informed him of what happened. He said, "Whoever is put to trial with daughters in any way, but then does good by them, they will be a barrier between him and the Hellfire." (*Sahih Bukhari, Sahih Muslim* and *At-Tirmidhi*)

This *Hadith* and others like it give cause for joy to every mother and father who have been blessed with a daughter, for through that daughter, they are shown a way that leads to Paradise.

A Proof of Allâh's Existence

A group of people went to Imam Shafi'i demanding proof for the existence of Allâh (the Exalted). He considered it for a moment and then replied that the proof is the leaf of the mulberry bush. This was puzzling to all. How can this particular leaf be a proof of Allâh's existence? Imam Shafi'i replied that the taste and substance of this bush is one; however, when a silkworm eats its leaf, it comes out of the worm as silk, yet when a bee does the same, what is produced is honey. Likewise, when the deer consumes it, what is produced is musk. He continued to explain that one should ponder upon the Creator of such a phenomenon - Who allows a variety of results to be derived from a single source.

The Interpretation of Her Dream

'Aishah ﵂ said that she saw a dream in which three moons fell into her dwelling. She asked Abu-Bakr ﵁ concerning what she had seen. He replied,

> "O 'Aishah, if indeed your dream is true, then the three best of Allâh's slaves will be buried in your house."

When the Prophet ﷺ died, he was the best of those three moons and he was the first of them. Thereafter Abu-Bakr and 'Umar ﵄ too were buried there.

The *Mufti* (the One Who gives Islamic Rulings) is like a Doctor

Imam Sha'bi ﷺ was asked about an issue and he replied, "I do not know." It was said to him, "Are you not ashamed of stating that you do not know, especially being the Islamic jurist of Iraq?" He said, "But the angels were not ashamed when they said that they have no knowledge except what Allâh taught them."

"We have no knowledge except what You have taught us." (Qur'ân 2:32)

Many learned people have said that one should learn to say the phrase: 'I do not know.' It has been said: "If you say: 'I do not know,' they will teach you until you do know; and if you say: 'I do know,' then they will ask you until you do not know!"

'Uqbah bin Muslim said that he was a companion of Ibn 'Umar ﷺ for thirty-four months and he was often asked questions regarding Islamic issues to which he would say, "I do not know." Sa'eed bin Musayyib in giving a *Fatwa* (Islamic ruling) would almost always follow up his Islamic ruling with the utterance: "O Allâh, keep me safe and keep others safe from me (referring to any errors that might have resulted from his ruling)."

And Imam Shafi'i was asked about an Islamic issue and he remained silent and it was said to him, "Will you not reply?" He answered, "Not until I know whether virtue is in my silence or in my giving a reply."

Ibn Abi Layla said that he met one hundred and twenty

from the *Ansar* (inhabitants of Al-Madinah who welcomed those who migrated from Makkah to Al-Madinah). When a question was put forth to one of them, he would refer it to another (from the *Ansar*) who would in turn refer it to another until finally the question returned to the first of them. This illustrates the humility and reluctance they felt in issuing a ruling for fear of not having complete knowledge. Also, if anyone of them were to relate a *Hadith* or issue a ruling or respond to a question, he would always prefer that it was his brother making it instead of him.

Abul-Husain Al-Azdi said of people that gave rulings that if a similar issue was presented to 'Umar bin Khattab ﷺ during the time of the Companions, he would have gathered the participants of the people of the Battle of Badr and sought counsel from them. In contrast to these times, such was the weight and importance given to making rulings or replying to Islamic issues.

Qasim bin Muhammad was asked about a certain issue and he replied, "Indeed I am not too familiar concerning this matter." And the one who questioned said, "Indeed, I have come to you and I do not know anyone other than you." Qasim replied, "Do not look at the length of my beard or the vast number of people that surround me. By Allâh, I am not learned in this issue." He continued, "By Allâh, it is more beloved to me that Allâh cuts my tongue than for me to speak concerning that of which I have no knowledge thereof."

Salman wrote to Abud-Darda' once (after the migration) stating: "I've heard that you have taken it upon yourself to serve others as a doctor. Beware of being from those who claim to have a skill, but in actuality end up harming others with their lack of knowledge or understanding."

The Firsts

The first to use chemistry to produce medicines were the Muslims. It was Razi who first used the salts in minerals (magnesium, zinc, iron) for medical purposes.

Ibn Zayyat, a famous Muslim geographer, who died in the year 1198, was the first to outline a map of America. This map was discovered in 1952, in the Escroyal Library in Madrid, after which a professor at Barcelona University, Dr. Khawan Khirtith, authenticated it.

The first female martyr in Islam was Sumaiyyah bint Khayyat, the mother of 'Ammar bin Yasir, the eminent Companion of the Prophet.

The first and only one to be born inside the Holy Ka'bah was Hakim bin Hizam Al-Azdi.

The first battle that took place between the Muslims and the Romans was the Battle of Mu'tah, in the year 8 H.

The first to mint coins (dirhams and dinars) was the Umawi Caliph Abdul-Malik bin Marwan.

The first naval victory that Muslims achieved was Dhat As-Sawari in the year 34 H. Abdullah bin Abi Sarh led the Muslim navy. This took place on the shores of Lycia during the days of Caliph Uthman bin Affan. The Byzantine fleet, led by Emperor Constantine II was defeated.

The first caliph to order books of other languages to be translated into Arabic was Abu Ja'far Al-Mansur.

The first selfless sacrifice in Islam was of 'Ali bin Abi Talib, for he volunteered to sleep in place of the Prophet ﷺ in his bed on the night of the migration to Al-Madinah.

The Angel of Death

It is related that a young, pious man from the Children of Israel used to sit with Sulaiman عليه السلام and attend his gatherings. During one of these sessions, the Angel of Death entered upon them. Upon seeing the angel, the young man's face turned yellow and he trembled with fear and uttered,

> "O Prophet of Allâh, I am afraid of this man, so order the wind to take me to the people of India."

The Prophet Sulaiman did so. Shortly thereafter, the Angel of Death came to the Prophet in amazement. Sulaiman asked the angel why he was so bewildered and he replied that he had been ordered that day to take the soul of a young man that was in Sulaiman's company, but that it was to be taken while he was in the land of India. He continued to explain that he was surprised to find him in Sulaiman's gathering though his soul was to be taken in India. Sulaiman explained that upon seeing the Angel of Death, the young man became agitated and wanted the wind to carry him away to India.

Similarly, Hasan said that no day passes without the Angel of Death looking upon people's faces, studying them five times, and those he finds engaged in merriment or committing sin, he exclaims disapprovingly: "Poor, pitiable slave who is heedless of what is intended for him (death). Do as you please, for indeed I have for you a wink (of the eye) by which I will cut off your aorta."

The Soul of the Son of Adam

Ibn Qayyim ﷺ wrote in his highly esteemed book, *Al Fawa'id*: "How perfect is Allâh! In the soul of man is the pride of *Iblis,* the jealousy of Qabil, the insolence of the people of 'Ad, the tyranny of Thamud, the temerity of Namrud, the arrogance of Pharoah, the wrongdoing of Qarun, the trickeries of the people of Sabt, the rebelliousness of Al-Walid, the ignorance of Abu Jahl, and the impudence of Haman. The soul of man also has many characteristics of beasts. He has the avarice of a crow, the gluttony of a dog, the display of the peacock, the filth of the hog, the malice of the camel, the predatory nature of the lion, the venom of the snake, the frivolity of the ape, the greed of the ant, and the deception of the fox."

The rigid training of the soul exercises these conditions; however, if one allows any of these traits to linger and prevail, one then becomes akin to the ones cursed by Allâh and akin to the beasts possessing lowly characteristics. A person who allows these traits to dominate his soul is not that commodity in the contract described by Allâh (the Exalted):

> "Verily, Allâh has purchased of the believers their lives." (Qur'ân 9:111)

Such a commodity (soul) must be refined by Faith and purified by repentance and attentiveness in worship. The commodity must also be protected from defects or from being destroyed so as to allow the buyer to accept it.

Allâh's Prophet in Jail

In the book, *Ruhul-Ma'ani,* the author Al-Alusi related that Anas ﷺ said that Allâh (the Exalted) revealed to Yusuf ﷺ: "Who saved you from death or murder when your brothers intended to kill you?" He replied, "You, O my Lord." And He then said, "And who saved you from the well when they threw you in it?" Yusuf replied, "You, O my Lord." Allâh (the Exalted) then said, "And who saved you from the woman when she intended to have you?" He said, "You, O my Lord." Allâh asked, "Then why is it you forget me and turn to a son of Adam?" The Prophet replied, "O my Lord, it is a word that my tongue has spoken." Allâh (the Exalted) replied, "By My *'Izzah* and My *Jalal,* I will forsake you and leave you in prison for a number of years!"

Then who better to seek favor from than Allâh (the Exalted), the All-Mighty, the All-Knowing?

The Intelligent Questioner

It is said that a beggar went to a rich man from Khurasan and asked for help. He heard him say to his servant, "O Gold, say to Gem, to say to Jewel, to say to Sapphire, to say to this beggar that we do not have anything." The beggar raised his hands to the sky and said, "O my Lord, say to Jibril, to say to Israfil, to say to Mikail, to say 'Izrail to take the soul of this miser."

The Sufficient Answer

One year, during his caliphate, Hisham bin Abdul-Malik came for *Hajj* and requested to see someone from the Companions and he was told that their generation had passed. He further requested to see someone from the *Tabi'een,* the second generation after the Companions. So they brought to him Tawus Al-Yamani, who upon his arrival removed his shoes and placed them on the edge of the carpet. His greeting to Hisham bin Abdul-Malik was not like that one would utter to the leader of all Muslims, rather it was a simple *'Assalamu 'Alaik'* (peace be upon you). Also according to normal custom of showing reverence and honor, he did not call the Caliph according to his relation to his son or daughter - i.e., by saying, for instance, Abu Muhammad or Abu Fatimah. He continued by asking, "O Hisham, how are you?" Upon hearing this, the Caliph became irritated. He stated, "O Tawus, why would you behave in such a manner?" Tawus replied, "What have I done?" The Caliph referred to Tawus' removal of the shoes on the carpet, and to his inappropriate and irreverent greeting. Finally Tawus had not ascribed his name to his son's, but rather insolently addressed him simply as Hisham!

Tawus said, "As for removing my shoes, that is a practice I maintain five times a day before praying to my Lord and He does not mind. As for my not addressing you as Leader of all Believers, it is my understanding that not all the believers are pleased with you as a caliph and I dislike lying. Finally, I did not ascribe you to your son, rather I simply addressed you as Hisham because Allâh spoke to his beloved Prophets in the Qur'ân as 'O Dawud', 'O Yahya' and 'O Musa', and he referred to His enemies in the manner of ascribing them to their sons, i.e., "Perish the two hands of Abu Lahab."

The Sermons of the Wise

'Ali bin Abi Talib ﷺ said, "I advise you with five... None of you should hope except from His Lord and none of you should fear except his sin, and none should be shy (when faced with a question) to reply humbly with 'I do not know.' And none should hesitate to acquaint themselves with the matter that they are ignorant about. One should know that patience to *Iman* is like the head to a body: if the head is cut off, the body perishes as well. Also whoever desires richness without having wealth and abundance and without having a large clan, then let him turn from the depravity of sin to the honor of serving Allâh."

Hasan said, "Whoever fears Allâh, He will make all things fear him. And whoever fears people, Allâh will make him fear everything."

Each Person spends from that which He has

Al-Masih bin Maryam ﷺ passed by a gathering of Jews who spoke evil words to him to which he responded with kindness. It was said to him, "Why do you reply to their evil with good?" And he answered, "Each person spends from that which he has."

Do not hasten to make a Ruling

Imam Sha'bi ﷺ said, "I was sitting with Shuraih, a famous judge, when a woman came to us crying profusely and complaining about her absent husband. I exclaimed to Shuraih that I saw her as one who was wronged and whose rights have been deprived from her." The judge replied to Imam Sha'bi, "What brings you to this conclusion?" Imam Sha'bi then said that the abundance of her tears indicated that she had been wronged. Shuraih, in his wisdom stated, "Do not rule except after the matter has become clear for indeed the brothers of Yusuf ﷺ came to their father crying when in fact they were the ones who were the wrongdoers."

Five Matters

The Prophet ﷺ said: "I was given five matters that no other Prophet before me was given. The first is that I was given victory with terror (i.e., people felt fear and terror) equivalent to the distance it would take one to travel in a month (that is how widespread the terror and awe had become). Secondly, the entire earth has been made a mosque for me and its soil is pure. Thirdly, the spoils of war have been made lawful to me. Next, I have been given intercession, and finally, each Prophet before me was sent specifically to a certain people, while I was sent to all of mankind." (*Sahih Bukhari*)

Competing to attain Virtue

It is related that there occurred between Husain bin 'Ali bin Abi Talib ﷺ and his brother Muhammad bin Al-Hanafiyyah some differences (disagreement) and they both parted, one angry with the other. Muhammad reached his home, took out a scroll and wrote:

"In the Name of Allâh,
the Most Gracious, the Most Merciful.

From Muhammad to his brother Husain:

Indeed, you have honor that is unattainable for me and superiority that I can never know. Upon receiving this scroll, wear your robe and shoes, come to me and be pleased with me. Be aware of allowing me to precede you to that virtue which you are more worthy of. And upon you is peace."

When Husain ﷺ read the letter, he wore his robe and shoes, met his brother and made peace with him. From this we can learn that one should initiate attaining virtue and hasten to seek conciliation with the one that he differs with.

The Manager at the Office

In a book written by Raghib Al-Isfahani, Maimun bin Mehran said that he was with the Caliph 'Umar bin 'Abdul-'Aziz ﷺ, who asked his guard at the door, "Who is at the door?" The guard replied that it is a man who claims to be the son of Bilal, the one who called the prayers for the Messenger ﷺ. The Caliph permitted him to enter and asked him to relate something of the Prophet. Ibn Bilal said that his father related to him that he had heard the Prophet ﷺ say: "Whoever is given authority in a matter that is related to the people and then creates a barrier (referring to the guard) between him and them, Allâh will place a barrier in front of him on the Day of Judgement." 'Umar quickly asked the guard to leave his post and return to his home. No one ever saw a guard at 'Umar's door again. He stated that there couldn't be anything more unfavorable to the leadership of a people than the harshness of guards and the inaccessibility of the rulers themselves. The wicked acts of the citizens can only become more widespread in the land, knowing that a ruler is difficult to gain access to. It has been said that a leader prevents people from speaking to him either because of the evil that is in him or from sheer stinginess.

A Good Deed that is not accepted

Asma'i related: "I was with a man from the inhabitants of Sham (Syria) and was attempting to appease him in a certain manner when a vendor with a bucketful of pomegranates passed by. To my surprise, my companion who was of the noble aristocrats of Sham quickly snatched a pomegranate and slipped it into his sleeve. I could not believe what my eyes had witnessed, until we happened upon a beggar. This man from Sham retrieved the hidden pomegranate from his sleeve and handed it to the beggar. I questioned him about this strange action." He replied, "Do you not understand that taking the pomegranate was one evil deed and giving it to the beggar equated to ten good deeds?" Asma'i responded,

> "Do you not know that the taking of it was an evil action and the good of giving it was not accepted of you because it was *Haram* (forbidden)."

True Bravery

Thabit Al-Bunani related from Ibn Abi Layla that Ibn Umm Maktum, who was blind, said,

> "O my Lord, reveal to me my excuse (for not participating in *Jihad*)." And then this Verse was revealed:
>
> "Except those who are disabled (by injury or are blind or lame, etc." (Qur'ân 4:95)

He would participate in battles later on in his life and say, "Give me the banner, for I am blind and will not be able to flee, and make me stand between two rows."

Each one of us has a duty to Allâh and a role that befits him – and we must remember that He (the Exalted) alone is worthy to be served.

Hammad bin Salamah said that Thabit informed him that Sala and his son participated in a battle. He said to his son,

> "O my son, go forth and fight and when I think of you as gone, I will seek my reward from Allâh." His son did so and was martyred. Sala, too, went forth in the battle and was martyred. Upon hearing this, many women gathered around Sala's wife, Mu'adhah, who said to them, "Welcome to all of you if you have come to congratulate me, but if you have come with any other intention, then return from whence you came."

A Most Valiant Effort!

Abu Dujanah, a well-known Ansari Companion was a brave fighter. In the battle of Uhud he fount so courageously that the Prophet ﷺ awarded him his sword. He used to wear a red band around his head before the war, and that was the sign that he has decided to fight until his death.

After the death of the Prophet ﷺ, during the caliphate of Abu Bakr As-Siddiq رضي الله عنه, Abu Dujanah went out as a soldier in the huge Muslim army that went forth to confront the army of the apostates, who were gathered under Musailimah the Liar. Abu Dujanah displayed the same bravery he possessed as he fought under the leadership of Prophet Muhammad ﷺ. When the Muslims were not able to penetrate a fortress occupied by the apostates, Abu Dujanah requested that his companions help him over the wall of the fortress so that he may open the door from within. His companions expressed their fear, for he would be alone amongst the enemy. Abu Dujanah became angry and insisted that they carry out his request. So they did. Despite a broken ankle, Abu Dujanah bravely fought his way to the door, let the Muslims in, and continued his battle against the apostates. He was finally overcome and fell as a distinguished and honored martyr in the Battle of Yamamah (Yamamah is in Saudi Arabia near Riyadh city).

How Arthur Alison became a Muslim

Some newspapers related the account of how Professor Arthur Alison, Head of the Electrical and Electronic Engineering Department of the University of London, accepted Islam. He participated in the First Islamic International Conference on the Medical Inimitability in the Qur'ân, it was held in Cairo in September, 1985. As one of the speakers of the conference, he presented a paper on spiritual and psychological methods of therapy in light of the Noble Qur'ân. He presented another paper on sleep and death in the light of the Noble Verse:

> "It is Allâh Who takes away the souls at the time of their death, and those that die not during their sleep. He keeps those (souls) for which He has ordained death and sends the rest for a term appointed." (Qur'ân 39:42)

After presenting his lectures, Professor Alison attended lectures presented by other speakers, which mainly dealt with the many miracles of the Noble Qur'ân; he was impressed with the religion of Islam - which he found to be a religion of knowledge and enlightenment. He began to ask the other attendees many questions about Islam, and he became more and more certain that Islam is the religion of truth and is the final religion revealed to mankind. It didn't take long before he openly announced on television that Islam is the true religion and the religion that is innately accepted by the hearts of men.

Professor Alison took a shower (which one takes before entering the fold of Islam) and then pronounced the testimony of Faith, speaking in the clear and lucid tones of the believer: "None has the right to be worshiped but Allâh, and Muhammad is the Messenger of Allâh."

The Professor said, "If the scholars of the West understood Islam, they would have entered into the fold of Islam as I did. I found that the disparity between Islam and other religions or creeds that I had hitherto studied was great indeed: Islam never contradicts knowledge and the sound mind, so I believe with certainty that it is the religion that is revealed from Allâh, the One."

The 'Uthmani Ruler and the Old Woman

It has been related that an old woman entered the hall of the ruler Sulaiman Al-Qanooni, complaining to him about his army that stole her livestock while she was sleeping in her house. The ruler said to her reproachfully, "You should have stayed up and taken care of your livestock!" She glared at him and quickly responded, "I thought that you were awake, watching over us, my leader, and so I slept with a peaceful mind." The ruler said, "The truth is with you!"

Jawaiyu and His Journey to Guidance

He is an architect from Ghana who embraced Islam, and this is his story:

Jawaiyu grew up in a fanatical Christian family, but from a very young age he was impressed with the manners and behavior of his Muslim neighbors. He states that from the time he was a child, he had strong leanings toward Islam; he would stealthily observe the behavior his neighbors when his parents weren't looking. He would notice how his neighbors would take care of their appearance before going to pray, and he was impressed with the elevated manner in which they dealt with each other. He once said, "Brotherhood, love and cooperation - I found the culmination of these qualities in my Muslim neighbors. We were blessed with their care, generosity and kindness - which to them are known as neighborly rights - even though we weren't Muslims."

His desire to be one of them increased through time, though he had to hide that inclination for a long time because of the severity of his parents. And though he outwardly with them, he inwardly rebelled more and more as the days went by.

After graduating, Juwaiyu found employment in a large company that sent him to one of their branches in Niger. Since the majority of Niger's inhabitants were Muslim, he didn't feel as if he were a foreigner, especially because of the wonderful treatment that he received from his hosts;

so this was the second picture of Islamic hospitality that Juwaiyu saw in his life.

The inner rebelliousness of Juwaiyu continued to increase, and he began to ask himself whether Islam was its cause. And he found comfort as soon as he finally decided to free himself from the shackles of his ignorance and embrace the religion of light, guidance and success. Muhammad Juwaiyu later said that during that period he saw a dream, in which he was performing the rites of *Hajj* and visiting the Mosque of the Prophet, and with him were his wife, his son and his youngest brother. Suddenly, as he was trying to make his way through the crowd of pilgrims, someone began to clear a path for him, and so he led his son, his brother and his wife through the opening that was made for him.

At that point he had still not embraced Islam, but he hurried to meet with Muslim scholars, hoping to ascertain from them the meaning of his dream. They informed him that his dream gave glad tidings of him accepting Islam. After a few days, he saw another dream in which he saw a large mosque. In it, he saw two men praying, whom he did not know. He again went to the scholars, who gave him the same answer as they did the previous time. Before announcing his acceptance of Islam, he moved to the capital city of Ghana, where he was the guest of a Muslim businessman, Al-Haj Karamba, who was a most generous host. On the second day of his sojourn in the capital city, he openly proclaimed his acceptance of Islam in the mosque.

Muhammad Juwaiyo said, "I was not able to hold back

tears of joy; a number of Muslims surrounded me, each waiting his turn to congratulate me. I became even happier when Al-Haj Karamba presented me with a plane ticket for the holy lands, so that I could fulfill my dream. And all praise is for Allâh, through Whose blessings good deeds are accomplished."

A Lost Journey turns into One of Faith

Muhammad Ayyub, a non-Muslim from France, traveled to Pakistan, hoping to acquire a certain kind of poison that he found difficult to acquire in his home country. At the young age of 18 he went out to search for slow death poison - better known to be classified under drugs. On the individual level, his is a common example of what has resulted from turning away from the laws of Allâh; each time a new hallucinatory drug is discovered, the more desperate and miserable becomes the state of the individual. For the confused soul, one dosage leads to two, which leads to three... And that is why the young man of this narrative decided to make his journey.

Throughout the flight, he was dreaming of smoking drugs and the effect that would have on making him forget his miserable personal situation. Yet matters were decreed differently from what the young man had intended: circumstances were to lead him to a pure and purposeful existence.

His new life, however, was not to be precipitated by a

lecture or sermon; rather what changed his life was living and mixing with Muslims. Although people in Pakistan are poor in the material sense, a sense of spiritual calmness pervades through almost each one of them. Because of that, he discerned the fundamental difference between his society and the Muslim one. From those simple folk, he learned the difference between a man with a purpose and a man who is nothing more than an automaton or a man who thinks only of himself and material gain. Muhammad witnessed nobility and character as well as the spirit of brotherhood.

When he returned to France, the direction of his search changed: he began to search for Islamic books, either written in French or translated into it. He found two books, one explaining the meanings of the Noble Qur'ân and the other relating the Prophet's biography. Slowly, his priorities and way of thinking changed; after two years passed, he decided to make a return trip to Pakistan. And there, in 1970, he proclaimed his entry into the fold of Islam, and he began studies in an Islamic University in Karachi. He remained there as a student for eight years, learning the various sciences of Islam. He became proficient in three new languages - Arabic, Urdu and Persian. When he returned to France, he began inviting others to the truth, and today he is still very active in the field of propagating Islam to others.

The Leper, the Baldheaded Man and the Blind Man

Both Bukhari and Muslim relate in their compilations from Abu Hurairah ﵁ that he heard Allâh's Messenger ﷺ say:

Indeed there were three from the Children of Israel - the leper, the baldheaded man and the blind man - and Allâh (the Exalted) decided to test them, so he sent to them an angel, who went first to the leper, and said, "What is most beloved to you?" He said, "Good color and good skin, for the people are disgusted by me." The angel touched over him and his affliction went away: he was now given good color and good skin. The angel asked, "And what wealth is most beloved to you?" He said, "Camels," or he said, "Cows." (He wasn't sure, either it was the leper or the baldheaded man who said, camels, while it was the other who said cows.) He was given a pregnant camel, and the angel said, "May you be blessed with it."

He then went to the baldheaded man and said, "What is most beloved to you?" He said, "Good hair and wish to be cured of this disease; indeed people are repelled by me." Then the angel touched over him; his affliction went away, and he was given good hair. The angel then asked, "And what wealth is most beloved to you?" He said, "Cows." The angel gave him a pregnant cow and said, "May you be blessed with it."

He then went to the blind man and said, "What is most beloved to you?" He said, "For Allâh to return to me my sight, so that with it I can see people." Then the angel touched over him and Allâh returned to him his sight. The angel asked, "And what wealth is most beloved to you?" He said, "Sheep." So he gave him one pregnant sheep and the livestock of each one of them reproduced, so that the first had a valley full of camels, while the second had a valley full of cows, and the third had a valley full of sheep.

Then the angel came to the leper in the shape of a man, and said, "I am a poor man who has run out of means during his travel. Today, I will not find that which I need to continue my travel except through Allâh and then through you. I ask you by the One Who has given you good color and good skin and wealth, to give me one camel upon which I may complete my journey." He said, "Indeed the rights (of others upon me) are many (i.e., I have a large family for whom I must provide)." The angel said to him, "It seems that I know you; were you not a leper, who people found to be repulsive? A poor man, and Allâh gave you?" He said, "Indeed, I have inherited from my forebears." He said, "If you are lying, then may Allâh change you back to your previous state."

He then went to the baldheaded man, again in the guise of a man, and said the same words that he said to the leper. The baldheaded man responded in the same manner that the leper did. The angel said, "If you are lying, then may Allâh change you back to your previous state."

He then went to the blind man, yet again in the shape of a man, and said, "I am a poor man who is cut off from his journey. Today, I have no means for reaching my destination except through Allâh and then through you.

I ask you by the One Who has returned to you your sight, to give me one sheep with which I may complete my journey." He said, "Indeed I was blind and Allâh returned to me my sight, poor and he made me rich, so take whatever you desire, for by Allâh I will not hold back anything from you today that you take for Allâh." The angel said, "Keep your wealth, for indeed you were only tested; indeed Allâh is pleased with you and is angry with your two companions." (*Sahih Bukhari* and *Sahih Muslim*)

A Wife can be a Source of Rewards and Gains

Ibn Mas'ud related that the Prophet said: "When a man spends on his family seeking the reward for that from Allâh, then it is charity on his behalf." (*Sahih Bukhari*)

Sa'd bin Abi Waqqas related that Allâh's Messenger said, "Indeed, whenever you spend on an expenditure, seeking Allâh's Countenance for doing so, you will be rewarded for it - even for what (i.e., the food) you put in the mouth of your wife." (*Sahih Bukhari*)

Abu Dharr related that Allâh's Messenger said, "In the private part of each one of you there is charity." The Companions asked, "O Messenger of Allâh, does one of us fulfill his desire and still get rewarded?" He said, "Yes, do you not see that if one of you were to use it for *Haram* - there would have been a sin upon him? And similar is the case of the one who uses it for *Halal* (purposes) - he has his reward." (*Sahih Muslim*)

Sudden Death

There have been many incidents in which people suddenly die in circumstances that portend evil; such cases have often been witnessed by the righteous, whose Faith increased in consequence, thus making them more prepared for the Hereafter. For example, Ibn Rajab related from 'Abdul-'Aziz bin Abi Rawwad, who said,

> "I was with a man who was dying and who was being prompted to say the *Shahadah*: None has the right to be worshiped but Allâh. His last words were, 'He is a disbeliever by what you say.' I asked about him and found out that he was an alcoholic."

'Abdul-'Aziz said,

> "Protect yourselves from sins, for it were sins that were his ruin."

Qurtubi related from Rabi' bin Sabrah bin Ma'bad Al-Juhani, a pious person from Basrah:

> "I met people from Sham, who reported that it was said to a man who was dying, 'Say: None has the right to be worshiped but Allâh.' And his response was, 'I drink (alcohol), so give me something to drink.'"

And Ibn Qayyim رحمه الله related in *Al-Jawab Al-Kafi*,

> "It has been said to some of them, 'Say: None has the right to be worshiped but Allâh.' They answered, 'Ahh Ahh, I am not able to say it.'"

The ill-used Cow

A mother asked her family doctor, "Why don't women of this generation find enough milk to breast-feed their children?" The doctor remained silent for a moment, and then said, "Imagine cows in the field that are constantly driven at high speeds. Each night, when they return to the barnyard, they will not be able to give forth milk; Madame, such is the state of mothers today."

Yes, such is the state of mothers today: a mother in these times leaves home in the morning just as men do, striving with all of her strength, persevering through the heat of the sun or through the cold of the winter, toiling - either of her own accord or under coercion, because at the end of the day, or at the end of the month, she needs her paycheck.

How will the woman just described be able find milk in her breasts in order to suckle her babies? Furthermore, how can she find time to look after her children, to bestow upon them her love, to give them her full attention?

And how are our children expected to be trained when their mothers are far away from them? Or to feel satisfied in that they are receiving compassion, especially when we consider that the only one to look after them is a babysitter or a nanny?

Therefore we should not be surprised when we find that the mothers of today are not giving birth, or are not raising, true men, men who aspire after the greater aims of life, men who contribute greatly to the Muslim nation. Today, we can only read about such men in books of history.

The Jealous King

Imam Sha'bi ﷺ, a distinguished scholar from the early generations of Islam, related the following incident:

'Abdul-Malik bin Marwan once sent me to the king of Rome. When I reached him, he asked me a number of questions, and I answered each one of them. In general, emissaries would not stay with him for a long time; however, in my case, he detained me for a number of days, until I myself requested permission to leave. When I determined to leave, he said to me, "Are you of the household of your king?" I said, "No, I am simply a common man from among the Muslims." He whispered something to (one of his guards), and then a card was given to me. He said, "When you hand over the letters you have with you to your king, give him this card as well." When I returned home, I handed over many letters to 'Abdul-Malik but I forgot to give him the card. Only at a later time did I remember, and I hastened to give it to him. After reading it, he said to me, "Did he say anything to you before giving you this card?" I said, "Yes, he asked me: 'Are you of the household of your king?' I told him no, but rather that I am simply a common man from among the Muslims." I was parting from the caliph, but when I reached the gates, I was called back to him. When I was again standing in front of him, he said, "Do you know what is on this card?" I said, "No." He said, "Read it." On it was written:

I am amazed at a people who have among them such a man, yet they have chosen another as their king!

I said to him, "By Allâh, had I known what was written on it, I would not have carried it with me! He only said this because he has not seen you." 'Abdul-Malik said, "Do you know why he really wrote it?" I said, "No." He said, "He was jealous of me for having you, so he tried to change my heart against you, hoping that I would kill you and so that the Muslims would not benefit from your knowledge." The news of what happened reached the king of Rome, who said, "He was right in knowing my intention."

A Supplication Answered

Abu 'Abdullah bin Ja'far, better known as Al-Balkhi, relates: "One day, heavy winds and torrential rains destroyed the field of a woman I knew who lived in the desert. People went to console her, and all she did was to raise her gaze to the sky and say: 'O Allâh, all hope is in You, You are the best to replace that which is lost, and in Your Hand is a replacement for what has been destroyed. So deal with us in a manner that is befitting of You, for our provision is from You, and we turn for all of our hopes to You.' Only a short time passed before a very affluent man, whom we did not know, came to us. And when we told him what had happened, he bestowed upon her 500 dinars."

Nuruddin – the Ruler – Standing before a Judge

Nuruddin Mahmud was a just and brave leader; he called people to Islam and exhorted them to attend Islamic courts. He used to say, "Before the *Shari'ah,* there is no difference between a man of status and the common man."

He became known for this statement to the extent that businessmen and men of high standing in society stopped going to courts, of course because they knew that they were now on an equal footing with others.

One day, as Nuruddin was out practicing the arts of war, he saw a man talking to another and pointing to him (i.e., to Nuruddin). He sent a guard to ask what was the matter, and he found out that the man was a messenger from the judge, who had come to inform Nuruddin that someone had a complaint about him and wanted to take the matter up before a judge. Nuruddin sent a letter to his judge, saying,

> "Deal with me as you would with any other person who comes to you for a ruling."

When he reached the judge, he stood side by side with the plaintiff, in the same manner that any other defendant would stand. We would be hard pressed in our times to imagine a ruler doing the same.

Salman's Journey to the Truth

Salman was raised in a village in the land of Faris (Persia). He lived a life of ease and comfort, for his father was extremely affluent. At the same time, the father worked hard to raise his son upon the religion of the Majus; however, Salman made friends with a people who were upon the religion of Jesus ﷺ. He took to liking their ways and their beliefs, so he asked them about the roots of their religion, and they told him that they were established in the land of Sham (Syria).

Salman's father tried to prevent him from continuing on his new path; he even locked him in the house, tied him up, and beat him. Salman managed to escape, and he went to the land of Sham. There he kept company with a Christian scholar, who was abstemious in his ways; he was constantly fasting and would frequently stand for prayer. When he was about to die, Salman asked him, "Who should I keep company with after you?" He directed him to a man in Musal, describing him as one who neither changed nor distorted the Bible. Salman remained with him until he too was about to die, when Salman asked him whom he should keep company with after him. He said, "There exists no man who is upon what I am upon except for a man in Nasibin. So, Salman went to that man and remained with him until he too was on the verge of dying. He then directed Salman to yet another man in 'Umuriyyah, and when that man was about to die, he said to Salman, "O my son, there is no one left on the face of the earth who adheres to what we are upon; however, the time is near when a Prophet will appear in the land of the Arabs. He will be sent upon the religion of Abraham and he will migrate to a land that is replete with date-palm trees, and there are signs that he is known by: he doesn't eat from charity, yet he eats from a gift, and between his shoulders is the stamp of Prophethood. Salman migrated to the land of the Arabs, but among the caravan he was traveling with were those who betrayed him and sold him to a people who then went on to sell him again to a man from the tribe of Banu Quraizah.

When Salman saw dates in Yathrib (Al-Madinah), he remembered what his final companion said when he described the place to where the Prophet was to migrate. Salman Farisi ﵁ said that when Allâh's Messenger ﷺ migrated to Yathrib:

"I was perched on the top of a date-palm tree, and it was an extremely hot day. As I was in that state and my owner was seated under that tree, a man from the Jews approached and said, 'May Allâh fight with the children of the tribe, for a man has come to them from Makkah, claiming that he is a Prophet, and they are gathered with him at Quba.' As soon as I heard what he said, I was overcome with wonder and joy, and I hurried down the tree. I demanded from him that he repeat what he said; however, my owner beat me, but during that very night I took some dates that were rightfully mine and then I went, walking to Quba. When I reached there, I asked permission to meet with Allâh's Messenger, and he gave me permission to enter. I entered to meet the Messenger and his words had a wonderful effect on my heart."

Salman addressed Allâh's Messenger ﷺ, saying, "Indeed it has reached me about you that you are a righteous man and with you are needy Companions; this is something that was with me, which was intended for charity." Allâh's Messenger ﷺ proffered what was given to him to his Companions, yet he ate nothing from it. Salman spoke to himself: "This is one of the signs," and love for the Prophet began to creep into his heart.

When the Messenger ﷺ moved from Quba to Al-Madinah, Salman came to him one more time, and again he brought dates with him. He said, "This is a gift for you." The Prophet ﷺ ate from it and his Companions ate from it as well. Salman said to himself: "And this is the second."

Salman later went to Allâh's Messenger ﷺ for a third time. When he went to him this time, Allâh's Messenger ﷺ was burying one of his Companions in Al-Baqi' graveyard. He was standing at the edge of the grave, remembering Allâh and supplicating. He was wearing two garments, through which Salman was trying to gain a peak at his back. When he prolonged his stare, the Messenger ﷺ knew his purpose and raised his garments over his back. Salman saw the stamp of Prophethood and knew that the promised Prophet of Allâh was standing in front of him. He went to the Messenger ﷺ, both kissing him and crying at the same time. He, of course, embraced Islam immediately. The Prophet ﷺ asked him to relate his story, and after Salman related it, the Prophet ﷺ was so well-pleased with it that he asked him to relate it to his Companions as well.

He was True to Allâh and so Allâh was True to Him

Shaddad bin Al-Had related that an Arab came to the Prophet, believed in him and followed him. He said to the Prophet ﷺ, "I will migrate with you." And the Prophet ﷺ appointed some of his Companions to take care of him. Later on, after a battle, the Prophet ﷺ distributed the spoils of war, and he allotted a share for that very man. Others were charged with the trust of handing over his share to him and when they tried to give it to him, he said, "What is this?" They said, "A share that the Prophet has allotted for you." He took it, went to the Prophet ﷺ, and said, "What is this?" He said, "This is your share which I have allotted to you." He said, "It is not for this that I have followed you; rather I have followed you so that I may be struck here - and he pointed to his throat - with an arrow, and then die, and then am made to enter Paradise." The Prophet ﷺ said, "If you are true to Allâh, He will be true to you." After a short time passed, the Muslims went to fight the enemy. A man was carried from the battleground to the Prophet; he was struck with an arrow in his throat. The Prophet ﷺ said, "Is this he?" His Companions said, "Yes." He said, "He was true to Allâh, and so Allâh was true to him." The Prophet ﷺ then shrouded him in his garment and prayed over him. This was heard from his prayer: "O Allâh, this is Your slave; on Your path did he migrate, and he was killed a martyr, and I am a witness to that."

Qarun

Ibn Abi Hatim related from Qatadah, and 'Abd bin Humaid related from Malik bin Dinar that Qarun was every day swallowed by the earth the length of his height. 'Abd bin Humaid related from 'Ikrimah that when Qarun was being swallowed, Musa ﷺ was near him, and the former said, "O Musa, invoke your Lord to have mercy on me." Musa did not answer him, and Qarun was completely swallowed by the earth. Then Allâh (the Exalted) revealed to Musa,: "He sought help from you, but you didn't help him. By My Honor and Might, had he said, 'My Lord,' I would have had mercy on him."

Ahmad related in *Az-Zuhd* from 'Aun bin 'Abdullah Al-Qari - a governor of 'Umar bin 'Abdul-'Aziz - the following narration that had reached him: Indeed Allâh (the Exalted) ordered the earth to obey Musa regarding Qarun. When Musa met him, he said to the earth, "Obey me," and it swallowed Qarun until his knees. He repeated, "Obey me," and it swallowed him completely, so that he was hidden from sight. Allâh (the Exalted) revealed to him: "O Musa, how severe is your heart. By My Honor and Might, had he sought help from Me, I would have aided him." Musa said, "My Lord, it was my anger for You that made me do as I did."

And Who is the Fool?

A man of great wealth and status built for himself a house, adjacent to which was a small and shabby house, not of much worth, which was owned by an old woman. Her rich neighbor needed her house in order to embark upon an expansion project that he had in mind, and so he offered her an exorbitant amount of money in order to purchase her house, but she refused to sell it.

It was said to her that the judge would freeze her assets because of her foolish persistence in not taking a large amount of wealth, especially considering the fact that her house was worth very little in the first place.

She said, "And why does the judge not freeze the assets of the one who wants to spend and waste such a large amount of money for a house of so little worth?" She refused to sell her house and she was able to silence everyone by the strength of her argument.

True Generosity

Allâh's Messenger ﷺ said, "Spend, O Bilal, and do not fear from the Owner of the Throne to be given little." Mamun said to Muhammad bin 'Ibad Al-Mahlabi, "You spend extravagantly." He answered, "To abstain from being generous is tantamount to having bad thoughts about the One Who is worshiped." Allâh (the Exalted) says:

> "And whatsoever you spend of anything (in Allâh's cause), He will replace it. And He is the Best of providers." (Qur'ân 34:39)

Asma' bint Yazid Al-Ansariyah

Muslim bin Asad related from Asma' that she went to the Prophet ﷺ while he was seated with his Companions. She said, "...I came as an emissary to you from a group of women. Indeed Allâh has sent you to both men and women, and we believe in you and in your Lord. Indeed, we women are limited and constrained, though we are the pillars of your houses, from us do you fulfill your desires and lusts, and we also carry your children. Indeed, you men have been favored over us by the congregational Friday prayer and by all other congregational prayers, by visiting the sick, by attending funeral prayers, by performing pilgrimage after pilgrimage, and better than all of that - *Jihad* in the way of Allâh. When men go out to perform *Hajj, 'Umrah,* or *Jihad,* we protect for them their wealth, spin for them their garments, and raise for them their children. Shall we not then share with you in this recompense and reward?"

The Prophet ﷺ turned to his Companions and said, "Have you ever heard any speech of a woman that is more beautiful than this woman's questioning regarding the affair of her religion?" They said, "O Messenger of Allâh, we never thought that a woman should be guided to something similar to this." The Prophet ﷺ turned to her and said, "Understand this, O woman, and teach this to those women whom you left behind: For a woman to be a good spouse to her husband, for her to seek his pleasure, for her to follow and cooperate with him, is equal to all of that (i.e., all of the rewards that men get for their toils or for the deeds mentioned above)."

She left and was making *Tahleel* (i.e., she was testifying: None has the right to be worshiped but Allâh).

The Kind of Tricks Used by the Generous Ones

Mu'awiyah sent many gifts of jewelry, perfume, and dishes made of gold and silver to 'Ubaidullah bin 'Abbas, and he sent them with his guard. When the guard delivered the gifts, he continued to stare at them for a long time before leaving. 'Ubaidullah asked, "Is there anything you desire from this?" He said, "Yes, by Allâh, there mingles in my soul a desire for these things that which was in the soul of Ya'qub for Yusuf!" 'Ubaidullah laughed and said, "Then all of this is yours!"

The guard said, "I fear that this news will reach Mu'awiyah, and then he will be angry." 'Ubaidullah said, "Stamp it with your own seal, then give it to the treasurer, and he will bring it to you in the night." The guard said, "By Allâh, indeed this is a trick befitting of the generous ones; in fact, it even surpasses exceptional levels of generosity. I hope not to die until I see you in his place – i.e., in the place of the ruler." 'Ubaidullah thought that he was being trapped, and he said, "Leave such speech; I am from a people who fulfill their promises and who do not go contrary to their agreements."

Allâh was indeed Pleased with Their Deed!

A man went to the Prophet ﷺ and said, "O Messenger of Allâh! Indeed I am extremely hungry." The Prophet ﷺ sent a message to one of his wives, asking, "Do you have any food with you?" She said, "No, by the One Who has sent you with the truth, all I have with me is water!" He then sent messages to all of his wives, asking the same question, and the answer of each one of them was, "No, by the One Who has sent you with the truth, all we have with us is water." Allâh's Messenger ﷺ said to his Companions: "Who will be a host tonight, may Allâh have mercy on him?" A man from the Helpers (the *Ansar*) called Abu Talhah رضي الله عنه stood and said, "I, O Messenger of Allâh."

He went to his house and asked his wife, "Do you have any food with you?" She said, "All I have with me is a little bit of food for our children." He said, "Give excuses to them, and then try to make them go to sleep! And when our guest comes, make him think we are also eating as he puts his hand forward to eat. Then go to the lamp and pretend that you are fixing it, but instead put it out. And give him the impression that we are eating, so that our guest eats and fills himself."

She did what her husband asked her to do: she made her children sleep hungry, she placed the food before the guest, she stood to turn the lamp off - but she was giving the impression of simply adjusting the lamp. Then she sat with her husband and with the guest for the meal. They sat idle as the guest ate.

On the following day, he went to Allâh's Messenger ﷺ, who said to him: "Tonight Allâh laughed, or wondered at your action." And then the following Verse was revealed:

> "And give them preference over themselves, even though they were in need of that." (Qur'ân 59:9)

The Silent Charity

Muhammad bin 'Isa related that a young man would often go to 'Abdullah bin Mubarak; he studied under him, carried out certain errands for him, and would listen to him relate *Hadith* narrations. One day, 'Abdullah went to the city where the young man was living, and when he didn't find him he asked after him. He was told that the young man was imprisoned for a loan that he could not repay. 'Abdullah said, "And how much does he owe?" He was told that the young man owed 10,000 dirhams. 'Abdullah searched out for the creditor, and when he found him, he gave him 10,000 dirhams, but he made the man take an oath that he wouldn't inform anyone as long as he (i.e., 'Abdullah) was alive that he gave him the money.

When the young man was released from prison, it was said to him, "Abdullah bin Mubarak was here and was asking after you, but he has already left." The young man hurried off in search for him and when he found him, 'Abdullah asked, "Young man, where were you? I could not find you." He said, "Yes, I was imprisoned because of a debt that I could not pay." He said, "Then how were you released?" He said, "A man came and paid my debt for me, yet I do not know who he is." 'Abdullah said, "Young man, praise Allâh for the blessing of having your debt repaid." And the creditor never informed anyone of what really happened until after 'Abdullah died.

It has been related that Abu Ja'far Al-Hadhdha said, "I heard Ibn 'Uyainah say: If your inner reality is the same as your outward appearance and deeds, then that is uprightness; if your inner reality is better than your outward appearance, then that is superiority; and if your outward appearance is better than your inner reality, then that is wrongdoing."

The Wife of the Caliph Nurses a Pregnant Woman

As was his custom, 'Umar bin Khattab ﷺ, the Leader of the Believers, went out at night to look after the needs of the people and to make sure that everyone was safe. As he passed by an open area in Al-Madinah, he heard the moans of a woman coming out from a small and shabby house, at the door of which was a man seated. 'Umar greeted him and asked him how he was. The man said that he was from the desert and had come, seeking to reap some generosity from the Leader of the Believers. 'Umar asked him about the woman and the moaning noises, and the man, not knowing that he was speaking to the Leader of the Believers, said, "Go away, may Allâh have mercy on you, and do not ask about that which does not concern you."

However, 'Umar persisted in asking the same question, offering to help if he could. And so the man informed him, "Indeed she is my wife, who is about to give birth, yet there is no one here to help her." 'Umar left the man, returned to his house in a hurry, entered, and said to his wife, Umm Kulthum ﷺ, "Will you take reward that Allâh has brought to you?" She said, "And what is that goodness and reward, O 'Umar?"

No sooner did he inform her of what happened than she stood and took all that she needed to help the woman deliver her baby and all that the newborn would need as well. Meanwhile, the Leader of the Believers took a pot and with it some fat and grains. He and his wife hurried off together until they reached the same shabby house. While Umm Kulthum went in to help the pregnant woman, the Leader of the Believers remained outside with the husband, and cooked the food that he brought with him.

From inside the house, Umm Kulthum called out, "O Leader of the Believers, give glad tidings to your companion that Allâh has provided him with a young boy." The man was amazed to find out that it was the Leader of the Believers who was seated with him and who was cooking food with him; and the wife was shocked to learn that it was the wife of the Leader of the Believers who came to meet her and help her in her shabby house.

Giving Charity to One's Husband

Zainab Ath-Thaqafiyah ﷺ, the wife of 'Abdullah bin Mas'ud ﷺ, related that Allâh's Messenger ﷺ said: "Give charity, O community of women, even if it is from your jewelry that you give."

She returned to 'Abdullah bin Mas'ud and said, "You are a man who is poor, and indeed Allâh's Messenger ordered us to give charity, so go to him and ask whether it is considered charity for me (to give you). Otherwise I will give it to others." 'Abdullah said, "You yourself ask Allâh's Messenger (about it)."

She went, and found a woman from the Helpers (*Ansar*) waiting at the door of Allâh's Messenger ﷺ, she had came also for a similar purpose. People were in awe of Allâh's Messenger ﷺ and so when Bilal ﷺ came out to them, they said to him: "Go to the Messenger of Allâh and inform him that two women are at the door, asking whether they will be rewarded for charity that they give to their husbands and to orphans that are living with them in their homes? But do not inform him of who we are."

Bilal went in to meet Allâh's Messenger ﷺ and he asked him their question. Allâh's Messenger ﷺ said, "Who are they?" He said, "A woman from the *Ansar* and Zainab." Allâh's Messenger ﷺ said, "Which Zainab?" He said, "The wife of 'Abdullah bin Mas'ud." Allâh's Messenger ﷺ said, "(Inform them that) they have two rewards: the reward of relationship, and the reward for charity." (*Sahih Bukhari* and *Sahih Muslim*)

A Comparison to the Generosity of Hatim

A man from the *Ansar* went to 'Abdullah bin 'Abbas ﷺ and said, "O Abu 'Abdullah, a son was born to me today, and I named him after you...but his mother has died." 'Abdullah said, "May Allâh bless you with your endowment and reward you for your tragedy." He called his agent and said, "Go immediately and purchase a young female slave for the child, so that she may suckle it, and give 2000 dinars to the father, so that he can spend it in raising his son." He then said to the man from the *Ansar*, "Return to us after some days pass, for you have come to us at a time when we have very little wealth." He answered, "Had you preceded Hatim (a man from the Arabs used as an example for generosity) by a single day, the Arabs would not be mentioning him today."

Perhaps My Brother has an Excuse

Abu Qulamah Al-Jirmi was an eminent *Tabi'i* and a distinguished Imam and jurist. He once said in a sermon: "If you hear something that you do not like about your brother, then try your best to seek out an excuse for him. And if you do not find any excuse for him, then say: perhaps my brother has an excuse that I do not know about."

A Ruler Who was Generous and easily Accessible

During the caliphate of 'Umar bin 'Abdul-'Aziz, a woman traveled from Iraq to come and meet him. When she arrived at his abode, she asked whether there was a guard to prevent people from going inside to meet him. They told her, "No, enter if you wish." The woman entered and saw Fatimah, the wife of 'Umar. She was sitting down at the time, spinning some cotton. The woman extended greetings of peace; Fatimah returned the greetings and told her to come inside.

As soon as the woman sat down, she began to look around, and was surprised to find that there was nothing of value or of importance in the house. Without realizing that she was speaking out loud, she said, "I came to build and furnish my house from this house, which I have found to be empty and barren." Fatimah said, "The emptiness and barrenness of this house allows for the construction and adornment of houses such as yours." 'Umar entered the house, gave greetings of peace, and then asked his wife about the woman. He took out a bunch of grapes, chose the best ones, and gave them to his wife, so that she could then offer them to the visitor. He then approached her and asked, "What is your need?"

She said, "I am a woman from the inhabitants of Iraq, and I have five daughters who cannot work and who have with them no material possessions. I came to you hoping that you might be willing to help them." He began to cry, took out his inkstand and papers, and wrote a letter to the governor of Iraq. He asked the woman the name of her eldest daughter, and when she told him, he wrote down an amount that was to be given to her. Upon realizing that, the woman praised Allâh (the Exalted), he then asked her the names of her second, third, and fourth daughters. The woman informed him and praised Allâh. When she realized that he had bestowed money upon all of them, she became so happy that she supplicated for him.

She left his house with the paper that she was to give to the governor of Iraq, and after a long travel, when she finally reached her home, she went to the governor to give him the piece of paper. When she gave it to him, he began to cry for a long time, and then he said, "May Allâh have mercy on the writer of this letter." She said, "Has news come to you of his death?" He said, "Yes." She screamed, but he told her not to worry, and that he was going to give the allotted portion to her in any case.

Maintaining a Balanced Lifestyle

'Ali bin Fudail related that he heard his father say to Ibn Mubarak, "You order us to seek little from this world, yet we see you trading in merchandise. Please explain how you reconcile one with the other?" He said, "O Abu 'Ali, I do so only to protect myself (from begging), to be generous to my family, and to use wealth to help me in obedience to my Lord." 'Ali said, "O Ibn Mubarak, if you achieve all of that, then your way of earning and spending are both noble indeed!"

The Truly Generous Ones

It has been related about a house from the early generations of Islam that it had in it only a single bunch of grapes. The owner of the grapes gave them to his sister, who in turn gave them to her sister, who in turn gave them to another sister, who in turn gave them to her mother, and her mother kept them safe for her husband, who gave them to his son, who was the original owner of the grapes. Such was the generosity of that house - the grapes were passed on from one to another until they finally returned to the first!

It has also been related that a group of hungry people from the early generations of Islam had with them a small amount of barbecued meat, and nine of them shared that food among themselves, while each of them said, "Give it to such and such person, for he is more deserving!" Thus would it be passed around until finally it returned to the first!

Advice for Every Ruler

Harun Rasheed requested a sermon from one of the pious scholars. He said, "O Caliph, for you to accompany a person who makes you afraid of the Hereafter is better than one who gives you safety here, only to have you face fear on the Last Day. Know that the person who reminds you of your responsibility to your flock is more sincere to you than one who comforts you with the knowledge that you are of the noble family of the Prophet and forgiven for your sins (which is not true!)." Harun Rasheed began to weep at these statements until those around him felt pity for him.

Do not scold the One Who asks of You

A story has been related about a man who one day sat with his wife to eat a barbecued chicken. A beggar then knocked on the door, and when the man went to answer it, he scolded the beggar and drove him away. It was the Will of Allâh that afterwards that same man should become poor and should be bereft of all material possessions; because of his poverty, he had to divorce his wife. She married another man, and one day she was sitting with him to eat a barbecued chicken, when someone knocked on the door. The man said to his wife, "Give this chicken to the man at the door." When she opened it, she was shocked to realize that it was her first husband. She gave him the chicken and returned, crying. Her husband asked her what was the matter, and she informed him that the man at the door was her previous husband. She then told him about the story of the beggar that her previous husband had scolded and sent away, and her husband said, "By Allâh, I was that beggar."

The Continuation of Your Deeds

Abu Hurairah ﷺ related that Allâh's Messenger ﷺ said, "When a person dies, his deeds are cut off except for three: from charity whose benefit continues, knowledge that is benefited by, and a righteous son who supplicates for him." (*Sahih Muslim*)

Make My Braids into a Bridle for a Horse that is going in the way of Allâh

After a certain battle, the Romans took some Muslim women as prisoners. It was said to Mansur bin 'Ammar, "Would that you sat in the gathering of the caliph, Harun, and exhort the people to *Jihad*." He went and exhorted the people to *Jihad*, and while he was speaking, a sealed package was thrown to him. He found written upon it: "Indeed I am an Arab woman, and news has reached me of what the Romans have done with Muslim women; then I heard you exhort people to go into battle, and so I wanted to give something from my body - my braids. I cut them off and put them in the sealed package. I ask of you to make them into a bridle for a horse that is going in the way of Allâh! Perhaps Allâh will have mercy on me because of that."

Mansur could not hold back his tears, and those around him began to cry as well. Harun Rasheed, the caliph, determined that the Muslims should go for *Jihad*, and he announced that the army should begin preparations for war. The army attacked and was able to free the prisoners, and the chaste and virtuous Muslim women were free again.

The Generosity of the Poor

'Abdullah, the nephew of Muslim bin Sa'd, said: I wanted to make *Hajj,* and before I left my uncle gave me 10,000 dirhams saying, "When you arrive at Al-Madinah, give this to the poorest household that you find over there." When I arrived at my destination, I asked the people to point me to the poorest house. I was led to a certain house, and when I knocked on the door, a woman opened it, and said, "Who are you?" I said, "I am a man from Baghdad, and I was given 10,000 dirhams, which I have to give to the inhabitants of the poorest house in Al-Madinah. You have been described thus, so take it." She said, "O 'Abdullah, the one who gave you the money stipulated that it should be the poorest household, and those who live in our neighbor are poorer than us." I left her and went to the house that she pointed out to me, and when I knocked on the door, a woman opened it, and I said to her the same words that I said to the previous woman. She said, "O 'Abdullah, we and our neighbors are at the same level of poverty, so divide the money between us and them."

The Most Difficult of Deeds

'Ali ﷺ said, "Among deeds, there are four that are most difficult to adorn oneself with: 1) Forgiveness when angry; 2) Generosity in hard times; 3) Chastity when alone; and 4) Speaking the truth to the one that fears it."

Another Case of Tremendous Generosity

'Abdullah bin Ja'far ﷺ, who was famous for his generosity, one day passed by a garden. He saw a slave gathering dates in it. He witnessed that the son of the owner came to him with two loaves of bread, after which the slave sat down to eat. A dog approached the slave, and it was wagging its tail. The slave threw one of the two loaves of bread in the direction of the dog; it came in a hurry and ate it, but it continued to wag its tail. And so the slave threw to it the second loaf of bread as well, after which he stood and continued his work!

'Abdullah bin Ja'far was so amazed at what he saw from the slave that he approached him and asked, "O young man, how much nourishment is provided to you every day?" He said, "The amount that you witnessed." He said, "Then why did you give all of it to the dog?" The slave said, "Indeed we do not live in a land that is inhabited by dogs, and so I knew that the only thing that led this dog here was hunger. That is why I preferred it to myself." 'Abdullah asked, "And what will you do for yourself today?" The slave said, "I will spend the night in hunger."

'Abdullah said, "The people reproach me for being too generous, and yet this young slave is more generous than me!" 'Abdullah bin Ja'far then went to the owner of the slave, asking to buy him. The owner asked, "And why do you wish to buy him?" He informed him of what he saw from the slave, and he told him that he wanted to buy the slave in order to free him. He also said that he wanted to buy the garden, to give it as a gift to him. The owner said, "Do you wish to do all of that for him, just because of that one deed? Indeed we see such wonderful deeds from him every day! I bear witness that he is free for the Countenance of Allâh and that the garden is a gift from me to him!"

Who is Most Generous?

Haitham bin 'Adi related that three people got into an argument beside the Ka'bah; they couldn't agree as to who was the most generous person of their era. The first claimed that it was 'Abdullah bin Ja'far; the second said it was Qais bin Sa'd; and the third said it was 'Arabah Al-Aousah. When their argument became more intense and when their voices were raised to the level of shouting, a man said to them, "Why does not each one of you go to his companion and see what he will give to him, and through that test a correct judgment can be a arrived at." The first man went to Ibn Ja'far and said, "O son of the cousin of the Messenger of Allâh, I am a traveler who has run out of resources and who has no means by which to continue his journey." At that moment, Ibn Ja'far was on his mount; he descended from it, and said, "Climb it, for it is yours, and all that is on it is yours also. Take what is in the bag and do not betray the sword, for it once belonged to 'Ali." The man returned with the camel to his companions, and they found 4000 dinars in it and other things as well, and most excellent of all, the sword of 'Ali. The second man then went to Qais bin Sa'd, and he found him to be sleeping. However, his female slave was there and she asked, "What do you need from him?" He said, "I am a traveler who has run out of resources and who has no means by which to continue his journey." She said, "What you need is easier than waking him up. Here is a bag, and in it is 700 dinars; there is nothing else in this house. But go to the stables and take for yourself one camel and one slave." Sa'd later said, "You should have woken me up, so that I could have given him that which was sufficient for him." Yet he was so pleased with what his female servant did that he freed her. The third man went to 'Arabah Al-Aousah, and when he reached him he found him to be leaving his house, heading in the direction of the mosque for prayer. He was leaning upon two slaves because he was blind. The man said to him, "O 'Arabah." He said, "Speak." He said, "I am a traveler who has run out of resources and who has no means by which to continue his journey." 'Arabah said, "...Take these two slaves." He said, "I will not do so." 'Arabah said, "If you do not take them, then I will free them in any case. If you wish, I will free them; and if you wish, you may take them." After being without the two slaves, 'Arabah continued to find his way by leaning on the wall. The man returned with the slaves to the two other men; the deeds of all three were praised, yet they decided that the most generous of them all was 'Arabah Al-Aousah, for he gave all that he owned.

Brothers, each similar to the Other

Malik Ad-Dar related that 'Umar once gave 400 dinars to a servant and said, "Take it to Abu 'Ubaidah, then stay with him for an hour in his house and see what he does." The servant took the money to him and said, "The Leader of the Believers orders for you to take this." Abu 'Ubaidah said, "May Allâh join ties between him and his relations." He then said (to his female servant): "Come here young girl! Take this 7 to such and such person, this 5 to such and such person..." and so on until all of the money was finished. The servant returned to 'Umar and informed of what happened. 'Umar had already prepared a similar amount for Mu'adh bin Jabal, and he sent the servant to him in order to deliver the amount. Mu'adh said, "May Allâh join ties between him and his relations." He then said (to his female servant): "O young girl! Take this and give such and such amount to this house and such and such amount to that house..." Mu'adh's wife came forward and said, "By Allâh, we ourselves are poor, so give to us also." All that remained in the bag were two dinars, and he gave them to her. The servant returned to 'Umar and informed him of what had happened. 'Umar was extremely pleased with what he heard and he said, "Indeed, they are brothers, each similar to the other."

From the Piety of Abu Hanifah

Abu Hanifah and a man from Basrah were partners in a business. On one occasion, Abu Hanifah sent 70 expensive garments to him, sending with them a note which read: "One of them is defective, and it is such and such garment, so when you sell it, make sure that you point out the defect." The man sold it for 30,000 dirhams, and when he came with the money to Abu Hanifah, the latter asked, "Did you point out the defect?" He said, "I forgot." Abu Hanifah took nothing from the profit, but instead gave it all in charity.

No One Else eats with My Spoon

Muhammad 'Abduh related that a European person asked, "Why do you not eat with a spoon?" He said, "My spoon is my hand and my fingers. Whereas I alone use my spoon to eat, no one else being able to use it, and I alone being responsible to wash it, you cannot be sure whether your spoon (that is made from steel) was washed or not, nor do you know if the one who used it before you was healthy or sick."

Charity is Better than a Voluntary *Hajj*

Ibn Kathir related the following in his famous history book, *Al-Bidayah wan-Nihayah*: The scholar - who was also a businessman - 'Abdullah bin Mubarak, set out to perform *Hajj*. As he was passing by a certain region, he noticed a bird that had fallen from the sky and died, so he ordered that it be thrown in a heap of garbage. Later on, when he passed by that very heap of garbage, he saw a young girl coming out of her home, going to the pile of garbage, taking the dead bird, and leaving with it, hurrying back to her home. He went to her and asked her about what she did, and she said, "My brother and I live here, and we own nothing except for our clothing. We have no sustenance except for what is thrown in that heap of garbage; for the past few days, even the dead carcass has become permissible for us. Our father used to have a lot of wealth, but he was wronged, his wealth was taken away from him, and he was killed." Ibn Mubarak ordered for the supplies of the trip to be taken back to his home, and he said to his agent, "How much do we have in terms of spending money?" He said, "1000 dinars." 'Abdullah said, "Take from that 20 dinars, which should be enough for our return journey, and give the rest to her, for that is better than our (voluntary) *Hajj* this year." He then returned home. And that is why the Egyptian scholar Muhammad Ghazali was of the view that to spend money on the needs of the Muslims is better than a voluntary *Hajj*. He said, "To fulfill a need of the Muslims is a communal obligatory deed, and the obligatory deed is given precedence over the voluntary deed."

Our Pious Predecessors and Their Aversion to Fame

Habib bin Abi Thabit related that Ibn Mas'ud ﷺ went out one day and a group of people followed him. He said, "Do you need anything?" They said, "No, but we wished only to walk with you." He said, "Return, for it is humiliation for the one who is following and a trial or temptation for the one who is being followed."

Harith bin Suwaid related that 'Abdullah said, "Had you known what I know about myself, you would have poured dirt on my head."

Bistam bin Muslim related that when a man was walking with Muhammad bin Sirin, the latter would say, "Do you need anything?" If he needed something, then Muhammad would give it to him, but if he continued to walk with him, he would repeat, "Do you need anything?"

Hasan said, "I was with Ibn Mubarak one day when we came to a fountain, from which a group of people were drinking. We went closer to drink, and because people didn't recognize him, they considered him just as any other person in the crowd, and so they tried to push their way by him. When he came out of the crowd, he said, 'Life is not to truly live except like this.' Meaning, the ideal life is one wherein one is neither known nor revered."

Hasan also related that when Ibn Mubarak was in Kufah, a book on the rites of *Hajj* was being read to him. When a certain view was read out loud regarding an issue, he said, "And that is our view." He then asked, "And who wrote down what I said?" Hasan told him who it was. Ibn Mubarak took the book and continued to wipe out the words that were written from him until they were completely obliterated. He then said, "And who am I that my speech should be written down?"

Moderation in Joking and Laughing

Anas ﷺ related that a man went to the Prophet ﷺ and said, "O Messenger of Allâh, carry me (i.e., provide me with a mount)." The Prophet ﷺ said, "We will have you carried on the child of a female camel." He said, "And what shall I do with the child of a female camel (i.e., it is too small)!" The Prophet ﷺ said, "Are camels given birth to except by female camels (i.e., meaning that it could be an adult camel and still be the child of a female camel, since all camels are given birth by female camels)?"

And Suhaib ﷺ related, "I went to the Prophet ﷺ and in front of him were bread and dates. He said, 'Come near and eat.' I began to eat from the dates, and the Prophet ﷺ said, 'You are eating dates and one of your eyes is sore?' I said, 'I am chewing from the other side.' Allâh's Messenger ﷺ smiled."

Why One seeks out Knowledge

'Aun bin 'Umarah said that he heard Hisham Ad-Dastuwai say, "By Allâh, I am not able to say that I have ever went out on any day to seek out *Hadith*, seeking thereby the Countenance of Allâh."

Dhahabi said: By Allâh, neither can I. Our pious predecessors used to seek out knowledge for Allâh; they excelled and became Imams whose examples are followed. From them there is a group who at first did not seek knowledge for Allâh, but then became upright. They took account of themselves, and knowledge itself dragged them to sincerity while they were still on the road. Mujahid and others said, "We have sought out this knowledge when we did not have a very strong intention; later on, Allâh provided us with (a good) intention."

Others have said, "We sought out this knowledge for other than Allâh, but it refused to be dedicated for other than Allâh," and that too is good. Then they spread that knowledge with a good intention.

Another group sought out knowledge with wrong intentions - for a worldly aim or to be praised, and for them is that which they intended. The Prophet ﷺ said, "Whoever goes forth in battle, intending (even) a cord, then for him is that which he intended (i.e., no reward does he receive from Allâh if his intention is not correct)." You should see that this group did not enlighten themselves with the light of knowledge, nor did anything occur in their souls, nor did their knowledge lead to any significant result in terms of action. The scholar is only he who fears Allâh (the Exalted).

Another group achieved knowledge, were given positions, but then did wrong; they did not limit themselves to their knowledge, they perpetrated great sins, so woe unto them, for they are not scholars!

Others did not fear Allâh (the Exalted) in their knowledge: they resorted to sophistry and spurious argumentation, issuing rulings of doubtful permissibility, relating strange narrations, while others showed even greater temerity by fabricating *Ahadith*. Such as these were exposed by Allâh (the Exalted), their knowledge went away, and their destination became the Hellfire. All of the above-mentioned groups related much in terms of knowledge.

A group came after them whose deficiencies in knowledge and in action were clear to all. And they were followed by a people who ascribed themselves to knowledge outwardly, but who excelled in only small matters, which deceived them into believing that they were superior scholars. It never crossed their minds that they were seeking closeness to Allâh (the Exalted), and that is because they never saw a true scholar whom they could emulate. And so they became like the ignorant masses. The highest that any of them aspired to was to gather expensive books to store and to look at one day. We ask Allâh to save us and to forgive us.

Some have said (during Dhahabi's times), "I am not a scholar and I have never seen a scholar."

A Just and Pious Ruler

It has been related that 'Umar bin Khattab appointed Sa'eed bin 'Aamir as the governor of Hims. When 'Umar visited that region, he said, "O people of Hims! How do you find your governor to be?" They complained to him, saying that they had four complaints about him: 1) "He does not come out to us until late in the morning." 'Umar said, "That is grave indeed! And what else?" 2) "He answers anyone during the night." 'Umar said, "Grave indeed! And what else?" 3) "One day during every month, he does not come out to us!" 'Umar said, "Grave indeed! And what else?" 4) "Every so often, he is in a miserable and wretched state."

'Umar gathered both Sa'eed bin 'Aamir and those who complained about him, in order to issue judgment regarding those accusations, which if proven to be true, would prove him to be an unfit governor.

When 'Umar gathered everyone, he said, "What is your complaint regarding him, O people of Hims?" They said, "He does not come out to us until late in the morning." 'Umar said, "And what do you say, O Sa'eed?" Sa'eed said, "By Allâh, O Leader of the Believers! Although I hate to mention it, my family has no servant. So, I am responsible for making the bread (from the early stages of the process to the very end), and then I make ablution, after which I go out to the people."

'Umar said, "And what else do you complain about

regarding him, O people of Hims?" They said, "He does not answer anyone in the night." 'Umar said, "And what do you say, O Sa'eed?" He said, "Although I hate to mention it, O Leader of the Believers! I have indeed made the day for them and the night for Allâh."

"And what else do you complain about him?" They said, "One day during every month, he does not come out to us." "And what do you say, O Sa'eed?" He said, "O Leader of the Believers! I have no servant who may wash my garment, and I have no other garment to replace it, so I wash it until it dries and then I go out to them at the end of the day."

'Umar then asked, "And what else do you complain about him?" They said, "Every so often, he is in a miserable and wretched state." "And what do you say, O Sa'eed?" He said, "I witnessed the death of Khubaib Ansari in Makkah; the Quraish cut parts of his meat into pieces. They then carried him to the root of a tree and crucified him. They said, 'Do you wish that Muhammad was in your place, and that you were with your family and with your child?' He said, 'By Allâh, I do not wish that I was with my family and my child, nor that Muhammad was pricked by a thorn!' Whenever I remember that day and how I did not help him in the state that he was in – I was a disbeliever at the time and did not believe in Allâh, the Almighty – I start to think that Allâh will never forgive me for that sin, and then I enter into a state of extreme misery."

'Umar said, "All praise is for Allâh, Who has not made me fail in my perceptiveness." He then sent for 1000 dinars to be given to Sa'eed, and he said, "Use this to help you in your affair!"

Sa'eed's wife said, "All praise is for Allâh, Who has given us enough so that we do not need your (i.e., Sa'eed's work in the house) services anymore." He said, "Do you wish for better than that? We give it to someone who will bring it to us when we are in most need of it."

She said, "Yes." He called someone from his household that he trusted in, and he put the money in a bag, saying, "Go with this money to the widow of such and such man, with this amount to the orphan of such and such parents, with this money to such and such poor person, and with this money to such and such person who was afflicted." Very little was left with him, and he said to his family, "Spend from this!" He returned to his work, and his wife said to him one day, "Will you not buy a servant for us! What happened to that wealth?" He answered her, saying, "It will come to you when you are in need of it most!"

The Virtues of seeking Forgiveness from Allâh

Three men came to Husain bin 'Ali ﵁; the first complained about a paucity of rain, and Husain answered, "Increase in seeking forgiveness from Allâh." The second complained of being barren and not having children. Husain said, "Increase in seeking forgiveness from Allâh." The third man complained about arid conditions and a lack of fertile soil, and Husain ﵁ said, "Increase in seeking forgiveness from Allâh." Those seated with him said, "O son of the Messenger of Allâh (i.e., grandson): each one of these three had a different complaints, yet you gave them the same answer." He asked him whether he had not read the Saying of Allâh (the Exalted):

> *"Ask forgiveness from your Lord; verily, He is Oft-Forgiving; He will send rain to you in abundance; and give you increase in wealth and children, and bestow on you gardens and bestow on you rivers."* (Qur'ân 71:11)

The Believer versus the Polytheist

A disbeliever once said to a believer, "Do you not say that nothing afflicts you except that which Allâh has written upon you?" The believer answered, "Yes." He said, "Then throw yourself down from the peak of this mountain, and if Allâh decrees safety for you, you will be saved." The believer said, "Listen, indeed it is Allâh Who tests His slaves and not the slave who tests his Lord."

The Intelligence of Khidr

The righteous man Khidr, said to Musa ﷺ, "O one who has spoken to Allâh, I am amazed that you blamed me for sinking a ship when I was only trying to save its passengers... Have you forgotten that you yourself were saved from drowning the day that your mother placed you in the water? And you blamed me for killing the young boy because the boy hadn't killed anyone himself... Have you forgotten the day when you killed a man from the family of the Pharaoh, and you said, 'O my Lord, indeed I have wronged my own self, so forgive me,' and He forgave you? O one who has spoken to Allâh, you have blamed me for erecting a wall without taking any recompense... Have you forgotten the day that you gave drink to the sheep of the two daughters of Shu'aib without taking any recompense? So, my three for your three."

The Removal of Knowledge and the Spread of Ignorance

Anas bin Malik رضي الله عنه said: Shall I not relate to you a *Hadith* I heard from Allâh's Messenger ﷺ, for none shall come after me to relate it to you from those who heard it first hand: "From the signs of the Hour is for knowledge to be removed, for ignorance to become widespread, for fornication to become rampant, for alcohol to be imbibed, for men to perish and women to stay, until the point that for each fifty women there will be one male guardian." (*Sahih Bukhari* 1/178 and *Sahih Muslim* 16/221)

The Color of the Dog that was with the People of the Cave

Allâh (the Exalted) said:

> "And of knowledge, you (mankind) have been given only a little." (Qur'ân 17:85)

It is said that a scholar named Muqatil bin Sulaiman became afflicted with pride and haughtiness because of his knowledge. One day, he said, "Ask me about anything under the Throne until the bottom of the earth." A man stood and asked, "I will ask you about a matter that is much less significant than all of that, about a cave on earth. Allâh (the Exalted) mentioned it in His Book. Inform me about the dog that was with the people of the cave: what color was it?" Muqatil immediately came back to his senses and was brought down to humility, for he could not find an answer.

Supplication

Sufyan bin 'Uyainah said that he heard a Bedouin say on the night of *'Arafah*: "O Allâh, do not prevent me from the good that is with You because of the evil that is with me, and if You do not accept my toils and my labors (then I am indeed an afflicted man), then do not prevent me from the reward of the afflicted one for his affliction."

Imam Shafi'i and the One Who debated with Him

A man who wanted to argue simply for the sake of an argument, decided to enter into a debate with Imam Shafi'i, and so he said, "O Imam, how can the Devil be created from fire and at the same time be punished by Allâh with fire?" Imam Shafi'i smiled; he then extended his hand to the ground and took a rock made from dry clay, which he threw at the man. It struck the man in the face, which he contorted, indicating both his pain and anger. Imam Shafi'i calmly said, "Has it hurt you?" He said in anger, "Yes, it has hurt me." He said, "How is it that you were created from clay, and it was clay that made you feel pain?" The man did not answer but he immediately grasped that the Devil was made from fire and that Allâh will punish him with fire.

Worldly Possessions

It was said to 'Umar bin 'Abdul-'Aziz, "O leader of the believers, you have much wealth in your hands, but we do not see you owning even those things that your house is in need of." He said, "A house should not be furnished in the fleeting world; there is an abode to which we have transported our best possessions, and after a short while we are moving there - i.e., the Hereafter."

What has made this Nation important throughout History

Isam Al-'Attar, a famous caller to Islam, said, "O Arab nationalists, we did not spring to prominence in history through the likes of Abu Jahl or Abu Lahab, but instead with Muhammad, Allâh's Messenger, with Abu Bakr, and with 'Umar...We were not made to rule the earth with the *Mu'alliqat As-Sab'ah* (seven famous poems that were once attached to the Ka'bah); rather, we were made to rule by the Noble Qur'ân. And we didn't convey to people the messages of Lat and 'Uzza; rather, we conveyed to them the Message of Allâh, the One."

Three Qualities that will be held against the One Who possesses Them

Transgression:

> "O mankind! Your rebellion (disobedience to Allâh) is only against your own selves." (Qur'ân 10:23)

Plotting and deception:

> "But the evil plot encompasses only him who makes it." (Qur'ân 35:43)

Not fulfilling one's promises and contracts:

> "Then whosoever breaks his pledge, breaks only to his own harm." (Qur'ân 48:10)

The Truthfulness of the Scholar and the Forbearance of the Ruler

Abu Muslim Khaulani went to meet Mu'awiyah, who was the caliph at the time. The former said, "Peace upon you, O employee." The people surrounding the ruler became angry, but the experienced ruler simply said, "Leave him, for indeed Abu Muslim knows what he is saying." Abu Muslim continued, "The example of you is that of an employee who is charged over a flock - to raise them well, to provide them with milk, to provide for the young members so that they grow properly, and to fatten the skinny ones. If he does that, then he deserves his salary and more; but if he doesn't do that, he is punished and of course receives no payment. Do not consider the caliphate to be simply gathering wealth and then spending it freely; indeed, it is in reality making sure that people follow the ways of Allâh; and people do not mind toiling all day long as long as the source and spring is pure and good. And the situation of the caliph vis-à-vis the people is that of the spring, for all that they want is for it to be pure."

The Transient Nature of this World

A righteous man was given news that one of his companions had died, and so he went to the family of the deceased to console them. When he arrived there, they were screaming and crying in very loud voices. He said, "Indeed the one we lost was not your provider; the One Who provides for you is Ever-Living and never dies. The one you lost did not block off the holes in the ground that belonged to you, for all he did was fill his own hole (i.e., fill his own grave). Indeed, each one from you has such a hole, and each one of you, by Allâh, will fill his hole. Indeed when Allâh (the Exalted) created the world, He decreed destruction for it, and death for its inhabitants. No experience permeates a household except that that household then becomes filled with a lesson. And no group gathers among themselves except that they will soon be parted, and then it is Allâh (the Exalted) Who will be the One Who inherits the earth and all that is on it. Whoever from you is crying, then let him cry over himself, for the destination of your companion (i.e., the deceased) is the destination of all people tomorrow."

Magnanimity

Ar-Rabi'atur-Raiy said, "Magnanimity consists of six characteristics: 3 as regards to when one is at home, and 3 as regards to when one is on a journey. As for when one is on a journey - spending from one's provisions, good manners, and pleasantry with one's companions. As for when one is at home - recitation of the Qur'ân, adhering to the mosques, and chastity of one's private parts. 'Umar ﷺ said, "There are two kinds of magnanimity: the outward kind and the inward kind. The outward kind is maintaining a good appearance, and the inward kind is chastity."

Learn the Good Supplication

Someone once said, "If you wish to learn how to supplicate, then listen to the supplication of the Arabs." Sa'eed bin Musayyib said that once Hullah bin Ashyam passed by him, and as he couldn't control his urge to go to him, he went and said, "O Abu Sahba, supplicate to Allâh for me." He said, "May Allâh make you keen for that which remains and sparing in that which is fleeting; may He grant you surety of Faith, without which the soul finds no comfort and upon which the religion of a person depends."

How You deal with Others is how You will be dealt with

A wise man once said to his son, "My son, do not become resentful when you are afflicted with trials, for indeed that is tantamount to having bad thoughts about one's Lord, and also, it gives pleasure to one's enemy. Do not mock others, for indeed by Allâh, every time I ever mocked anyone, I was afflicted in the same way as the person who I mocked. In this world, man is a target of arrows that come to him successively: some pass him by, some fall short, some fall to his right and others to his left, and some strike him. Know that for every deed, you are rewarded, and how you deal with others is how you will be dealt with. And whoever is dutiful to his parents, his children will be dutiful to him. Avoid greed and ambition, for both represent poverty in the present. Fear Allâh as much as you are able. And if you are able to make today better than yesterday and tomorrow better than today and your secrets better than your outward deeds, then do so. Beware of deeds that you have to apologize for, for one never has to apologize for goodness. When you stand for prayer, perform the prayer of one who is saying farewell, as if you feel that you will never afterwards pray again (i.e., that you will die). Adhere to modesty, and you will be of its people. Do not inflict harm upon others; rather give them good, and forgive if you are able to. Do not be miserly if you are asked for something and do not tarry when one seeks help from you. Whoever is stingy, then Allâh will make things narrow for him; and whoever gives, then Allâh will give him a replacement for what he gave."

Luqman the Wise was a black Man

Auza'i related that a black man went to the most distinguished man among the *Tabi'een* (successors of the Companions), Sa'eed bin Musayyib, in order to ask him some questions. Sa'eed said, "Do not be sad because you are black, for among the best of people three were Black: Bilal bin Rabah - the caller to prayer of Allâh's Messenger; Mahja' - the freed slave of 'Umar bin Khattab; and Luqman Hakim (the Wise) - for he too was black-skinned, he was from Nubia, which lies between Egypt and Sudan, and he had very large lips."

A man went to Luqman the Wise, and said, "Are you Luqman? Are you the slave of Bani Nuhas?" He said, "Yes." The man said, "You are the black shepherd?" He said, "As for my skin being black, that is apparent, but what is it about me that amazes you?" He said, "That people come to visit you in throngs, that they crowd at your door, and that they are pleased with your speech." He said, "O my cousin, if you do as I say, then you will be the same." He said, "And what is that?" Luqman said, "Lowering my gaze, holding my tongue, honoring my guest, preserving the rights of my neighbor, and refraining from that which does not concern me - that has made me become as you see me now."

Ibrahim and Namrud

Zaid bin Aslam related that Namrud had with him great supplies of food, and people would go to him to seek provision from him. Ibrahim ﷺ was one of those who went to him, and between him and Namrud there took place the famous debate that Allâh (the Exalted) related in the Qur'ân:

> "When Ibrahim (Abraham) said (to him): 'My Lord (Allâh) is He Who gives life and causes death.' He said, 'I give life and cause death.' Ibrahim said, 'Verily! Allâh causes the sun to rise from the east; then cause it you to rise from the west.' So the disbeliever was utterly defeated. And Allâh guides not the people, who are *Zalimun* (wrongdoers, etc.)." (Qur'ân 2:258)

He didn't give Ibrahim any food, and when the latter returned to his family, he went to a sand-hill and filled two sacks with dirt, with the intention of preoccupying his family when he returned to them. When he returned home, he put down his possessions, and then leaned on something and fell asleep. His wife, Sarah, went to the two sacks and found them to the filled with good food. With that food, she began to cook. When Ibrahim woke up, he was surprised to find the food that she had prepared. He said, "Where did you get this from?" She said, "From the food that you brought with you." And he knew that it was Allâh Who provided that provision for them. Then Allâh (the Exalted) sent an angel to the aforesaid tyrant king, ordering him to believe in Allâh, but he refused. The angel called him to believe a second time, and he refused again; then a third time, and still he refused. The angel said, "Gather your armies and I will gather mine." Namrud gathered his army together at the time of sunrise, and Allâh sent to him mosquitoes, so many in number, that the people of the army could not even see the sun. Then Allâh gave power to the mosquitoes over them: they ate their flesh and blood, leaving them as decomposed bones. One of those mosquitoes entered into the nostrils of the king. Allâh punished him by it, and he was in so much pain that he would continually hit his head against objects (hoping to make the mosquito exit or simple because of sheer madness that resulted from the pain) until he finally died.

Allâh's Scales

Abul-'Abbas Sahl bin Sa'd As-Sa'idi said that a man passed by the Prophet ﷺ, who then asked a man who was seated with him, "What is your view regarding this (man)?" He said, "A man from the most noble of men; if he proposes, he is, by Allâh, worthy of being accepted for marriage; and if he intercedes, he is worthy of having his intercession accepted." Allâh's Messenger ﷺ remained silent, and then another man passed by, and Allâh's Messenger ﷺ asked, "What is your view regarding this (man)?" He said, "O Messenger of Allâh, this man is from the poor Muslims. It is befitting of him that if he proposes, he not be accepted for marriage; that if he intercedes, his intercession not be accepted; and that if he speaks, he not be listened to." Allâh's Messenger ﷺ said, "The latter is better than a number of people who fill the earth that are like the former."

Khalid bin Barmak and Qahtabah

The ruler or the leader of an army must always be diligent as well as vigilant, and he must also be blessed with powers of inference. It is related that Khalid bin Barmak was with Qahtabah, and both were seated within the limits of their army encampment. Khalid saw an entire flock of deer coming toward the camp and some were even entering the camp. He quickly ordered Qahtabah to prepare the army immediately, and when the latter asked why, he said, "The matter is more urgent than for me to explain the situation to you right now." The army was swift in getting their weapons ready and in climbing their mounts; no sooner were they ready than did the enemy begin their attack. However, Khalid's army was victorious over their enemy, and when the battle was over, Qahtabah asked Khalid, "How did you know that they were about to attack?" He said, "I saw the deer coming and even entering our camp. And I knew that, in general, deer run away from man and try to stay out of his way; therefore it must have been a great matter indeed that forced them to leave where they were and come upon us." Such is the vigilance required of a leader.

A Gentle Admonition

A man went to the caliph, Mamun, in order to advise and admonish him; however, he was very severe in his speech, so much so that the ruler was visibly affected by his words. When the man left the company of the caliph, he regretted his words and feared punishment from him. When he returned to his home, he found out that the caliph wanted to meet him, and so he returned to him in a state of fear and agitation. Mamun said, "Indeed, Allâh has ordered he who is better than you to be gentle in speech with he who is more evil than me. He said to Prophet Musa ﷺ when he sent him to Fir'aun:

> "And speak to him mildly, perhaps he may accept admonition or fear Allâh."

The man apologized for what he said, and he learned gentleness in speech from Mamun.

The Impenetrable Fortress

'Umair once entered Hims as its ruler, and following the way of Allâh's Messenger ﷺ, he began at the mosque, calling people to it. He climbed the pulpit, praised Allâh (the Exalted), and said: "O people! Indeed Islam is an impenetrable fortress and a solid door. The fortress of Islam is justice and its door is the truth. When the fortress is brought down and when the door is destroyed, then the sanctuary of this religion will be violated. The severity of the ruler is not in striking with a whip or killing with a sword; rather it is ruling with justice and taking by what is right."

The Way of a Muslim in His Life

The life of a Muslim must stand on seven foundations: adherence to Allâh's Book, following the way of Allâh's Messenger ﷺ, eating that which is lawful, refraining from harming others, staying away from sins, repenting frequently, and fulfilling the rights of others. In the past and present, the great Islamic jurists of this nation have confirmed that the Muslim's life must be based on the aforesaid foundations. Brother Muslim, you must remain firm upon those seven comprehensive foundations - by the Will of Allâh - until the day you die.

Imam Ghazali

It was once said to Imam Ghazali, "We hear about punishment that occurs in graves, but we open graves sometimes and find nothing that indicates punishment in them. We neither see fire nor snakes nor scorpions." The Imam paused for a moment, and then said, "Consider one who is sleeping and who is having a succession of nightmares. He sees a murderer following him, snakes chasing him, or fire that is burning him. How is that? Indeed sleep is a small example when compared to the greater sleep that occurs in the grave. And pain occurs in the grave to the one who deserves it even if we do not see it with these eyes of ours."

Safety comes Tomorrow

The rightly-guided ruler 'Umar bin 'Abdul-'Aziz - who was also considered to be an Islamic jurist - said in his last sermon: "O people, indeed, you have not been created without a purpose and you will not be left alone without being held accountable. And you have a final destination, where Allâh will judge among you. He will indeed be the loser who is outside of Allâh's Mercy, which comprehends all things. He is the loser who will be forbidden from Paradise, whose width is as the heavens and the earth. Know that safety tomorrow is for he who fears his Lord and sells a small amount to achieve abundance - for he who sells that which is perishing for that which shall remain... I say this to you, though I do not know of anyone among you who has more sins than me, and I ask Allâh to forgive both me and you." Such was the humility of good doers who were practicing Muslims. And indeed Allâh's Mercy is near the good doers.

Wise Sayings from Fudail and Ibn Mubarak

Fudail bin 'Iyad said: "If you are not able to fast or pray, then know that you are shackled and confined by your sins." Allâh (the Exalted) says:

> "Yes! Whosoever earns evil and his sin has surrounded him, they are dwellers of the Fire (i.e., Hell); they will dwell therein forever." (Qur'ân 2:81)

Ibn Mubarak said: "I saw that sins cause hearts to die, that base actions lead to their addiction, that avoiding sins is life for the heart, and that it is better for your soul for you to disobey it."

The Bedouin and Ibn 'Uyainah

It has been related that a Bedouin spent a long time in the company of Sufyan bin 'Uyainah, listening to the *Ahadith* that he related. When the Bedouin decided to return to his home country, Sufyan asked, "O Bedouin, what did you like most from my *Ahadith*?" He said, "Three *Ahadith* only: first the *Hadith* of 'Aishah from the Prophet that he liked sweets and honey; the second is the *Hadith* wherein he said that if dinner is served and the prayer has commenced, then begin with dinner; and the third is the *Hadith* of 'Aishah that it is not from righteousness to fast while one is in a journey."

I came seeking Help, not a Religious Ruling

One day a man accosted 'Umar bin Hubairah on the road and said, "O ruler of the Arabs, I want to perform *Hajj*." He said, "The path lies before you, and may Allâh make it easy for you." The man said, "I am unable to walk." 'Umar said, "Ride for a day and walk for a day." He said, "I do not own anything with which I may purchase or rent a mount." He said, "Then *Hajj* is not obligatory upon you." The man said, "O ruler of the Arabs, I came to you seeking help, not a religious ruling." 'Umar laughed and gave him 5000 dirhams.

He is Insane

A man went to Ibn 'Aqeel and said, "Whenever I plunge myself two or three times into a river to take a bath, I am not sure whether the water reached every part of my body, and am consequently unsure whether I have purified myself. What should I do?" He said, "Do not pray." "Why do you say that?" Ibn 'Aqeel answered, "Allâh's Messenger ﷺ said, 'The pen is raised from three: from the child until he reaches adulthood, from the one who is sleeping until he wakes up, and from the insane man until he regains his senses.' And whoever plunges himself into a river once, twice, and then three times, yet still feels that he has not taken a shower, is insane."

He Chose The Hereafter

Maslamah bin 'Abdul-Malik visited 'Umar bin 'Abdul-Aziz while he was on his deathbed, and he said, "O Leader of the Believers, you have always prevented your children from this wealth, and you have left them poor, though they need something for their upkeep. If you delegate me to provide for them, I will give them what they need." 'Umar said, "Sit down, help me sit up, and then call to me my children." He called them, and in total they were 12 boys. 'Umar looked from one to the other until his eyes became filled with tears. He then said, "O my children, I have left you in a good situation, and you will never pass by a Muslim or one who has a covenant with us except that you have an obligatory right over him. O my children, I was left with two options: between you remaining poor in this world and between your father entering the Hellfire. For you to remain poor in this world until the end of time is better than for your father to spend a single day in the Hellfire. Stand children, may Allâh protect you and provide for you." Maslamah said: "(After their father's death) 'Umar's children were never poor or in need."

Malik bin Dinar

He once said to some of his students: "When you perceive hardness in your heart, weakness in your body, and paucity in your sustenance - then know that you have spoken about that which does not concern you!"

True Honor

Allâh (the Exalted) said in the Noble Qur'ân that honor comes only through piety:

"Verily, the most honorable of you with Allâh is that (believer) who has *Taqwa* (piety, righteousness, the fear of Allâh, etc.)." (Qur'ân 49:13)

It is related that 'Umar bin Khattab ﷺ passed by a man who proudly said, "I am from the valleys of Makkah." He stood over him and said, "If you have religion, then you have honor; if you have a sound mind, then you have dignity, if you have knowledge, then you have respect; otherwise, you are on an equal footing with donkeys." And it has been said, "Honor during the Days of Ignorance was achieved by eloquent speech, by bravery, and by forbearance; and in Islam by religion and piety."

A Thief and a Message

Ibn Zuhair Al-'Anbari sent a messenger to his family with 30 sheep and a sack full of cooking fat. The messenger stole one sheep and skimmed some cooking fat from the top of the sack. When he reached the family, he said, "Do you have a message for him that I may convey?" The wife said, "Inform him that the month is waning and the fence that used to overlook us is broken." When the messenger returned to Zuhair, he gave him the message, and Zuhair, understanding his wife's secret message, knew what happened. He forced a confession out of the thief and made him return the sheep and the cooking fat.

"The Wicked Doer has sufficed Us all with His Evil"

Bakr bin 'Abdullah Al-Muzani related the following story: There was a man who was known for spending a lot of time in the courts of kings. He would stand beside a certain king and say, "Do good to the good doer with his goodness, for the evildoer will suffice you with his evil." Another man was jealous of him for his status and for his speech, so he decided to come between him and the King. He went to the King and said, "The man who stands beside you and says such and such, claims that you have bad breath." The King said, "And how do I know this is true?" He said, "Call him to you, and if he draws near you and places his hand on his nose so as not to smell your bad breath, then you will know that I have spoken the truth." The King said, "Go and I will see." He left the King and went to invite the other man to his house for dinner. During dinner, he fed him food that was heavy with garlic. The guest left and went to the King as was his custom, and said, "Do good to the good doer with his goodness, for indeed the evildoer will suffice you with his evil." The King said, "Come near me." He went near the King and placed his hand on his mouth, fearing that the King would smell the foul odor of the garlic. The King said to himself, "I do now realize that the other man had spoken the truth." The King then wrote a letter to a governor, instructing him as follows: "When the one who is carrying this letter comes to you from me, slaughter him and cut him up into pieces." He gave the man the letter, and as the man was on his way to meet the governor, the other man - who had plotted to destroy him - met him on the way, and said, "What is this letter?" He said, "A letter from the King for an endowment to be given to me." The other man said, "Give it to me as a gift." He said, "Alright, I give it to you as a gift." The man took the letter and went with it to the governor. The governor said, "It says in this letter that I have to slaughter you and cut you into pieces." The man said, "This letter does not belong to me. You must return to the King and clear up the matter." The governor said, "When the King sends a letter, one does not return to him to discuss his commands." And so he slaughtered him and cut him up into pieces. The other man returned to the King as was his custom and said the same phrase that he always said to him. The King was amazed and said, "What did you do with the letter?" He said, "Such and such person came to me, asked for the letter, and I gave it to him as a gift." The King said, "Indeed he told me that you claim that I have bad breath." He said, "I never said that." The King said, "Then why did you put your hand on your mouth?" He said, "Because that man had fed me garlic, and I disliked for you to smell it." The King said, "You have spoken the truth, return to your position beside me, for indeed the wicked doer has sufficed us all with his evil."

Charity And Sickness

In 1408, the newspaper *Al-Muslimun* (issue number 181, dated Dhul-Hijjah 8, 1408) related the following story: It is a real-life story whose hero is a Syrian doctor who was afflicted with cancer and who remedied it with charity. Dr. 'Isa Marzuqi relates that he was afflicted with cancer, a fact that is attested by the most eminent of doctors in Damascus; the amazing thing is that he was cured through charity. After many of his colleagues lost hope of his cure, the said Doctor returned to the hospital to assume his duties. The doctor's fiancée had refused to break off their marriage because of the sickness, and instead decided to wait patiently until he died. But instead of that happening he was saved. He later provided authenticated certificates from many eminent doctors that he had cancer in his left armpit; they also attested to the fact that later on, no traces of that cancer remained. In fact, the first doctor who diagnosed him said that at first, he expected him to die only after a few days.

Dr. 'Isa Marzuqi later said that he applied the words of Allâh's Messenger ﷺ: "Remedy your sick ones with charity." With that statement he still had hope, and so when he found out about a house whose breadwinner had died many years before, he decided to give them all the wealth he had, even though it was only a small amount. He sent the money to the poor family through a friend of his, asking him to tell them that the money was from a man afflicted with a death threatening sickness and that he was seeking a cure by giving charity, hoping for help from Allâh. The story ended with his cure, which perplexed many of the most skilled doctors in Syria. He later said that he chose that cure because he wanted to follow the way of Allâh's Messenger ﷺ. He also said, however, that he did not leave off treatment through normal medical methods; he believed in the Divine Preordainment, but that belief does not mean that one should turn away from doctors, nor does it mean that one should not take the appropriate, tangible steps that are needed to achieve a desired goal.

The Ruler and His Brother

A man stood before Al-Wathiq Billah and said, "O Leader of the Believers, join ties with and have mercy upon your relatives, and be generous to a man from your family." Al-Wathiq Billah said, "And who are you? For I never saw you before this day." He said, "I am the son of your grandfather, Adam." He said, "O young man, give to him one dirham." The man said, "O Leader of the Believers, and what should I do with this?" He said, "Suppose that I were to divide the treasury among your brothers from the children of my grandfather - would your share be equal to even a single grain?" The man then praised him for his intelligence, after which, he was given a much larger share.

Words of Wisdom

When Ibn 'Aun was bidding farewell to another man, he said: "Upon you is to fear Allâh, for the one who has *Taqwa* never feels loneliness."

Zaid bin Aslam said: "Whoever fears Allâh people will love him, even if they had previously hated him."

Imam Thauri رحمه الله said to Ibn Abi Dha'ib: "If you fear Allâh, He will be enough for you so that you do not need people. And if you fear people, they will not satisfy you in the least in terms of your total dependence on Allâh."

Sulaiman bin Dawud said: "We have been given what others have been given and more, and we know what others know and more, and we have found that nothing is better than the fear of Allâh in secret and in open, justice during times of happiness and sadness, and moderation in times of poverty and richness."

In *Az-Zuhd*, Imam Ahmad رحمه الله relates the following *Hadith Qudsi*: "Whenever one from creation seeks protection from another one from creation instead of from Me, I cut off all tangible support for him from the heavens and the earth; if he asks Me, I do not give him; if he supplicates to Me, I do not answer him; and if he asks forgiveness from me, I do not forgive him. And whenever one from creation seeks protection from Me instead of from My creation, his provision is guaranteed in the heavens and on the earth; if he asks Me, I give to him; if he supplicates to Me, I answer him; and if he asks me for forgiveness, I forgive him."

The Story of the Cow and the Dutiful Son

Among the Children of Israel there lived a very rich man; he had a cousin who was poor and who was also his only inheritor. The latter felt that the former was slow to die, and so he killed him in order to acquire his estate. He then carried him to another village and hid his body there. Pretending that he was seeking revenge, he took some people to Moses ﷺ, accusing them of the murder. They proclaimed their innocence before Moses, who was not sure of what really happened. They asked him to invoke Allâh to expose the true murderer. He ordered them to slaughter a cow, the story of which is related in the Qur'ân:

"They said, 'Do you make fun of us?'" (Qur'ân 2:67)

Meaning, 'we ask you about the murderer, yet you order us to slaughter a cow!' They said that because of the apparent disparity between the two matters and because they did not know the wisdom behind his request. Moses said:

"I take Allâh's Refuge from being among *Al-Jahilun* (the ignorant or foolish ones." (Qur'ân 2:67)

Meaning, 'I seek refuge in Allâh from being among those who mock the believers.'

When the people realized that the command to slaughter a cow was really from Allâh (the Exalted), they asked Moses to describe it for them. Had they went to any cow and slaughtered it, that would have been enough for them; however, they were severe upon themselves, and so Allâh was severe in dealing with them. And there was wisdom behind that.

Prior to that time, there was a righteous man whose son was still a young boy. The father owned a young cow, which he took to a field and said, "O Allâh, I leave this with You for safekeeping until my son grows up." The man died and the cow remained in the field. At the time of the story, the cow was neither old nor young, and it fled from all those who saw it or came near it. The son, now of age, was dutiful to his mother. He would divide his nights into three parts: he would pray for one-third of the night, he would sleep for one-third, and he would sit with his mother for one-third.

In the mornings, he would go to gather wood, which he would then carry on his back until he reached the marketplace, where he would sell the wood for whatever price Allâh willed. He would then give one-third of the profits to charity, he would eat from the proceeds of one-third, and he would give one-third to his mother.

One day, his mother said to him, "Your father has left behind for you a young cow, and he asked Allâh to keep it safe for you in such and such field, so go there and invoke the Lord of Ibrahim, Isma'il, Ishaq and Ya'qub to return that cow to you. The sign that it is the right cow is that when you will look at it, you will imagine that the rays of the sun are coming out from its skin." It was called the golden one because of its yellowness and its beauty.

The boy went to the field indicated to him. There he saw a cow grazing, and it was the very one that his mother described to him. He called out loud, "I ask you (to come) by the Lord of Ibrahim, Isma'il, Ishaq and Ya'qub." It came to him in a hurry until it was standing in front of him; he took hold of its neck in order to lead it. By the Will of Allâh, the cow spoke, saying, "O young man who is dutiful to his mother! Ride me, for that is easier for you." The young man said, "My mother did not order me to do that; rather she said: 'take it by its neck'." The cow said, "Go, for indeed, if you ordered for a mountain to be cut from its roots so that it would go with you, it would have gone with you because of your dutifulness to your mother." The young man then took the cow to his mother, and she said to him, "Indeed you are poor, you have no wealth, and gathering wood during the daytime is very difficult upon you, and so is standing in the night. So go and sell this cow."

The young man said, "And how much should I sell it for?" She said, "For three dinars, and do not sell it without first seeking counsel with me." The cow was as his mother said, worth three dinars; when the boy reached the marketplace, Allâh sent to him an angel, in order to see his ability and in order to test him - how dutiful was he to his mother, though Allâh had full knowledge of that.

The angel said to him, "For how much will you sell this cow?" He said, "For three dinars, and I stipulate the pleasure of my mother (in this transaction)."

The angel said, "I will pay six dinars, but you must not seek the counsel of your mother."

He said, "If you gave me money that weighed as much as this cow, I would not take it except with the pleasure of my mother." He then returned with the cow to his mother and told her of what had happened. She said, "Return and sell it for six dinars, but stipulate my pleasure."

He went to the marketplace and the angel came again and said, "You sought the command of your mother?" He said, "She ordered me not to sell it for less than six, on condition that I first seek her order."

The angel said, "Then I will give you twelve, on the condition that you do not first seek her command." He refused, returned to his mother, and informed her of what happened. She said, "Indeed the one who was coming to you is an angel in the shape of a man in order to test you." She instructed her son to ask him if he comes again: "Do you order us to sell this cow or not?" The young man did in fact pose that question, and the angel asked him to go to his mother and say to her: "Keep this cow! For indeed Moses, the son of 'Imran, will buy it from you for one was murdered from the Children of Israel. Do not sell it except for enough dinars that can fill its skin."

Allâh decreed that the Children of Israel had to slaughter that exact cow. As they continued to ask after the description of the cow that they were supposed to slaughter, Moses described the cow that belonged to the dutiful son, which was his reward for his dutifulness to his mother - a blessing, favor and mercy from Allâh. When he stipulated the said price, which was of course very high, they had no choice but to buy it from him.

Allâh ordered Moses to command his people to strike the corpse of the one who was murdered, and when they did that, he stood alive by the Will of Allâh. And he said: "Such and such person killed me," referring to his cousin, and then he died again in that very place. His murderer was thus prevented from inheriting his estate.

The Honest Opponent

'Amr bin Al-'Aas related: I led the Muslim army until we reached Alexandria. The ruler there said, "Send forth a man who will speak to me and to whom I will speak." I said, "None other than I shall go to him." And when I went to him, beside me stood my translator and beside him was his. Two podiums were erected for us, and he said, "What are you?" I said, "We are Arabs, and we are the people of Allâh's House. We were the most limited of people in terms of land and the most evil in terms of living - we would eat the flesh of a dead carcass as well as its blood. We used to have malice toward one another; and our lives were the worst kind that anyone lived, until a man from among us came out to us - he wasn't the greatest of us then in terms of honor nor did he have the most wealth - saying, 'I am the Messenger of Allâh to you.' He commanded us to perform deeds that we knew nothing about and he forbade us from those ways that we were upon. We disbelieved in him and rejected him until a people other than us came to him and said, 'We believe you and we will fight those who fight you.' We went out to fight him, but he was victorious over us. He also fought with neighboring Arabs and was victorious over them as well." The ruler of the other army said, "Indeed your Messenger has spoken the truth, and to us have come Messengers similar to him. We were upon their way until kings who used to deal with us according to their desires overcame us, and as such, the ways of the Prophets were abandoned. If you follow the way of your Prophet, you will not fight anyone except that you will overcome him. Yet if you do as we did, leaving the way of your Prophet, you will not outnumber us, nor will you be stronger than us."

The Intelligence of Al-Mahdi

Al-Mahdi was sitting in a general assembly that was organized for the people. A man entered, carrying shoes that were wrapped up in a large handkerchief. He said, "O Leader of the Believers, these are the shoes of Allâh's Messenger and I give them to you as a gift." Al-Mahdi took them from him and looked them carefully; he then ordered for 10,000 dirhams to be given to the man, who took the money and left. Al-Mahdi said to those who were seated near him, "Do you think I didn't know that Allâh's Messenger never touched nor even saw those shoes. Had we proclaimed him to be a liar, he would have said to the people: 'I went to the Leader of the Believers with the shoes of Allâh's Messenger, and he rejected them.' And those who believed him would have been more than those who rejected his claim, for the commoners are inclined to believe those like them and are keen to help the weak over the strong. Even if he was a wrongdoer, we purchased his tongue, accepted his gift, and believed his speech - and in our view, what we did is better and more likely to lead to success."

The Insightful Interpreter of Dreams

When a king was startled to consciousness after having seen a nightmare, he was in such a state of fright that he called every interpreter of dreams in his kingdom to inform him of the meaning of his dream.

In the dream, he saw himself seated upon his throne in the most dignified and handsome of poses, and suddenly he felt that his teeth were falling, one after the other, until no tooth remained in his mouth. When he related his dream to the interpreters, they all tried to calm his nerves through false speech and lies. They didn't inform him of the true meaning of the dream. At that point, the king still had doubts, and looking at the group in front of him, he saw two men who were seated in a corner and were quiet. He asked them about their silence, and one of them said, "It makes me sad to say, my king, that I must inform you that all of your children will die during your lifetime, which will make you sad, and then you will die because of that sadness." When the king heard this statement, the world became dark for him in his eyes and he was filled with rage; he lost his mind and said to his guard, "Take this man to prison." He then looked at the other man and said, "And you, what do you know?" He said, "O my king, my interpretation is that you will live for a very long time, longer than any other person from your family, and that is what your people wish and desire most." The king became happy and all grief was removed from him, and he gave an excellent reward to the man. But were we to reflect on what both men said, we would find the meaning of their words to be the exactly the same, but it was the intellect of the latter that saved him.

The Prisoner's Intelligent Ploy

Haris bin 'Abbad, one of the rulers of Andalus, was looking to capture 'Adi bin Abi Rabi'ah in order to exact revenge from him. His problem, and that of many of his guards, was that he didn't know what Ibn Abi Rabi'ah looked like. A prisoner said to one of the guards, "Will you free me if I show you to him?" He said, "Yes, I promise to do so." After an oath from him, he said, "I am 'Adi bin Abi Rabi'ah," and, remembering his promise and oath, the guard felt compelled to free him.

A Quick Save

One day, Al-Hajjaj went out hiking. When his companions left him, he was left alone in a field, where an old man from Bani 'Ijl came across his way. Al-Hajjaj asked, "From where, old man?" He said, "From this village." He asked, "And what is your opinion of the governors in this region?" He said, "They are the worst of governors: they oppress the people and deem lawful their wealth." Al-Hajjaj then asked, "And what is your opinion of Al-Hajjaj?" He said, "No one has ever ruled over Iraq who was more evil than him." He asked, "Do you know who I am?" He said, "No." He said, "I am Al-Hajjaj!" The old man said, "And do you know who I am?" He said, "No." He said, "I am such and such, son of such and such. I am the madman of Bani 'Ijl; every day I am afflicted with two fits of madness, and I do not know what I say during those fits." Al-Hajjaj laughed and gave him an endowment.

Shunn's Search for a Suitable Wife

Shunn was known for his exceptional intelligence among the Arabs. He one day said, "By Allâh, I will search through the lands until I find a wife similar to me, and then I will marry her." On one of his journeys he met with a man who wanted to travel to the same village that he wanted to go to, and so they accompanied one another. As they started their journey, Shunn asked, "Will you carry me or shall I carry you?" The man said, "O ignorant one, how can a rider carry a rider?" They continued until they reached a garden replete with ripe vegetables, and Shunn asked, "Do you think that these crops have been eaten or not?" The man said, "O ignorant one, do you not see these vegetables still here before you?" And they continued until they passed by a funeral procession, and Shunn asked, "Do you think that the man for whom this procession is marching forth is alive or dead?" The man said, "I have not seen anyone more ignorant than you; do you think that they would carry him to his grave alive?" When they finally reached the village, the man went into his home, while Shunn waited outside. The man had a daughter, named Tabaqah, and he told her the entire story of the man who was standing outside. She said, "When he said, 'Should I carry you or will you carry me?' he meant, 'Will you speak to me or will I speak to you so that we may pass the hours of our journey?' When he asked, 'Whether the crops have been eaten or not?' he meant, 'Did the owners of the crops sell them and then eat their proceeds or not?' And when he spoke of the dead man, he meant - did he leave behind any children or any great work to keep his remembrance alive or not." The man went outside and told Shunn what his daughter said. Shunn proposed, asking for her hand in marriage, and the father married her to him.

'Umar and Mu'awiyah

May Allâh have mercy on the Leader of the Believers, 'Umar bin Khattab ﷺ, who sought little from this world and who very much disliked to see manifestations of richness or extravagance from his governors. On one occasion he visited the governor of Sham, Mu'awiyah bin Abi Sufyan, who gave a warm welcome to him and arranged for a very large convoy. 'Umar was amazed and said, "By Allâh, he is the Kisra of the Arabs." He became very angry indeed and reproached his governor for being extravagant. Mu'awiyah responded, "In our land, there are many spies from the enemy. Therefore, we must show them the dignity and power of the ruler so as to instill fear into their hearts. But if you order me, I will do so, and if you forbid me, I will abstain." 'Umar said, "If what you say is true, then it is the opinion of a very intelligent and wise man. And if it is false, then it is the deception of a very literate and civilized man." Mu'awiyah said, "Order me, O Leader of the Believers." He said, "I neither order you nor forbid you."

Arguing over that which is Delicious

As a ruler and his wife were seated for dinner, they argued over which of two kinds of sweets was better and more delicious. On the same day, a famous judge came to meet the ruler, who invited him immediately to join them in their meal. When the judge arrived, the ruler informed him about the difference of opinion between himself and his wife over the two kinds of sweets. He demanded of the judge to rule between them, and the judge playfully said, "I cannot rule over that which is absent!"

And so the servants hurried to present before him the two different kinds of sweets. He extended his hand and ate from the sweet that the ruler loved more, and then he said, "A beautiful and delicious kind of sweet, and all praise is for Allâh, Who has made it sweet." Then he went to the other sweet, which the wife of the ruler loved more. He began to eat from it and he said, "A beautiful and delicious kind of sweet, and all praise is for Allâh, Who has blessed us to taste it." He continued to eat, from one kind and then from the other, until he could eat no more. And all the while the ruler and his wife were looking at him. When the judge finally finished after what seemed to be an endless amount of time, the ruler asked him which was better and more delicious. He said, "O ruler! I have not seen anyone more eloquent in arguing a case than these two. Each time I intended to rule for one of them, the other came forth with his proofs and arguments." All those who were present laughed and the disagreement came to an end.

Justice, even with the Enemy

When 'Umar bin 'Abdul-'Aziz assumed the duties of the caliphate, a party from Samarqand came to him, claiming that Qutaibah bin Muslim, the leader of the Muslim army, attacked them in a treacherous manner. 'Umar wrote to his governor over there, requesting him to appoint a judge to rule in the matter. He ordered that the Muslims should leave Samarqand should the judge rule in favor of its inhabitants. The judge - who was a Muslim - ruled that the Muslims should leave and that the leader of the Muslim army should then warn them of their attack, according to the principles of Islamic warfare, so that the inhabitants of Samarqand could make their preparations for fighting with the Muslims. When the inhabitants of Samarqand saw this - this unparalleled example of justice in history, they said that it is a nation that must not be fought, for their rule is a rule of mercy and kindness. And so they were pleased with allowing the Muslim army to remain.

Have you ever heard of such an instance in history when an army conquered a city, when those who were defeated complained to the victorious nation, and when a judge from that victorious nation ruled that the army attacked in a way that was not lawful and that they had to leave that city? I know of no such instance or example from any nation throughout history.

He ran from the Prayer

A Bedouin prayed behind an Imam who was reciting from the Qur'ân:

"Did We not destroy the first ones?" (Qur'ân 77:16)

The Bedouin happened to be in the first row, and upon hearing that Verse, he moved to a row that was further behind. Then the Imam recited:

"So shall We make later ones to follow them." (Qur'ân 77:17)

The Bedouin then moved to another row. Next, the Imam recited this Verse:

"Thus we will deal with the Mujrimun (polytheists, disbelievers, sinners, etc)!" (Qur'ân 77:18)

The Bedouin, whose name happened to be Mujrim, ran away from the congregation, saying, "By Allâh, I am his target." When some other bedouins met him, they said, "What is the matter, O Mujrim?" He said, "Indeed, the Imam destroyed the first ones and then the last ones, and he wanted to destroy me as well. By Allâh, I do not want to see him after this day."

Political Acumen

It was said to a ruler, "What has made you reach this level?" He said, "I forgave when I was able to exact revenge, I was soft even when I was severe, I was just even regarding my own self, and I left enough place in my love and hate so that I could still easily change from one to the other."

He deserved a Large Endowment

During the days of Hisham bin 'Abdul-Malik, a group of Arabs came to his court but were afraid to speak to him. Among them was a young man named Dirwas bin Habib, who was only 16 years of age at the time. Hisham spotted him among the group and said to his guard, "Now anyone who wishes to enter and meet me may do so - even young children!" Dirwas jumped forward and said, "O Leader of the Believers, we have been afflicted with three hard years - in the first our fat melted away, the second year ate away our flesh, and the third affected our bones. In your hands you have surplus money. If that surplus is for Allâh, then divide it among his slaves; and if it belongs to them, then why do you prevent that wealth from them? And if it is yours, then give it in charity to them, for indeed, Allâh rewards those who give charity." Hisham said, "In each of the three scenarios, the young man left no excuse for me." He ordered for the group to be given 100,000 dinars and for that young man to be given 100,000 derhams.

Choosing a Husband

A man asked Hasan bin 'Ali ﵁, "I have a daughter and people have proposed her, so to whom should I marry her?"

He said, "Marry her to one who fears Allâh, for if he loves her, he will honor her; and if he hates her, he will not wrong her."

A Bedouin at the Dinner Table of Al-Hajjaj

A Bedouin attended a banquet that was held by Al-Hajjaj. When the sweets were served, Al-Hajjaj let the Bedouin eat a bite and then announced, "Whoever eats this, I will cut his throat." Everyone who was present refrained from eating; the Bedouin, however, alternated between looking at the sweets and between looking at Al-Hajjaj; this continued for a while, until he finally said, "O Leader of the Believers, I kindly ask you to do well by my children." And then he quickly attacked the sweets.

Our Pious Predecessors and Their Dutifulness to Their Parents

Muhammad bin Sirin related that the price of a date-palm tree was as high as 1000 dirhams during the period of 'Uthman bin 'Affan ﷺ. Once during that period, Usamah went to a date-palm tree that belonged to him, pierced it, and took out its palm pith. Then he went and gave it to his mother to eat. People said to him, "What made you do this when you know that the price of a date-palm tree has reached 1000 dirhams?" He said, "My mother asked me for it (for the palm pith), and she has never asked me for anything that I was able to give her except that I gave it to her."

He had to choose between His Wife and Money

In Kufah, there was a woman whose husband was very poor. She said to him, "Travel in the lands and seek from Allâh's bounty, and perhaps you will be given provision." He went to Sham and earned 300 dirhams, with which he bought a beautiful camel. He mounted it, intending to return to Kufah. However, he was dismayed to learn that the camel was wild and disobedient, and at one point he became so angry at it that he hastily made a bad oath. He said that he would divorce his wife unless he sold the camel for one dirham the day he returned to Kufah. When he finally returned home, he greatly regretted what he did and he became miserable because of his hasty action. His wife asked him what happened and at first he denied that anything had occurred. But finally, in a fit of desperation, he told her the whole story, and that he had to choose between the camel that was worth 300 dirhams and between her, because if he was to keep his wife, he would have to sell the camel for only one dirham. She said, "I will find a way out of this for you, so that you neither break your oath nor lose anything." She picked up a cat and hung it around the neck of the camel with a rope and she said, "Go to the marketplace and say: this cat is for 300 dirhams and the camel is for one dirham only, and I will not sell them separately." When he went to the marketplace, a Bedouin was walking around the camel, saying, "How healthy it is, how beautiful it is, how noble it looks ... were it not for this partner that is on its neck!"

The Best of Women

A Bedouin was asked about women, and being a man who was experienced with them, he said: "The best woman is the tallest when she stands, the most prominent when she sits, and the most truthful when she speaks. She is the one whose anger subsides quickly, and whose laugh is a beautiful smile. When she does anything, she does it well. She obeys her husband and adheres to her home. She is honored among her people, yet insignificant in her own mind - affectionate and fertile, and all of her affair is good."

"I was hoping to find Something else!"

The ruler of Germany once visited Turkey. A member of the Turkish Congress wanted to show the German leader how civilized they had become. He prepared a group of schoolgirls to welcome him, and he dressed them up in a gaudy manner, and each one of them was to give him a bouquet of roses.

The German ruler was shocked to see the dress of the young girls, and he said to those in charge: "Indeed I was hoping to see the *Hijab* and modest dress in Turkey, which is in accordance to the ruling of your Islamic religion. And here I am witnessing lewd dress, which we are afflicted with in Europe, and which is leading us to the loss of family, to the destruction of societies, and to the ruin of children!"

He intended to repay His Debt and Allâh helped Him do so

The following story is related in *Sahih Al-Bukhari* from Abu Hurairah ﷺ from Allâh's Messenger ﷺ: A man from the Children of Israel asked another man from the Children of Israel to lend him 1000 dinars, and he answered, "Bring witnesses that I will make bear witness (to this transaction)." The first man said, "Allâh is enough as a Witness." He said, "Then bring me a guarantor." He said, "Allâh is enough as a Guarantor." The man said, "You have spoken the truth."

He gave him the money for a fixed term. The debtor traveled by sea and when he fulfilled the purpose of his journey, he was looking for a ship that he could board and return on to pay the debt at the appointed time. However, he was not able to find a ship, so he took a piece of wood, pierced it, and thrust into it 1000 dinars along with a letter to the creditor. Then he took it to the ocean.

He said, "O Allâh, You know that I borrowed 1000 dinars from such and such person, and he asked me for a guarantor. I said: Allâh is enough as a Guarantor. He was pleased with You, and he also asked for a witness. I said: Allâh is enough as a Witness, and he was pleased with You (as a Witness). And I have not been able to find a ship on which I could send him that which is due to him, so indeed I trust it to you."

He threw the piece of wood into the ocean until it was

swallowed by it, and then he went away. He then continued to search for a boat on which he could return to his country. The creditor went out looking - perhaps a boat would come with his wealth. He found a piece of wood - in which was the money - and he took it to his family as firewood. When he broke the wood open, he found the money and the letter.

Then the debtor returned, bringing with him 1000 dinars. He said, "By Allâh, I continued to search for a boat in order to return your wealth to you, but I did not find one until I found the one that I came on now." The other man asked, "And did you send anything to me?"... "For indeed, Allâh paid for you through the wood that you sent."

This is how Friendship should be

Abu Darda' ﷺ said to his wife, "If you see that I am angry, then appease me; and if I see that you are angry, I will appease you - otherwise why should we keep company with one another?" When this saying reached Imam Zuhri, he said, "That is how companionship should be."

Juraij, the Worshiper

The story of Juraij is significant, for it contains many very important lessons. Juraij was a righteous man who was a prolific worshiper from the Children of Israel; however, he angered his mother one day when she came to him three times, asking to speak to him. Each time, he was busy in prayer, and he was torn between answering his mother and continuing in his prayer, and each time he chose the prayer. She became angry and invoked against him with a supplication that Allâh answered. She supplicated that he should not die until he lives to see the faces of lewd women. Later on in his life, a woman accused him of fornicating with her and claimed that he was the father of her child. Then Allâh saved him because of his righteousness and his piety. But before that happened, people became angry against him because of the woman's claim, and they went to his abode and destroyed his place of worship. He made ablution, prayed, and then asked for the child to be brought forth. In front of all who were present, he asked the child, "Who is your father, O child." It spoke by the Will of Allâh, saying, "The shepherd." The people regretted having destroyed his place of worship, and said, "We will build your place of worship from gold." He refused, saying, "But rather (build it) from mud."

An Example of Piety

Tawus related from his father a story about a man who had four children. He became sick, and one of them said, "Either you take care of him during his sickness, and you will have nothing from his inheritance, or let me take care of him during his sickness, and I will have nothing from his inheritance!" The other children said, "No, you take care of him and you will have nothing from the inheritance." And so he took care of him until he died, and as he had promised, he did not take anything from his father's estate.

Later on, it was said to him in a dream, "Come to such and such place, and take 100 dinars!" During the dream, he asked, "Are there blessings in that money?" It was said to him, "No." When he woke up, he told his wife about his dream. She said, "Take the money, for from its blessings is that you will be able to clothe us and we will be able to live off of it."

On the following night, he saw a similar dream, in which it was said to him, "Come to such and such place, and take 10 dinars!" He said, "Are there blessings in that money?" They said, "No." In the morning he told that to his wife, and she said the same as she did the day before. He refused to take it, and on the third night, it was said to him, "Come to such and such place, and take one dinar!" He asked, "And are there blessings in it?" It was said, "Yes!" When he woke up, he went and actually found the dinar. He then went to the marketplace and saw a man carrying two fish; he asked, "How much are they for?" The man said, "For one dinar." He bought them and returned to his home. When he cut them open, he found in the belly of each a pearl, the likes of which no man from his land had seen before.

The Reward for visiting One's Brother

Muslim related from Abu Hurairah ﷺ from the Prophet ﷺ that a man went to visit his brother in another village. On his path, Allâh made an angel lie in wait for him, and when he reached that point, the angel asked, "Where do you wish to go?" He said, "I want to visit a brother of mine in this village." The angel said, "Does he have to give any blessing to you that you wish to collect?" He said, "No, except that I love him for Allâh." The angel said, "I am indeed a messenger from Allâh to you to inform you that Allâh indeed loves you as you love him (i.e., your brother)." (*Sahih Muslim* 2567)

The Signs of an Ignorant Person

Abud-Darda' ﷺ said: "The signs of the ignorant one are three: self-conceit, much talk in that which does not concern him, and forbidding others from something that he himself commits."

Dutifulness to One's Parents

'Abdullah bin Abi Aufa ؓ related: We were with the Prophet ﷺ and someone came to him, saying, "O Messenger of Allâh! A young man is dying, and it was said to him, say: 'None has the right to be worshiped except Allâh,' but he was not able to say it!"

The Prophet ﷺ asked, "Did he use to pray?" The man said, "Yes." Allâh's Messenger ﷺ stood and so we stood with him. He entered upon the young man and said, "Say: 'None has the right to be worshiped except Allâh'!" He said, "I am not able to." The Prophet ﷺ asked, "And why not?" The man said, "He was undutiful to his mother."

The Prophet ﷺ said, "Is his mother alive?" They said, "Yes." He said, "Then call her." They called her and she came, and the Prophet ﷺ said, "This is your son?" She said, "Yes." He said, "Suppose that a huge fire is kindled for him, and it is said to you, if you intercede for him, we will leave him free; otherwise we will burn him with this fire. Would you then intercede for him?" She said, "O Messenger of Allâh, in that case I would intercede." He said, "Then make Allâh and myself bear witness that you are indeed pleased with him." She said, "O Allâh, I make You bear witness and I make Your Messenger bear witness that I am indeed pleased with him." The Prophet ﷺ said, "O young man! Say: 'None has the right to be worshiped except Allâh alone and He has no partners,' and bear witness that: 'Muhammad is His slave and Messenger'." The young man spoke those words, and the Prophet ﷺ said, "All praise is for Allâh, Who has saved him through me from the Hellfire."

"If You choose Me as Your Leader, then You must obey Me"

Mus'ab bin Ahmad bin Mus'ab said that Abu Muhammad Al-Mirwazi passed through Baghdad, desiring to go to Makkah. I wanted to accompany him, and so I went to him and asked permission to join him in his journey, but he refused. Two years later, he came again, and again I went to him, greeted him, and asked permission to go with him. He said, "I stipulate one condition: that one of us is leader, and that the other one must not oppose him in his decisions." I said, "You are the leader." He said, "No, you be the leader." I said, "You are older and more worthy." He said, "Then do not disobey me." I said, "Okay." We started our journey, and whenever the time for a meal arrived, he would prefer me to himself, which I didn't like, but whenever I voiced my disagreement, he said, "Did I not stipulate that you should not oppose me?" That was our way, and I ended up regretting my keeping company with him because he would inflict much harm upon himself by taking care of me and by choosing me over himself at all times.

On some days during the journey, the rain came down heavily; whenever that had been the case he would make me sit down and cover me with a cloth in his hand, keeping me dry, but remaining wet himself. It reached the point that I wished that I had never went out with him in the first place, and I could not stand to see him continue to inflict pain on himself. This is how he was in all matters until we reached Makkah - may Allâh have mercy on him.

How to make Amends after a Domestic Dispute

Sahl bin Sa'd As-Sa'idi related that the Prophet ﷺ went to the house of Fatimah ؓ, but he didn't find 'Ali. He asked, "Where is your cousin (who was also her husband)?" She said, "There occurred between me and him something, and he was angry with me and went out." Allâh's Messenger ﷺ said to someone, "Find out where he is." The man said, "He is sitting down in the mosque." The Prophet ﷺ went there and saw that he was lying down; his robe was falling from his side, and there was some dust on him. The Prophet ﷺ began to say, "Stand, O Abu Turab; stand, O Abu Turab." Sahl said, "He later on had no name that was more beloved to him than that name."

When he was angry with his wife and went outside, it was an opportunity for 'Ali to calm down his anger, which could otherwise easily have gotten out of control. Contemplate the wisdom of the Prophet ﷺ; he went to 'Ali in the mosque and playfully called him Abu Turab (the father of dust - because he was covered with dust). He was making him feel better without asking for the details or the cause behind the difference of opinion. Fatimah did the same, for she did not tell her father the details of the fight between her and her husband, 'Ali; rather, she only said, "There occurred between me and him something, he became angry with me and went outside." There is indeed an important lesson to be learned here by all husbands and wives, as well as by their parents.

Hasan Basri

He advised some of his students admonishing them about avoiding the state of being proud. He said:

1) Do not deceive yourself into becoming too proud because you are in a good or righteous environment, for there is no place that is better than Paradise, and our father, Adam ﷺ, experienced there what is known to all.

2) Do not become proud merely because you worship often, for consider what happened to *Iblis* (Satan) after he spent a great deal of time worshiping.

3) Do not think yourself great because you have met with righteous people, for there is no man more righteous than the Prophet ﷺ, yet the disbelievers and hypocrites did not benefit by simply knowing him.

Generosity, Friendship, and Good Companionship

When the time for *Hajj* would come, Ibn Mubarak would gather his friends from Marw, and they would say, "We will accompany you." He would say, "Bring your expense money." He would take expense money from them for the trip and place that money in a box, which he would then lock away. He would take them to Baghdad and continue to spend on them, always feeding them the best of food and the best of sweets. And then, wearing the best of clothing, they would leave Baghdad until they would reach the city of the Messenger. He would say to each one of them, "Did not your family ask you to buy for them some of the merchandise of Al-Madinah?" When they reached Makkah, he would say to each one of them after the *Hajj* was over, "Did not your family ask you to buy for them from the merchandise of Makkah?" And he would buy for them whatever they wanted. He would leave Makkah and he would continue to spend on them until they returned home. Then the doors of their homes would be polished, and after three days passed, he would hold for them a banquet, for which he prepared special clothes for each one of them. After eating and enjoying themselves, he would call for the box of money. He would open it, and give to each man from them his bag of spending money, upon which was written his name, and each person would find that nothing was missing from what they originally put in those bags.

A Mother's True Love

Abu Hurairah ﵁ related that Allâh's Messenger ﷺ said: "There were two women and each of them had a son. A wolf came and took away the son of one of them. One said to the other, 'It took away your son.' And the other said, 'No, it took away your son.' They went to Dawud ﵇ for judgment, and he ruled for the older of the two. Then they went to Sulaiman bin Dawud ﵇ and informed him of what happened. He said, 'Bring to me a knife and I will cut him in two.' The younger of the two women said, 'Do not do so, may Allâh have mercy on you, for he is her son.' Then Sulaiman (knowing the love of a mother), ruled for the younger of the two women." (*Sahih Bukhari* and *Sahih Muslim*)

One's Recompense for going through a Calamity

Bukhari and Muslim related from Abu Hurairah ﵁ that Allâh's Messenger ﷺ said: "Whenever a Muslim loses three of his children, the Hellfire will not touch him, except to fulfill an oath." And that is referring to the Verse:

> "There is not one of you but will pass over it (Hell)." (Qur'ân 19:71)

This refers to passing over the bridge that is erected over the Hellfire - and may Allâh protect us from it.

Strike Him as He struck You

'Abdur-Rahman bin Al-Hakam (the brother of Marwan bin Al-Hakam) struck a freed slave from the inhabitants of Al-Madinah, whose name was Hannat. At that time, Marwan bin Al-Hakam was governor of Al-Madinah. Hannat complained to Marwan about his brother 'Abdur-Rahman.

The governor gathered both his brother and the freed slave together, and he said to the latter, "Strike him as he struck you."

Hannat said, "By Allâh, that is not what I wanted; my only intention was to teach him that above him is a ruler who will support me over him. And I have given it (i.e., the right to strike him) as a gift to you." Marwan said, "I do not accept it from you, so take your right." Hannat said, "By Allâh, I will not strike him, but rather I give it as a gift to you." Marwan said, "If you think that by striking him you will make me angry, you are wrong, for by Allâh, I will not become angry. So take your right." Hannat said, "Indeed I forgive it as a gift to you, and by Allâh, I will not strike him." Marwan said, "By Allâh, I will not accept it. If you forgive, then do so for the one who struck you or for Allâh." Hannat said, "I forgive it for Allâh."

I am the First to be led to the Truth

The Caliph, An-Nasir, decided to build a castle for one of his wives in Qurtubah; however, the location on which he wanted to build the castle was neighbored by a small home that was inhabited by orphans under the patronage of the judge, Mundhir bin Sa'eed. The Caliph asked to buy that small home. They said, "We will not sell it except by the permission of the judge."

The Caliph sent experts for an appraisal of the house, and the price that they estimated did not please the judge in the least. Not satisfied with the price, and fearing that the ruler would take it by force, the judge ordered for the house to be destroyed, and he sold the timber for a price that was greater than that which was estimated by the experts that were sent! When the Caliph found out what he did, he became angry and said to him, "And what made you do that?" The judge said, "I did what I did based on Allâh's Saying:

> 'As for the ship, it belonged to *Masakin* (poor people) working in the sea. So, I wished to make a defective damage in it, as there was a king after them who seized every ship by force.' (Qur'ân 18:79)

I sold the timber for more than the amount that was estimated by your experts, and yet the land remains for the orphans, so now pay a price that you see fit to pay." The Caliph said, "I am the first to be led to the truth, and may Allâh reward you well for us and for our nation."

The Final Command of the Ruler Muhammad Al-Fateh to His Son

Muhammad Al-Fateh, a Muslim ruler during the Ottoman Empire was known for his knowledge, bravery, justice, piety and humility. He was able to conquer Constantinople when many before him had failed. And at that time he was only 23 years old.

At the end of his life, he advised his son, saying: "Here I am dying, but I am not sorry, for I have left behind one such as you. Be just, righteous, and merciful. Give generously to the people and defend them without distinguishing between them. Spread Islam, for that is compulsory upon the kings of the earth. Give precedence to religion over all things and do not become tired in that pursuit. Do not appoint people who do not care about religion and who do not stay away from the major sins, those who have plunged themselves into wickedness and into evil innovations. Expand the borders of our nation through *Jihad* and watch over the wealth of the treasury, making sure that it is not wasted. Never extend your hand to the wealth of anyone from the people except by the right of Islam. Guarantee the weak for their strength and give freely your generosity to those who deserve it."

Qadi Abu Yusuf's Advice to the Ruler, Harun Rasheed

Qadi Abu Yusuf Ya'qub bin Ibrahim prefaced his book, *Al-Khiraj*, with these wonderful words, which he had written to the Leader of the Believers, Harun Rasheed:

"May Allâh prolong the life of the Leader of the Believers, and may He bestow continuous honor for him in order to complete that favor for him. And may He make the blessings that He gave to him continue into the blessings of the Hereafter, which are never depleted and which never go away. And may he be blessed with the companionship of the Prophet ﷺ.

O Leader of the Believers, indeed Allâh - and all praise is for Him - has made you to bear the responsibility of a great matter indeed, the reward for which is indeed great, and the punishment for which is the most severe of punishments. He has appointed you over the matter of this nation. In the morning and in the night, you are busy working for a great number of people that Allâh has made you responsible over and has entrusted you with and has tested you through. He has appointed you over their affairs, but the building does not remain whose foundation is not build upon *Taqwa,* and do not forsake those whom Allâh appointed you over from this nation, for strength is in action, by the Will of Allâh!

Do not delay today's deeds until tomorrow, for if you do so, you will have become lost: death often comes before hope. Spend your time with action before death, for there is no action after death.

The happiest of shepherds with Allâh on the Day of Judgment is the shepherd whose flock is pleased with him. And do not go astray, for your flock will go astray with you. Do not rule by desires and do not take by anger. If you see two matters before you, one being for the Hereafter and the other for this world, choose the one of the Hereafter over the one of this world, for the Hereafter remains while this world is fleeting. Regarding Allâh's affair, deal with people equally – both those who are near and those who are far. And do not fear the blame of anyone if you do something for Allâh. And be careful, for caution is in the heart and not on the tongue. Fear Allâh, which is achieved through caution and prevention. Whoever fears Allâh, He protects him. Enough misery and regret there is on the Day of Judgment for the one who knows what he does not do, on the day when feet will slip, when colors will change, when people will be standing for long, and when the accountability will indeed be severe." Allâh (the Exalted) says:

> "And verily, a day with your Lord is as a thousand years of what you reckon." (Qur'ân 22:47)

And He says:

> "That will be a Day of Decision! We have brought you and the men of old together!" (Qur'ân 77:38)

Wise Sayings

Rabi' bin Khuthaim said: "All that is desired not for Allâh, but for something or someone else, perishes."

Abu Hamzah Ath-Thumali said: "Ali bin Husain used to carry loaves of bread on his back during the nighttime, to give them in charity. And he would say: 'Indeed, charity that is given in secret extinguishes the anger of the Lord.'"

'Amr bin Thabit said, "When 'Ali bin Husain died, they washed him and found black stains on his back. They asked: 'What is this?' And they were told: 'He used to carry sacks of wheat during the nighttime on his back, and he would distribute them to the poor inhabitants of Al-Madinah.'"

Advice from Fudail bin 'Iyad

He once said in a sermon, addressing both the young and the old: "O group of young men! I have come across many crops that were defective even before they grew up! O group of old men! And are crops harvested except after they become ripe? And what are you waiting for? And what excuse do you have to present? What will the young and the old among you say, when the All-Knowing will say,

> "Did We not give you lives long enough, so that whosoever would receive admonition could receive it? And the warner came to you." (Qur'ân 35:37)

'Umar bin 'Abdul-'Aziz

'Umar bin 'Abdul-'Aziz ﷺ had a servant named dirham, who would gather wood for him and take care of his sheep. 'Umar one day asked him, "What do the people say, O dirham?" He said, "And what should they say – all of them are in a good state of affairs, while you and I are in a bad state of affairs." He asked, "And how is that?" He said, "I was with you before you became caliph, when your clothes were good, your mount was strong, and your food was wonderful. When you were appointed as ruler, I was hoping to relax and work less, but instead my work has become more difficult and you are always in a state of tribulation." 'Umar said, "You are free. Go away from me and leave me in the state that I find myself to be in until Allâh makes a way out for me from it."

He wants to prolong Those Two States

Walid bin 'Abdul-Malik was once in a mosque and everyone left it except for an old man who was weak in his old age. Those present wanted to help him leave, but Walid told them to leave him alone. He then went to the old man and said, "O *Shaikh*, do you love death?" He said, "No, O Leader of the Believers. Youth and its evil have left and old age and its goodness have come. When I stand, I begin to praise Allâh, and when I sit, I begin to remember Him. And whenever I enter into one of those two states, I wish for my sojourn in that state to be prolonged."

He followed the Way of Allâh's Messenger ﷺ

When 'Umar bin 'Abdul-'Aziz رحمه الله was appointed as caliph, he began with cases related to transgression against the rights of others. He began with his family and those closest to him. His family gathered together to meet with his aunt, whom he honored and revered. They asked her to intercede for them regarding that which he intended to do, and when she spoke to him about the matter, he said, "Indeed Allâh's Messenger ﷺ followed a way, and when he died, his Companions followed the same path that the Messenger ﷺ followed. When the matter was then taken up by others, they dragged it to the right and left of that path, and by Allâh, if my life is prolonged, I will return the matter to the path that Allâh's Messenger ﷺ and his Companions followed."

From the Wise Sayings of Luqman

"If you're in prayer, take care of your heart; if you're eating, take care of your throat; if you're in another man's house, take care of your eyes; if you are among people, take care of your tongue. Remember two matters and forget two matters: Remember Allâh and death; forget any good that you have done to another and any evil that was done to you by another."

The Opinion of a Woman saved the Army

The Mother of the Believers, Umm Salamah ﷺ, was endowed with sound opinions and an intelligent mind, which were of great use on the day of Al-Hudaibiyah. When the Prophet ﷺ completed the affair of the agreement at Al-Hudaibiyah, he said to his Companions, "Stand, slaughter (your sacrifice), and then shave your heads." Not a single person among them stood up, not even after the Prophet ﷺ repeated his command three times. Then Allâh's Messenger ﷺ entered upon Umm Salamah and mentioned to her the treatment he received from the people. He said, "The people have become destroyed." She said, "O Prophet of Allâh, do you want that? Go out, then speak not a single word to anyone from them, until you slaughter your sacrifice and then call your barber to shave your head." The Prophet ﷺ went out, spoke to no one from them, until he performed both of those actions - he slaughtered his sacrifice and called his barber to shave his head. When the people saw that, they stood and slaughtered their sacrifices. Then they began to shave one another's heads - they were so miserable for having first disobeyed the Prophet ﷺ that they almost hurt one another while shaving each other. That was a most sound opinion that Allâh inspired to Umm Salamah, and as a result, the problem was resolved and the Muslim Army was saved after having at first gone against the commands of Allâh's Messenger ﷺ.

A Mother's Advice to Her Daughter prior to Marriage

Harith bin 'Amr, the king of Kindah, proposed to marry the daughter of 'Auf bin Muhillim. Her mother said to her the following words on the day that she was to be taken to her husband:

"My daughter, if advice were to be left off to those of virtue, I would have abstained from advising you, but good advice is a reminder to the heedless and a helper to the wise. If a woman didn't need a husband because of the richness of her parents and because of their great need for her, then you would have been the richest of people in that regard; however, women were created for men and men were created for women.

My daughter, you are indeed leaving this house that you have been raised in, leaving to go to a man that you do not know and to a partner that you are not used to. Be a slave to him and he will become your slave, and preserve for him 10 qualities:

1, 2) Sincerity toward him by always been satisfied with your condition and good obedience to him.

3, 4) Be careful about his eyes and his nose: do not let him see you in a bad state and do not let him smell from you any odor except for the most fragrant of odors.

5, 6) Look after the time of his sleep and the time of his meals, for the continued state of hunger makes one weak and restless sleep leads to anger.

7, 8) Protect his wealth and look after his family – the key to wealth is good estimation, and the key to the family is good planning.

9, 10) Never disobey his command and never spread his secrets – the former embitters his heart and the latter will make you unsafe from his betrayal."

Eat, O Bedouin

During a battle in Constantinople, Mughirah bin 'Abdur-Rahman bin Harith bin Hisham was injured in the eye. He was a man who was known for his generosity, especially when it came to feeding his guests. It is related that a Bedouin came to him once and continued to stare at him without eating anything that was proffered to him. Mughirah said, "What is with you, Bedouin, that you do not eat as the people eat?" He said, "By Allâh, I am indeed amazed at the abundance of food that you serve, but I have doubts about your eye." Mughirah asked, "And what makes you have doubts about it?" He said, "I see that you are one-eyed and that you feed others. And I have heard one who was describing Dajjal in a sermon in the mosque (that he is one-eyed)." Mughirah laughed and said, "Eat, O Bedouin, for indeed the Dajjal will not be inflicted in his eye while he is fighting in the way of Allâh!"

Allâh blinded Them

Imam Qurtubi ﷺ said: "In the land of Andalus, I was once fleeing from the enemy. Two horsemen came after me, and it was a difficult situation indeed because I was in open terrain, without having anything to hide under or in. I began to recite the beginning part of *Surat Ya-Sin* and other Verses and chapters of the Qur'ân; and they passed right by me, returning thereafter from whence they came, and I heard one of them saying to the other: 'He is a devil (that he is able to hide in open terrain)!' Allâh blinded their sight so that they were not able to see me - and I praise Allâh with much praise for that."

Umm Habibah's Dream

Umm Habibah ﷺ said: I saw someone coming to me in my sleep and saying to me: "Mother of the Believers." I then woke up and interpreted it to mean that Allâh's Messenger ﷺ was going to marry me. Immediately after my period of waiting ended, a messenger from Najashi came to my door, seeking permission to enter. It was a young girl named Abrahah, she came in and said, "Verily, the king says to you: 'Indeed Allâh's Messenger wrote to me, saying that I should marry you to him.'" I said to the messenger, "May Allâh give you glad tidings." She said, "The king says that you should appoint someone to marry you off."

Do not attach Your Heart to Other than Allâh

Imam Ibn Taimiyyah ﷺ said: "Anyone whose heart is attached to the creation, hoping for someone from the creation to help him or provide for him or guide him, then his heart submits to them and to the degree that his heart submits to them he becomes their slave. This holds true, even if he is outwardly a ruler or a guardian over those whom he treats as masters. The wise one looks at realities and not at appearances. So if a man's heart is attached to his wife, even though that is permissible, his heart remains a prisoner to her, and she may rule over him as she pleases - though outwardly he is her master and her husband. In reality, he is her prisoner and her slave, especially if she knows how much he is in need of her and how much he is in love with her and how much he feels that she cannot be replaced by anyone else. At that point, she rules over him as the tyrant master rules over his subjugated slave, who cannot escape or go free. Indeed for the heart to be taken as a prisoner is a much greater matter than for the body to be taken as a slave or prisoner. Even a body that is a slave can have in it a serene and peaceful and happy heart. As for the heart that is a slave to other than Allâh (the Exalted), then that is true humiliation, imprisonment and slavery."

The Repentance of Abu Mahjan Ath-Thaqafi

Ibn Sirin related that Abu Mahjan Ath-Thaqafi, a great warrior, would constantly be whipped for drinking alcohol, but it happened so much that those in authority felt that they had no other choice but to the imprison him and tie him up. On the day of Qadisiyyah, the Muslims were having a hard fight. Abu Mahjan was in prison near the battlefield, he felt inside of him that the disbelievers were overcoming the Muslims in battle, and so he sent a message to the wife of Sa'd; the message read: "Abu Mahjan says to you - if you free him, allow him to ride on the horse, and give him weapons, he will be the first to return to you unless he is killed." She ordered for him to be untied, and he was given the horse and weapons. He wrapped his face with a cloth and went out until he reached the battlefield, and he fought valiantly, killing man after man, opponent after opponent. Sa'd looked at him and was amazed. He said, "Who is that rider?" Very quickly Allâh (the Exalted) made the Muslims victorious. As soon as the battle ended, Abu Mahjan hastened to return and put back the weapons. And when he returned, he tied his legs as they were tied before. When Sa'd returned, his wife asked, "How was the battle?" He began to inform her and said, "We faced a difficult situation for a while, and then Allâh sent a man on a horse. Had I not left Abu Mahjan tied up, I would have said that those were the (fighting) qualities of Abu Mahjan." She said, "By Allâh, indeed he was Abu Mahjan," and she related to him his story.

Sa'd called him, untied him, and said, "We will never again whip you for alcohol." Abu Mahjan said, "And I, by Allâh, will never drink it again. I refused to leave it off prior to this because you would whip me." And he never drank alcohol after that.

The Repentance of a Man Who dealt in Usury

Habib was a businessman who worked as a currency exchanger. He one day passed by a group of children who were playing, and they were saying to one another, "Here comes the one who eats usury." He lowered his head and said, "O my Lord, You have made my secret known to these children."

He returned from whence he came and a change overcame him. He cried, repented, and asked Allâh for forgiveness. He placed all of his wealth before him and said, "O my Lord, I indeed purchase myself from You with this wealth, so free me." When the morning came, he gave all of the wealth in charity. Then he devoted himself to worship, which he became so preoccupied with, that he was always seen to be fasting, standing for prayer, or remembering Allâh. News of his righteousness spread among the people until he became known as Habib, the worshiper. One day, he again passed by the same group of children that had previously belittled him because he dealt in usury. When they saw him this time, they said to one another, "Be quite, for Habib, the worshiper has come." He heard that, cried for a long time, and praised Allâh.

He Prevented Evil from Occurring

Ibn 'Asakir related from Abul-Husain An-Nuri that he once passed by many containers of alcohol. He asked, "What is this? And to whom does it belong?" He was told that it belonged to Al-Mu'tadid, the ruler at the time. He began to break open the barrels and spill all the alcohol, and he continued to do so until only one barrel remained. The police came, took him, and made him stand before Al-Mu'tadid, who said, "Who has appointed you to enjoin good and forbid evil?" He said, "The One Who appointed you as ruler, O Leader of the Believers." Al-Mu'tadid bowed his head, then raised it, and said, "And what made you do that?" He said, "Compassion for you – to remove harm from You." He again bowed his head and then raised it, saying, "And why did you allow for one barrel to remain?" He said, "I had broken the previous barrels in glorification of Allâh (the Exalted) and I was not thinking of anyone else, until finally, I reached the last barrel, when pride entered into my heart - that I was showing bravery in the face of someone similar to you, and so I abstained from breaking it." Al-Mu'tadid said, "Go, for I give you a free hand to prevent any evil that you see."

He rejected the Testimony of the Ruler

Ba-Yazid, who was the ruler at the time, went to give testimony in a courthouse, whose judge was Shamsuddin Muhammad Hamzah Al-Funari; however, the judge rejected the testimony of the ruler, and when the latter asked why, the former said, "You do not pray with the congregation."

First, we should contemplate why his testimony was rejected, and then ask ourselves, whether our testimony would be rejected for the same reason.

Second, we should appreciate the bravery of the judge, who derived his powers of judgment from Allâh's *Shari'ah,* and not from man-made laws. The ruler, who was as much impressed by the bravery of the judge as he was by his justness, built a (mosque) in front of his castle, and never thereafter missed prayer in congregation.

Choose well the Mother of Your Children

A Bedouin one day said to his children, "I did good to you not only when you were young or when you grew up, but also before you were born." They said, "Indeed we know that you have treated us well when we were very young and then when we grew up, but how is it that you treated us well even before we were born?" He said, "I chose mothers for you that will not disgrace or discredit you."

Allâh's Prophet, Yunus and the Whale

Allâh (the Exalted) said about His Prophet Yunus ﷺ in the Noble Qur'ân:

"And, verily, Yunus (Jonah) was one of the Messengers. When he ran to the laden ship, He (agreed to) cast lots, and he was among the losers. Then a (big) fish swallowed him and he had done an act worthy of blame. Had he not been of them who glorify Allâh, He would have indeed remained inside its belly (the fish) till the Day of Resurrection. But We cast him forth on the naked shore while he was sick, and we caused a plant of gourd to grow over him. And We sent him to a hundred thousand (people) or even more. And they believed: so We gave them enjoyment for a while." (Qur'ân 37:139-148)

Ibn 'Abbas ﷺ related that the ship was filled with goods, that they drew straws, and that they were overcome. This is referring to the fact that the waves were playing with the ship from all directions, and it was about to sink. So they drew straws to see who would be thrown into the river in order to lighten the load of the ship, and Allâh's Prophet, Yunus ﷺ, drew the shortest straw. He didn't only draw it once, but he drew it three times, but they did not want to throw him overboard. However, he undressed himself and threw himself into the sea in spite of their protests. Allâh ordered for a whale from the green sea to come quickly and swallow Yunus, but not to shatter any part of his body nor to break any of his bones. The whale came and swallowed him, and after settling in the stomach of the whale, Yunus thought that he had died. He then moved his head, legs, and other limbs, and he realized that he was in fact alive. He stood then and prayed from inside the belly of the whale, and one of his supplications was:

> "O Allâh, I have taken as a mosque for You a place that no one from the people has reached."

The First Time One Sins...

Ibn Hazm ﵀ related that a thief was brought to Abu Bakr ﵁, who said, "Cut off his hand." The thief said, "Forgive me, O *Khalifah* of the Messenger of Allâh, for I have never stolen prior to this." Abu Bakr said, "You have lied, for by the One Who has my soul in His Hand, Allâh does not suddenly take a believer on the first time that he sins."

Anas bin Malik ﵁ related that a thief was brought before 'Umar bin Khattab ﵁. The thief said, "By Allâh, I have never stolen before this." 'Umar said, "You have lied, by the Lord of 'Umar. Allâh does not take a slave at the first sin." It is said that 'Ali bin Abi Talib ﵁ said, "O Leader of the Believers, Allâh is more forbearing than to take a slave for his first sin." 'Umar then gave the order and the man's hand was cut off. Then 'Ali asked him to speak the truth – how many times before had he stolen? He said, "21 times."

He forbade His Soul from Desires

Ibn Hazm relates that a young, handsome man had a very close friend, and they trusted each other so much that all barriers of caution were removed from between them. The young man one day intended to spend the night at his friend's house; in the middle of the night, the host had an important errand to run outside of the house, and when he did not return, it was understood that he would probably return on the following day. His young guest, however, was still in the house, and so was the beautiful wife of the host, who was approximately the same age as the young man.

When she knew that it was not possible for her husband to return on that night, her heart yearned for the young man that was staying as a guest. She appeared before him in his room and invited him to take her. At first, he intended to do as she asked, and then his wits returned to him, and he did something strange indeed: he put his finger in the lamp, covered his finger with fire, and all the while he was saying to himself, "Taste this, and how can this be compared to the fire of Hell?" The woman was terrified to witness that scene, but ever so quickly she invited him again to herself and again his desire returned. But he did the same as before, and by the time that the morning came, one could have witnessed that the fire of the lamp had completely destroyed his finger.

Truth and Lying

Allâh (the Exalted) says in the Noble Qur'ân about the basic qualities of a believer:

"O you who believe! Why do you say that which you do not do? Most hateful it is with Allâh that you say that which you do not do." (Qur'ân 61:2,3)

Allâh's Messenger ﷺ was asked, "Can a believer be a miser?" He said, "Yes." He was asked, "Can a believer be a coward?" He said, "Yes." And he was asked, "And can a believer be a liar?" He said, "No."

It has been related that a man went to Allâh's Messenger ﷺ, and said, "O Messenger Allâh, indeed I do three sins in secret: (I drink) alcohol, fornication and lying. So inform me which of them I should abandon." He said, "Leave off lying." The man went away, and later desired to fornicate, but he thought to himself, "I will go to the Messenger of Allâh and he will ask me whether I fornicated? If I say yes, he will punish me. And if I say no, I will have broken the covenant and lied." So he abstained from fornicating, and the same occurred regarding alcohol. He returned to Allâh's Messenger ﷺ and said, "O Messenger of Allâh, indeed I have abandoned all of them."

My brother, do you not see then, that lying is the root of every wicked deed, and it leads to all other sins. You will not see anyone more miserable and wretched than the liar, and disbelief is the most severe kinds of lying, for it is lying upon Allâh (the Exalted).

Qutaibah and His Prisoner

Abu 'Ubaidah relates that a number of people were presented to Al-Hajjaj; they were all accused of rebelling against him, and so he ordered that they all be executed. Because the time of prayer had arrived, there remained one from them who was still not executed. Al-Hajjaj said to Qutaibah bin Muslim, "He shall remain with you and you will bring him to us early tomorrow."

Qutaibah said: I went and took the man with me, and as we were on our way, he said, "Qutaibah, do you wish to do a good deed?" I asked, "And what is that?" He said, "I have things that were trusted to me by people, and your companion, Al-Hajjaj, will surely kill me. Let me go free so that I may return each item to its rightful owner. And Allâh is my Guarantor that I will return to you tomorrow?" I was amazed at what he said, and I laughed at him. He then repeated for a second time the same words and said, "By Allâh, I will return to you." He continued and persisted in the same manner, until finally, I said, "Go." When he left, and when I could no longer see him, I returned to my senses and said: 'What did you do to yourself, O Qutaibah?' I returned to my family and spent the night, which seemed to last forever. In the morning, there was a man knocking at our door, and when I went to open it, there stood before me the same man from the day before. I said, "You have returned?" He said, "I made Allâh as a Guarantor and then why I should not return?" I took him with me, and when Al-Hajjaj saw me, he said, "Where is the prisoner, Qutaibah?" I said, "He is at the door." I brought him before the ruler and I informed him of the story. Al-Hajjaj gave him many piercing glances, and then said to me, "I give him to you as a gift." I left with him and when we had exited from the building, I said to him, "Go wherever you please." The man raised his head to the sky and said, "O Allâh, all praise is for You." He said nothing more and left.

She is in Paradise

Khalid bin Safwan saw a group in the mosque of Basrah, and he said, "What is this gathering?" He was told, "There is a woman who informs men about women who are available for marriage." He went to her and said, "I want to marry a woman." She said, "Describe her to me." He said, "I want her to be a virgin who is wise like a married woman, or a married woman who is innocent like a virgin; she should be sweet when she is near, splendid when she is at a distance, she should have lived a life of luxury and then became afflicted with poverty - so she has the manners of the rich and the humility of the poor. When we gather wealth we should be as the people of the world, and when we become poor, we should be as the people of the Hereafter."

She said, "I know of such a woman for you." He said, "And where is she?" She said, "In Paradise, so work to achieve her!"

The Doctor and the Digger

There was a man who had a very lazy servant. One day, he sent him to buy grapes and figs, and he took so long in returning from the errand, that the master's patience was running out. The servant finally came, but he only brought one of the two items that he was originally commanded to bring. The master beat him and reproached him severely and said, "When you go out to do something, you will be more productive if you try to do another task at the same time."

Some days passed and the master became sick, so he ordered his servant to bring a doctor. He took a long time to return, and when he finally did return he brought with him a doctor and another man as well. His master asked about the other man and the servant said, "You beat me and ordered me to do two things instead of one at a time, saying that it would be more productive. So, I came to you with a doctor, and if Allâh cures you, then that is fine; otherwise, this other man will dig for you your grave, for he is a grave digger!"

Begin with Yourself

A man went to Ibn 'Abbas ﷺ and said, "O Ibn 'Abbas, I want to enjoin people to do good and forbid them from doing evil." Ibn 'Abbas said, "And have you reached that level?" He said, "I hope that that is so." He said, "If you do not fear to be exposed by three Verses of Allâh's Book, then do so." The man asked, "And what are they?" He mentioned this Verse:

"Enjoin you *Al-Birr* (piety and righteousness and each and every act of obedience to Allâh) on the people and you forget (to practice it) yourselves." (Qur'ân 2:44)

And then asked, "Have you applied the implications of this Verse?" He said, "No." Ibn 'Abbas then mentioned the second Verse:

"Why do you say that which you do not do? Most hateful it is with Allâh that you say that which you do not do." (Qur'ân 61:2, 3)

After that he asked, "Have you applied the implications of this Verse?" He said, "No." He then mentioned the third Verse regarding Shu'aib ﷺ:

"I wish not, in contradiction to you, to do that which I forbid you." (Qur'ân 11:88)

And then he asked, "Have you applied the implications of this Verse?" He said, "No." Ibn 'Abbas said, "Then begin with yourself."

The Quality of fulfilling One's Promises is akin to a Bright Light

When Hurmuzan was brought as a prisoner before the Muslims, 'Umar bin Khattab ﷺ invited him to Islam, but he refused. 'Umar then ordered his execution, and when the sword was near him, he said, "O Leader of the Believers, would that you bring me a drink of water, for that would be better than to kill me while I am thirsty." He ordered for the water to be brought, and when it was in his hand, he said, "Am I safe until I drink this water?" 'Umar said, "Yes." He threw the glass down and said, "The quality of fulfilling one's promises, O Leader of the Believers, is akin to a bright light." 'Umar said, "I will give you respite until I look into the matter further; raise the sword from him." The prisoner then said, "I now bear witness that none has the right to be worshiped except Allâh and Muhammad is the Messenger of Allâh." 'Umar said, "Woe unto you ... and what made you delay?" He said, "I delayed, O Leader of the Believers, because I feared that it would be said that I only accepted Islam because I feared death." 'Umar said, "The intellect of people from Persia (Faris) is equal in weight to mountains."

Many Wives

There was a man from the Arabs who was known for always having many wives throughout his life, and it was said to him, "And how were you able to keep so many?" He said, "When we were young, they stuck to me because of my youth. Then I had wealth, and they were patient with me because of that. When my youth and wealth parted, all that remained were my good manners, and through them I live with my wives and they live with me."

His Dedication to Knowledge

Muzani said that it was stated to Imam Shafi'i رحمه الله, "How do you lust for knowledge?" He replied, "I hear a word of knowledge that I have not heard of before and each one of my body parts wishes that it had the faculty of hearing so that they, too, could enjoy the pleasure of hearing what my ears enjoy upon hearing new knowledge." It was further put to him, "Describe your eagerness to attain knowledge." He replied, "It is akin to the eagerness of a striving, miserly man who seeks to achieve pleasure through hoarding wealth." It was then asked, "How do you seek knowledge?" Imam Shafi'i responded, "I seek it like a weak woman seeks after her only child."

Rabi' said, "I heard of Imam Shafi'i saying during an illness that of all the books he had compiled, he wished that all of the creation learned of what those books contained without them being ascribed to him."

A Profound Saying of Ibn Qayyim

Ibn Qayyim ﷺ said: "When the slave wakes up as the night encloses upon him and his only concern is Allâh and how to please and obey Him, then Allâh takes upon Him to fulfill all of his needs and remove from him all that causes him anxiety. Allâh also makes his heart free to love Him only, his tongue free to remember Him only and his body free to serve Him only. However, when a slave of Allâh wakes up when the night encloses upon him and his main concern is the world, Allâh will make him bear the burdens of its anxiety, grief, and hardships. Allâh will entrust him to his own self and He will make his heart busy, sealing it from His love since it will be preoccupied with love for creation. Allâh will keep his tongue from His remembrance because it will be engaged with His creation; his body will be kept from obedience since it will be enslaved by its desires and services. And he will toil like a beast of burden toils in the service of another. And all who turn away from the worship, obedience and love of Allâh, will be put into trial with the worship, service and love for the creation." Allâh (the Exalted) says:

> "And whosoever turns away (blinds himself) from the remembrance of the Most Gracious (Allâh) (i.e., this Qur'ân and worship of Allâh), We appoint for him *Shaitan* (Satan/Devil) to be a *Qarin* (an intimate companion) to him." (Qur'ân 43:36)

Ibn Qayyim continues to say: "Seek out your heart in

three situations: first, when you are listening to the Qur'ân; second, when you are part of a gathering of remembrance; third, when you are alone and away from the world and its distractions. If you cannot find your heart in these three situations, then ask Allâh to bestow upon you a heart, for indeed you are bereft of one."

I have traveled to the East and West Twice

Sa'eed bin Musayyib said: "I used to travel for days and nights at a time to search out for a single *Hadith*."

Abul-'Aaliyah Rafi' bin Mehran, who died in 93 H, said: "We used to hear a narration from the Companions of the Prophet ﷺ when we were in Basrah and we were not pleased until we traveled to Al-Madinah to hear it directly from their mouths."

In his book, *Al-Manhaj Al-Ahmad,* Abul-Yemen Al-'Ulaimi Al-Hanbali, said of Imam Ahmad bin Hanbal رحمه الله, as he compiled his biography that the Imam sought out *Ahadith* when he was only sixteen years of age. He went to Kufah in the year 183 H and that was his first journey. He traveled to Basrah in 186 H and to Sufyan bin 'Uyainah in Makkah in the same year. It was also the first year that he performed *Hajj*. He went to Abdur-Razzak in San'a', Yemen in 197 H, accompanied by Yahya bin Mu'een.

The scholars traveled far and wide, suffering great hardships to seek out *Ahadith*.

He sinned for a long Time but then repented

It has been related that during the time of Musa عليه السلام, the Children of Israel were afflicted with a drought. The people went to Musa and said, "O one who has spoken to Allâh, invoke your Lord for us to provide us with rain." He, accompanied by the people, went out to the desert; they numbered 70,000 or more. Musa supplicated for rain and for Allâh's mercy, but nothing happened, except that the sky seemed to be even drier and the sun seemed more oppressive with its heat.

Musa عليه السلام was surprised and asked his Lord for the reason behind that. Allâh inspired to him, "Indeed, among you is a slave who has been challenging Me with sins for the past forty years. Call out to the people until he comes out from among them, for because of him you were prevented (from rain)." Musa said, "My Lord, I am a weak slave and my voice is weak. How can my voice convey (to them) when they are 70,000 or more in number?" Allâh inspired to him, "From you is the call and from Us is its conveyance." Musa stood as a caller and said, "O sinning slave, who has challenged Allâh with sins for the last forty years: come out from among us, for because of you, we have been deprived from rain. The said sinner turned to the left and to the right, seeing no one coming out from among them, which made him realize that he was the one who was wanted. He spoke to himself, "If I come forth from among this group of creation, then I will have exposed myself. But if I sit with them, then they will be deprived because of me." He put his head in his garment, regretting his evil deeds. He said, "My Lord, I have disobeyed You for forty years and You have given me respite. I have come to You in obedience, so accept from me." He no sooner finished his speech than a white cloud appeared and the rain came down in abundance. Musa said, "My Lord, why did You give us drink when none from among us came out." Allâh said, "O Musa, I have given you rain because of the same man who was the reason why I prevented you from rain (i.e., the man who repented)." Musa said, "My Lord, let me see this obedient slave." Allâh said, "O Musa, I did not expose him when he was disobeying Me, then do you expect Me to expose him while he is obedient to Me?"

Words of Wisdom

Junaid was asked about thankfulness and he said: "To not use one of Allâh's blessings for the purpose of disobeying Him."

Hasan Basri said: "I met with people who deemed the world to be less important than the earth underneath their feet. One of them would own only enough sustenance to maintain his body, yet he would still say, 'I will give part of this in the way of Allâh!'"

For what Sin was She murdered?

It is related that when a man from the Prophet's Companions fell into a continual state of depression, Allâh's Messenger ﷺ said to him, "What is wrong with you that you are sad?" He said, "O Messenger of Allâh, during the Days of Ignorance, I indeed perpetrated a sin so great, I fear that Allâh will not forgive me...!" Allâh's Messenger ﷺ said, "Inform me about your sin." He said, "O Messenger of Allâh, I was from those who killed their daughters." He continued, "Then a daughter was born to me, and my wife interceded on her behalf, pleading with me that I should leave her alone, and so I left her until she grew up and became of age. She became one of the most beautiful of women and many proposed to her. I was overcome by a fit of fanaticism and my heart could bear neither to marry her off nor to leave her in the house without a husband. So I said to my wife, 'I want to go to such and such tribe to visit my relatives, so send her with me.' She was pleased with that (arrangement) and she then adorned her with (nice) clothing and jewelry. She took many promises from me that I should not be treacherous with her. I took her to a well, and she sensed that I wanted to throw her inside, so she hugged me, crying and saying, 'My father, what do you wish to do to me?' I had mercy on her then, but when I looked into the well, I was again overcome by a fit of fanaticism. She hugged me and said, 'My father, do not waste the trust of my mother.' I began to look once at the well, then once at her, at which time I had mercy on her, but the Satan overcame me (in the end), and I took her and threw her upside down into the well. She was calling from the well, "O my father, you have killed me.' I remained there until her voice broke off, and I then returned." Allâh's Messenger ﷺ, as well as his Companions, cried, and he said, "Had I been ordered to punish anyone for what they did during the Days of Ignorance, I would have punished you."

The generosity of 'Aisha ﵂, the Mother of the Believers

Rarely throughout history has anyone possessed the generosity that 'Aisah ﵂ was blessed with. Two similar examples highlight that quality: on one occasion, Mu'awiyah ﵁ sent 1000 dirhams to her, and on another, Ibn Az-Zubair ﵁ sent her a similar amount. On both occasions, she could not even wait until nightfall before distributing the money to the poor and needy. And on both occasions, she neglected to keep anything for herself or for her servants. After she finished distributing the money that Ibn Az-Zubair ﵁ had sent to her, one of her servants came to her and said, "O Mother of the Believers, were you not able to have saved a single dirham [from that amount], so that you can buy meat for us?" 'Aishah ﵂ answered, "Do not be harsh with me. Had you reminded me, I would have done so."

He was seeking the Pleasure of Allâh

Walid bin 'Abdul-Malik wanted to make *Hajj* and he thought that a large and elaborate structure should be sent before him, on which he intended to be carried around the Ka'bah, and his nearest relatives and friends should sit with him as well. He ordered for the structure to be carried on camels from Sham and he sent a number of horsemen with it. They transported it until finally the leader of the expedition erected the structure in the Prophet's Mosque.

The people were shocked at what they saw, and after long discussion, they decided to take the matter to Sa'eed bin Ibrahim bin 'Abdur-Rahman bin 'Auf, a pious and brave scholar. He relates the following part of the narrative:

People came to me, informing me of what had happened. I ordered them to burn the structure down, but they said that they were not able to do so, for with the structure came 1000 horsemen from Sham. I called a servant and said, "Bring my armor," and he came to me with the armor of my grandfather, 'Abdur-Rahman bin 'Auf, the same armor that he wore during the Battle of Badr. I mounted my mule and headed toward the structure, and on that day, every man from the Quraish and from the *Ansar* accompanied me. I said, "Bring me fire," and when fire was brought, I burned down the structure. News of that of course reached Walid, who called me to him, ordering me to have someone replace me in my duties as the local judge. I did so, feeling not the slightest amount of fear. When I reached Sham, I remained at the door of the

Caliph for an entire month without being given permission to enter, until finally, I ran out of expense money. One evening, as I was in the mosque, a young man who was drunk entered. I asked, "Who is that?" I was told, "His uncle is the Leader of the Believers, Walid bin 'Abdul-Malik." I immediately said, "Bring me a whip." I stood and whipped the drunkard 80 times in the mosque, though I had full knowledge that his uncle was the Caliph, whom I was waiting to meet with. I no sooner completed the task of punishing him than I mounted my mule again, intending to return to Al-Madinah. The young drunk was taken to his uncle, and he said in amazement, "Who did this to him?" It was said, "Your Judge from Al-Madinah, O Leader of the Believers: it was Sa'eed bin Ibrahim." He said in anger, "Bring him to me."

When he was brought back, the Caliph said, "O Abu Ishaq, what did you do to the son of my sister?" Sa'eed said, "O Leader of the Believers, you have appointed me as a judge, and I saw a right of Allâh being wasted – a drunk man wandering in the mosque, while visitors from abroad and people of status were inside of it. I hated to think that people would leave you thinking that you abandoned punishing people according to the *Shari'ah*, and so I punished him." The Caliph took him by his hand, supplicated for him, and ordered for wealth to be given to him." He never even mentioned the affair about his structure being burned, which was the very reason why he invited him in the first place. Sa'eed pleased Allâh (the Exalted), not caring about the anger of the ruler, and so Allâh (the Exalted) was pleased with him and made the ruler be pleased with him as well. We ask Allâh (the Exalted) to make Muslims today follow the way of our pious predecessors.

The Story of Rukanah

Ishaq said that Rukanah was the strongest man among the Quraish. One day he was alone with Allâh's Messenger ﷺ in one of the valleys of Makkah, and the Prophet ﷺ said to him, "O Rukanah! Will you not fear Allâh and accept that which I invite you to?" He said, "If I knew that what you say is the truth, I would have followed you." Allâh's Messenger ﷺ said, "See now, if I would overcome you in wrestling, would you then know that what I say is the truth?" He said, "Yes." The Prophet ﷺ said, "Then stand so that I may wrestle with you."

Rukanah stood and they wrestled. The Prophet ﷺ was quick to take Rukanah down, so that the latter was unable to do anything! He said, "Repeat that, O Muhammad!" They wrestled once more, and the Prophet ﷺ defeated him again. He said, "O Muhammad, by Allâh, this is indeed strange - do you overcome me!" The Prophet ﷺ said, "And something more wonderful, if you wish, I will show you - if you fear Allâh and follow my order." He said, "And what is that?" The Prophet ﷺ said, "I will call for you this tree that you see and it shall come to me." Rukanah said, "Then call it." He ﷺ called it and it came until it was standing directly before Allâh's Messenger ﷺ, who said to it, "Return to your place."

It returned to its place. Then Rukanah returned to his people and said, "O sons of 'Abd-Manaf! I have never seen one more skilled in magic than he!" He then informed them of what he saw.

In another narration, the Prophet ﷺ defeated him three times, and each time, for 100 sheep. When the third time came, Rukanah said, "O Muhammad, no one has made me lie on my back before you. None was more hateful to me than you, but now I bear witness that none has the right to be worshiped but Allâh and that you are indeed the Messenger of Allâh." Allâh's Messenger ﷺ then returned to him his sheep.

The Importance Of Acknowledging Our Sins

Al-Auza'i related the following incident. Once when the people of Damascus went out to pray for rain, Bilal bin Sa'd went out with them. When they reached the designated spot where they were to pray, Bilal called out to the people: "Do you not acknowledge your sins!" They all answered in one voice: "Yes, indeed we do." Bilal then said, "O Allah, indeed you said: "No ground (of complaint) can there be against the *Muhsinun* (good doers)" (9: 91). We have indeed acknowledged our wrongdoing, so forgive us and provide us with rain." It rained on that very day, and thus did a long dry spell come to an end.

Don't Flaunt the Faults of Your Brothers

Once when Al-Kisai and Al-Yazidi were gathered before the ruler, Ar-Rashid, the time for *Maghrib* prayer set in, and they had to choose someone among them to lead the prayer. It wasn't a difficult choice, for Al-Kisai was a well-known reciter of the Qur'ân; until this very day, he is known as one of the Seven Famous Reciters. After the prayer commenced and after he finished reading the "Opening Chapter" of the Qur'ân, Al-Kisai then proceeded to recite "The Disbelievers Chapter":

"Say: (O Muhammad to these disbelievers): "O *Al-Kafirûn* (disbelievers in Allah, in His Oneness, and in His Angels, in His Books, in His Messengers, in the Day of Resurrection, and in *Al-Qadar*, etc.)!" (Qur'ân 109: 1)

Although this is one of the shortest chapters of the Qur'ân and one that is memorized by most young children, Al-Kisai made a mistake in his recitation of it. When the prayer was over, Al-Yazidi exclaimed, exhibiting a great deal of surprise, "The Reciter and *Imam* of Kufa being confused about, making a mistake in, and forgetting the 'Chapter of the Disbelievers!'"

When it came time to perform the '*Isha* prayer later in the night, Al-Yazidi did not wait but instead put himself forward to lead the people in prayer. As soon as the prayer commenced, his voice began to tremble, and he forgot that Chapter of the Qur'ân which is easiest to remember of all, "The Opening Chapter":

"All the praises thanks be to Allah, the Lord of all that exists" (Qur'ân 1: 1).

When the prayer was over, Al-Kisai turned to Al-Yazidi and said, "Hold back your tongue and do not speak, or else you will be put to trial. Indeed, it is guaranteed for one to be put to trial when he opens his mouth [to flaunt the faults of others]."

"She Is Definitely No Good for You"

Ash-Sha'bi related that he one day heard Al-Mughirah bin Shu'bah ﷺ say, "The only person who ever defeated me in anything was a young man from the clan of Banu Al-Harith bin Ka'b. That occurred when I proposed to a woman from Banu Al-Harith. When I did so, a young man from the same clan was seated nearby and heard everything I said. He then approached me and said, 'O leader, she is definitely no good for you!' I said, 'O son of my brother, what is wrong with her?' He said, 'I once saw a man kiss her!' I immediately withdrew my proposal, but then I later found out that that very same young man had married her. I went to him and said, 'Did you not tell me that you saw a man kiss her?' He said, 'Yes, I once saw her father kiss her!'"

Divine Preordainment

Her husband's death came as a great shock for her, yet she moved on with life, toiling long hours for the son her husband left behind. Not wanting to introduce a strange man into her son's life, she refused many marriage proposals, thus remaining the boy's mother, father, and friend, all in one. Every day when he returned home from school, she would, without exception, be waiting for him at the door of their home. Despite being a single mother, she gave him a good upbringing, educating him, disciplining him, and instilling into him noble characteristics. He was always a grade "A" student, and when he finished high school, he resolved to travel abroad and study in a prestigious foreign university. His mother shot down the idea as soon as he presented it to her, for she could not bear to be separated from her only child. The boy loved her, but as with all other teenagers at the age of 18 or so, he was predominantly occupied with thoughts about his future. And so he secretly applied to the university of his choice, and of course being accepted - for he was a fair catch for any university - he secretly made plans to travel, hoping that, by informing his mother at the last minute, she would give in and allow him to go.

The day before he was to depart, he told his mother about his plans. She was deeply saddened but kept her true feelings hidden from him. She was desperate to keep him but didn't know how. In a fit of desperation, she stealthily made her way to her son's room and removed his passport and plane ticket, both of which he had already placed inside of his traveling purse. On the following morning, the son bade farewell to his mother and left. Much to his chagrin, he later found out that he didn't have his passport and plane ticket with him; but it was too late, for he had already reached the airport and his plane was ready to take off. Of course, he knew that it was his mother who hid his things. He could do nothing then but return angrily to his home.

When he reached his home, he went straight to his bedroom and fell asleep. The mother, meanwhile, was in the kitchen, busily preparing lunch for her son, knowing that he would return shortly. She did not perceive that her son had actually returned and was in his bedroom: She was too busy cooking and listening to the radio. To be sure, she was shocked to hear the radio announcer say that a plane had just crashed, and when he mentioned the flight number, she realized that it was the very plane that her son had planned to board. She was supremely happy, feeling that her son now had no reason to be angry with her, for she had just saved him from certain death. She walked around the house, looking for him, hoping that he had already returned. She was very eager to tell him what had happened. When she opened his bedroom door, she did in fact find her son - lying dead on his bed, having died from a heart attack or from some other unknown cause.

A Trustworthy Man

A businessman who lived centuries ago related the following story:

My business was doing so well one year and I had earned so much money that I decided to take a break from business and dedicate some time to worship. I joined a group that was heading off to make the yearly pilgrimage to Makkah. I took along two bags, which I tied around my waist. In them I kept money and some precious jewels in case need should arise during the journey.

When I stopped to relieve myself at some point during the journey, my belt loosened from the waist and the bags fell to the ground. But I only realized that the bags were missing many miles later; we traveled far enough that I had every reason to lose hope of finding the bags again. But losing the money and the jewels had no effect on me whatsoever; after all, I was still rich, and I knew that since I was traveling to worship Allah ﷻ, He would soon recompense me for what I had lost.

After the pilgrimage was over and I was back in my homeland, my situation in life worsened. Every business venture I embarked upon ended up in failure, until I finally lost everything. Feeling the disgrace of failure and penury, I fled with my family from my homeland, and we wandered for many years in a state of poverty. The hardship of poverty became even more difficult to bear when one night my wife gave birth to a baby boy, for my wife had lost much blood and needed medical attention as well as food. All that I had with me, however, were two small coins. It was a rainy night, and so despite my wife's weakness, I conducted her to an abandoned inn, where I asked her to rest while I went out in search of food and help. I wandered aimlessly for a while until I came across a store; I didn't go inside, however, for what could I hope to buy with only two small coins. Seeing my miserable state, the storekeeper came out and began talking to me. When I told him my situation, he felt sorry for me and in exchange for the two coins I had, he gave me milk and oil, both of the best kinds. He also lent me a container, in which I placed the supplies. I then headed back towards my wife, feeling contented in that I could at least give her some nourishment. Nothing was going right, though; I slipped on the way, the container shattered as it fell to the ground, and all that was in it spilled onto the ground. There I sat, a miserable and wretched creature. Although I had endured poverty for many years, I was never so hopeless and downtrodden as I was at that point in time. I began to cry; apparently, I was crying out loud, for a man opened the window of his home, near to where I was seated, and said, "Woe unto you! Why are you crying? And why do you not let us go to sleep?"

I explained to him my story, or just that part of it that took place in the last two days or so. He looked at me in surprise and said, "All of this crying for two small coins!" I became even more miserable after hearing what he said. I answered, "By Allah, I am not crying over the money I lost; I am crying out of mercy for my wife and my own self. At this very minute, my wife is dying of hunger. By

Allah, I performed pilgrimage in such and such year and I owned such and such amount of wealth, and I lost a great deal of that wealth when I lost two bags containing money and precious jewels. I didn't care about that loss then. Do you think now that I will cry over two small coins! Indeed, I ask Allah to protect me from such ignominy. And do not insult me, or else you might become afflicted as I am afflicted now."

The man, getting excited for some reason, said to me, "Describe your bags to me." I then approached him and with tears falling from my eyes, I said, "Here I am standing in the rain, and to add insult to injury, you want to ask me about bags. How will that benefit me?" He insisted that I describe them to him, and when I indicated to him that I was about to leave, he held on to me and I had no choice but to fulfill his request. After I describe the bags and their contents to him, he asked me to enter and said, "Where is your wife?" I told him that she was resting in an abandoned inn; he then sent his servant to go and fetch her. When my wife arrived, she was taken to the female members of the household, who then took care of her, providing for her every need. Their generosity was not limited to my wife, for I was given a new set of clean garments to wear; I was told to take a shower and then to wear them. When I was clean and was finished freshening up, the man said, "Stay with me for a few days." He was so hospitable and kind that I ended up staying for ten days. Each day he gave me 10 dinars, explaining that they were gifts. I must admit that I was somewhat taken aback; he first seemed cold to me when I was standing out in the rain, and now he was so very kind and generous.

On the 10th day, he began to talk more openly with me, perhaps noticing that I finally felt at home under his hospitable care. He asked me what I did for a living, and I told them that I had once been a businessman. He said that he had some money to invest, and he wanted to know whether I would be willing to do business on his behalf and thus become his partner. I immediately agreed. He took out 100 dinars, gave them to me, and finalized the agreement. Not only had he been a hospitable host, but also he now gave me a new source of income. I thanked Allah for having made me rich again.

The man then asked me to sit down, after which he proceeded to take out two bags, the very same bags, I was surprised to see, that I had lost many years ago. He said, "Do you recognize these?" When I saw the bags, I quickly fainted. One hour passed before I finally regained consciousness. He then said to me, "I have been keeping this safe for so many years. On the night that I met you, when you gave an account of your story, I had asked you to describe the bags for me. Upon hearing your description, I immediately knew that I had finally found the owner of the bags. But seeing your miserable state, I did not want to tell you about your bags right away, fearing that the shock would be too much for you. And so I asked you to stay with me, and each day I gave you 10 dinars not from my own wealth, but from your wealth – from your own bags. Take your bags and all of your money and jewels, and forgive me for having deceived you, though I only did so for your welfare." I thanked him and prayed for him. I then took the bags, returned to my homeland, and using his money as well as mine, I began to do business again. Only a few years passed by before my newly found friend/business partner and I and became very rich and prosperous. And all praise is for Allah, Lord of all that exists.

The Positive Effects of Giving Charity

A long time ago her son went missing from her; he was gone for so long a time that she finally lost all hope of ever seeing him again. One day, she sat down to eat. Breaking off a piece of bread from a nearby loaf, she was about to put it into her mouth, when all of a sudden a beggar appeared at her door and asked her to feed him. Not only did she give him the remaining part of the loaf of bread, but she also gave him the morsel that she was about to put into her mouth. Putting the loaf back together as best as she could, she handed it over to the beggar, and since she herself was relatively poor, she remained hungry for the rest of the day. After a few days passed, her son returned and they both rejoiced at their meeting. They sat down together, and he began to give an account of the many hardships he endured since the time he had gone missing.

He said, "Perhaps the worst thing that happened to me

occurred when I was walking in the valleys of such and such place, only a few days ago. A lion approached, and instead of trying to attack the donkey that I was riding upon, it leapt straight at me, throwing me off my mount. As fast as it could, the donkey raced off, and I was left as easy prey for the lion. It began to tear away at my clothes with its ferocious claws. I was so afraid that I almost fainted. The lion then leaned over me, getting ready for a lethal strike, but a huge man, whose face and garments were both white, suddenly appeared and drew the lion's attention away from me. He came, and without the use of any weapons, he pulled the lion away from me and wrestled it to the ground. Then looking at the lion with a menacing expression, he said, 'Stand, O dog, a morsel for a morsel!' The lion immediately got up and raced away. After seeing the lion speed away, I returned my gaze to the man, but he was no longer there, and I couldn't find him afterwards. I stayed where I was for a number of hours, until my strength returned to me. Realizing that the lion had done no harm to my body, I got up and walked away, until I joined up with a traveling party. I told my story to them, but there is one part of it that I was, and still am, extremely confused about: what did the man mean when he said, 'A morsel for a morsel'?" At this point during the narrative, his mother stared straight ahead of her with an incredulous expression, realizing that the man came to save her son at approximately the exact same time that she had given up her morsel of bread to the beggar.

Unparalleled Generosity

'Abdullah bin Ja'far ﷺ was so famous for his generosity that he became known by the title, "Father of the Poor." One day, he walked by a garden and saw in it a slave harvesting dates. At that very same moment, the son of the slave's owner came, bringing with him two loaves of bread. The slave took them and then sat down to eat. But before he could eat even a morsel of bread, he saw a dog approaching in his direction; in a pitiable state of health, the dog was moaning and wagging its tail. The slave threw one of the two loaves in the direction of the dog, which immediately pounced upon the bread and ate it up. It was not satisfied, however, for it approached nearer, still wagging its tail. To'Abdullah bin Ja'far's great surprise - for he was watching all of this from a distance - the slave then threw the second loaf of bread in the direction of the dog, which proceeded to quickly eat it up.

The slave then stood and continued with his daily labor. Amazed by what he saw, 'Abdullah bin Ja'far ﷺ approached the slave and addressed him: "What amount of food are you given each day?"

"Only that which you saw," said the slave.

"Then why did you give both of the loaves to the dog?" asked 'Abdullah ﷺ.

"Indeed, our land is not one that is inhabited by dogs, and

so I knew that the dog must have come this far only because of hunger. And that is why I preferred it to my own self."

"Then what will you do about yourself for the rest of your day?"

"I will go hungry this night," said the slave.

'Abdullah bin Ja'far ﷺ then said to himself, "The people censure me for my generosity! Yet this slave is more generous than I am." He then went to the owner of the slave and asked to purchase him. The owner asked, "And why do you want to buy him?" 'Abdullah bin Ja'far ﷺ then informed him about everything that he had witnessed; he explained that he wished to buy him only so that he could then free him. He also voiced his intention of buying the garden and giving it to him as a gift. The owner said, "You want to do all of that for him, simply based on the one deed that you witnessed from him; indeed, we witness wonderful acts from him every single day. I bear witness that he is indeed free for the Countenance of Allah ﷻ and that the garden is a gift from me to him!"

The Most Just, The Most Merciful

It is related that a woman once went to the Prophet David ﷺ and said, "O Prophet of Allah, is your Lord just or unjust?" David ﷺ said, "Woe unto you, woman; indeed, He is Most Just and never acts unjustly." He then asked her, "What is your story?"

She said, "I am a widow; I have three daughters, and I provide for them from what I spin with my needle and yarn. Yesterday, I wrapped my yarn in a cloth and went with it to the marketplace, intending to sell it and use the proceeds to buy provisions for my children. But while I was walking to the marketplace, a bird suddenly swooped down and took my yarn and my cloth, after which it flew away. I sat there in a sad and miserable state, faced with the reality that I owned nothing that I could use to provide for my children."

As the woman was with David ﷺ, telling him her story, someone knocked on the door, asking permission to enter. Ten men then entered; each one was a businessman, and each one had 100 dinars in his hand. They said, "O Prophet of Allah, give this money to someone who is deserving of it." David ﷺ asked, "What prompted you to bring this money here?"

They said, "O Prophet of Allah, we were traveling in a sea vessel, when the waves began to roar tempestuously, and our ship began to sink. Then suddenly, as if out of nowhere, a bird came and dropped a red cloth that contained yarn inside of it. Using those materials, we quickly worked to repair the hole in the ship that was causing us to sink. Not much time passed before the winds and waves calmed down and the hole was repaired. We then made an oath to Allah ﷻ that each one of us would give 100 dinars in charity. This is that money, which you may give as charity to whomsoever you please." Turning to the woman, David عليه السلام said, "A Lord Who does business for you on land and in the sea, yet you make Him out to be unjust!" He gave her the entire 1000 dinars and said, "Spend it on your children."

Another Story about the Positive Effects of Giving Charity

The governor of Egypt once summoned Ibn Al-Furat to come to him. When the two men were face to face, the governor said, "I always had evil intentions regarding you. So much hatred do I harbor in my heart against you that I am always making schemes to capture you and banish you from these lands. But do you know what prevents me from doing so? For many nights now, I am seeing you in my dreams; you are always preventing me from reaching you, using a loaf of bread to keep me back. And when I order my guards to kill you, you fend off their various blows with a loaf of bread that is in your hand, so that neither blow nor arrow reaches you. Now tell me the story behind this loaf of bread."

Ibn Al-Furat said, "O governor, ever since I was very young, my mother would come to me every night and place a loaf of bread underneath my pillow. Then in the morning she would give it away in charity on my behalf, and she never stopped doing so until she died. Then I continued to do the same myself, every night placing a loaf of bread underneath my pillow, and then in the morning giving it away in charity." The governor was greatly affected by what he heard; he said, "By Allah, I will never even think about harming you after this day. I now think well of you and love you very much."

Who Should I Obey?

The school day ended, and the young girl returned to her home; but she wasn't her usual happy self. No, today a cloud of sadness covered her face. Her loving mother immediately perceived that something was wrong, that something was bothering her dearest child. She calmed her daughter down and asked her what was wrong. The young girl said, "Mother, my teacher warned me that she would have me expelled from the school if I continue to wear the long clothing that I always wear."

"But they are the clothes that Allah wants you to wear," said the mother.

"Yes, mother, but my teacher doesn't want me to wear them."

"Good point, my dearest daughter. Your teacher doesn't

want you to wear them, and Allah wants you to wear them... who then will you obey? Will you obey Allah, Who has created you, given you your form, and blessed you with countless favors? Or will you obey a created being, who has not the power to either benefit or harm her own self?"

"Rather, I will obey Allah," said the girl.

"Good, my dearest daughter, for you are in the right," said the mother.

On the following day, the teacher flared up in anger when she saw the young girl challenging her authority by wearing the very same clothes that she had prohibited her from wearing. She continues to reproach and threaten the child, until the young girl broke down crying, no longer being able to show a brave face to her teacher and to her fellow classmates. When she would not calm down but instead continued to cry, the teacher was bewildered, not knowing how to make her stop. Then the young girl called out, "By Allah, I do not know who it is that I should obey: you or Him?"

"And who is He?" asked the teacher.

"Allah. Should I obey you and wear what you want me to wear and make Him angry in the process? Or should I obey Him and disobey you? Indeed, I will obey Him ﷻ, come what may! " The teacher was struck silent, and on the following day she invited the girl's mother to come and visit her. When the two were face to face, the teacher said, "Indeed, your daughter has taught me the greatest spiritual lesson that I have ever learned in my entire life."

The Devil-like Thief

The events of this strange story took place in Al-Yamamah, which is located in the middle of the Arabian Peninsula, and which today is a part of Saudi Arabia. It was the end of the first century of the Islamic calendar, during the reign of Al-Walid bin 'Abdul-Malik.

Times were hard in the town of At-Tihamah, which was located in the region of Al-Yamamah. For months people in that town had lived in a constant state of fear and terror. They slept uneasily, and they were terrified when they would walk the streets. Each one of them was afraid that he was going to be next in the ongoing list of victims.

There wasn't any gang that was wreaking havoc on the town, nor a group of murderers that was prowling its streets. Rather, it was a single man who for months now was robbing people of their sheep and their money, yet no one stopped him; in fact, no one even dared to stop him.

One day, a group of hardy youths decided that, if the authorities were not going to do anything, then they would patrol the streets and apprehend the criminal. The robber walked openly in the streets during the day and the night; such was his confidence concerning his strength and cunning. When the youths confronted him, a brief struggle ensued, brief because the robber was able to take down his opponents with the strength of a lion and the skill of a trained warrior. The youths fled, and after news of what happened spread, no one else then dared to stand in the robber's way. People began to say, "Indeed, he is no regular robber; instead, he is a devil wearing the garment of a robber." People began to spread strange stories about the robber, some of which were true while others were false. He was the talk of the town, and the stories that were spread about him made him out to be a powerful, evil otherworldly being.

It is mainly because of those stories and the spreading of those stories that the town became seized by terror and fear. Even the guards and policemen of the town were frightened. News of the situation reached the ruler of Iraq and the East, Al-Walid bin 'Abdul-Malik. He was furious and could find no reason to excuse the impotency of his appointed governor in Al-Yamamah; after all, how could he and the police force under his authority fail to apprehend a single man who made no attempt to keep his whereabouts secret. Al-Walid bin 'Abdul-Malik wrote a letter to the governor, ordering him to kill the menace or to send him to the capital city as a prisoner. And he warned the governor that, if he failed to capture the robber, he would replace him with a stronger and more competent governor.

The governor of Al-Yamamah actually knew who the robber was, and he even knew his name – Jahdar. But he felt bewildered concerning what he should do about him, because every single one of his police officers was either too afraid to go after Jahdar or too unskilled. However, the matter was now altogether different, for he feared losing his job. As is usually the case in desperate situations, desperate measures needed to be taken in order to resolve the problem. And since all of his previous attempts to apprehend Jahdar ended up in failure, he realized that he now had to resort to trickery and deception.

Having finally come up with an idea, the governor chose two of the strongest and smartest youths that he knew, and he agreed to pay them a lofty reward if they successfully brought Jahdar to him, whether in chains or in a coffin. The plan was simple enough, but its execution required both strength and cunning.

They were to go and pretend that they were robbers like Jahdar. The plan actually held promise because Jahdar probably wouldn't recognize them since they did not live in At-Tihamah but in another town in the Al-Yamamah region. When they reached At-Tihamah, they asked the locals about Jahdar, and to their surprise, the locals knew where he could be found, though most of them had never actually seen him. The youths went to him and began to tell him about their background. They said that they were amateur robbers who had a few successes in stealing from others. They explained that they heard about his feats and bravery, and so wanted to meet him in person. They then proposed to work under him in order to learn from him his tricks and strategies. As apprentices to the master robber, they promised to give him a large percentage of every successful robbery. They said that they understood why he might be suspicious of them, but that he had nothing to fear from them; he could even test them for a while to make sure that they would remain loyal to him.

Otherwise, if he refused, he would lose out because they would work for themselves and reap the rewards of their labors themselves, without him having any share whatsoever.

Jahdar was neither afraid nor suspicious, so sure and confident was he regarding his ability and strength. That confidence, which often served as his best quality, this time turned out to be a great fault. For Jahdar never imagined that any human being would even dare to challenge or deceive him. And so he accepted the proposition of the two youths, and thereafter tested their loyalty a number of times. He was in fact quite impressed by their skill and bravery, and they soon became a close-knit gang with Jahdar as their leader. They worked so well together that Jahdar began to imagine himself as soon becoming the richest of the rich in the Al-Yamamah region.

When the two youths were sure that they had gained the trust of Jahdar, they prepared to move into phase 2 of their plan - actually apprehending the scoundrel. They did not have to wait long for their opportunity, for on one of the ensuing nights, Jahdar fell asleep, and feeling safe under the protection of his two lieutenants, he put both his sword and his dagger at some distance from his bed. After all, why should he need any weapon while he was among friends. Pretending to be asleep as well, the two youths waited until Jahdar fell into a deep sleep. Every few minutes, they stole glances at him and at each other, fearing that he was aware of their plans or would catch them in the act. They felt that they had reason to fear, for on many occasions they witnessed the cunning and skill of their leader.

But then finally the older of the two signaled that they should take advantage of the opportunity. Moving with lightning-like speed, they took out two strong ropes and tied Jahdar' s hands and legs. Then they tied his arms to his body very tightly, so much so that the tightness of the rope almost broke his ribs. It is then that he woke up with a start, looking around him with complete and utter amazement. As much as he tried to escape, his attempts were of no avail, for he was made completely immobile by the many ropes that were tied around him. Refusing to speak, perhaps from his anger and pride, he closed his eyes, as if in reproach of the two traitors. They tied a piece of cloth around his eyes, so that he could not know what was happening around him or what paths they were traveling upon. And despite the tension of the ropes, his silence and submission made the two youths more afraid than ever. They feared that his silence was tantamount to gloating; for perhaps he had one trick left up his sleeve and would soon surprise them by freeing himself from his bonds and attacking them. Many long intense hours passed, but finally they reached the governor of Al-Yamamah, happy with their success and with the prospect of the huge reward that was promised them; and they were also happy to have finally saved the people of At-Tihamah from a most devil like robber.

When he saw the two youths approaching with the

prisoner walking before them, the governor let out a call of joy: "All praise is for Allah... all praise is for Allah... how brave indeed the two of you are... may Allah bless you." Of course, more than anything else the governor was content in the knowledge that Al-Walid bin 'Abdul-Malik would be pleased with him and that his job as governor was still safe. Without wasting any time, the governor sent a rider to Al-Walid bin 'Abdul-Malik in Iraq with a message containing the good news.

When the people heard that the infamous robber had been apprehended, they crowded the streets, each wanting to have a good look at Jahdar as he was being led through the streets in chains. Everyone imagined him to be a giant, a man with huge muscles, but when they actually saw him, they were shocked to see that he was skinny and of medium height. They also imagined him to look like the Devil, but in appearance he was clearly an ordinary man. Al-Walid bin 'Abdul-Malik sent the rider back with the message that Jahdar was to be brought before him.

Jahdar was then transported to Iraq, and when he was taken to the court of the ruler for judgment, he was greeted, so to speak, by the faces of many army generals and ministers, all of whom wanted to see the man who had created so much mischief in At-Tihamah. Al-Walid gave the prisoner a long hard stare, and he was surprised to see that, though the man had come to his imminent doom, he kept a brave face, showing no sign of fear.

"Are you Jahdar?" asked Al-Walid.

"Yes... I am Jahdar bin Rabi'ah."

"And what were your motives for committing your many crimes?"

"The oppression of the times, the boldness of my heart, the emptiness of my pockets, and the cowardice of the people," answered Jahdar. Both his boldness and his eloquence, unusual in such a tight situation, made an impression upon the mind of Al-Walid.

Al-Walid continued to question him: "Do you know what the consequences are of your actions?"

"Were you to choose me to be one of your soldiers, you would see from me many brave and impressive deeds," said Jahdar, avoiding the ruler's question.

"You, one of my soldiers!" Said Al-Walid. "Indeed, robbers are only good at stealing, so do not have hopes for anything other than your certain punishment."

But Jahdar did not give up. "Were you to witness my wisdom in difficult matters, you would see from me that which would please you," said Jahdar.

To the surprise of everyone, Al-Walid said, "If you insist, we will test you."

"May Allah honor the ruler! I will take on any test you have to throw at me."

"But it is a difficult test that I have in mind for you," said Al-Walid. "Death is easier than it."

"Let the ruler command as he pleases," said Jahdar.

"It is not a test in the normal sphere of warfare," said Al-Walid.

"I am prepared for any test," said Jahdar.

"It is not a test that involves any human being," said Al-Walid, adding to the suspense.

"Even if you pit me against a jinn, I will still accept the test."

"It is not with a jinn."

"O leader, from this moment onwards, I promise to be under your obedience. Test me with anything that you wish."

"Then here is your test," said Al-Walid. "I will put you in a closed area with a fierce lion. And you will have with you no weapon save a sword. If the lion kills you - and a painful death it will be - you will have received your punishment. But if you kill it, then we will have forgiven you."

"May Allah makes matters well for the ruler, for the time when you will forgive me draws near," said Jahdar.

"Do not be too hasty with your happiness," said Al-Walid. "For there is a surprise that will be awaiting you." Choosing the fiercest and strongest of lions, Al-Walid prepared the surprise, namely, to make the lion go hungry for three straight days, thus almost guaranteeing that Jahdar would not escape from it.

Whether it was to make an example of Jahdar or for some other reason, the authorities informed the people about the situation, and they were given permission to attend the event. On the appointed today, the weather was scorching hot, but people still came, not minding the heat or the huge crowd. Such an event, which might have been common in the Roman Coliseum, was quite unique for those who attended. The attendees despised Jahdar for his many crimes, but they felt sorry for him when they saw the lion roaring inside of his cage; the lion looked especially terrifying since it had not eaten for three days, and had a look of desperation and hunger on its face.

Al-Walid gave the signal and the lion was released. It sprang out, searching for its long-awaited meal. This lion was particularly huge, with a large head, sharp teeth, and blood-red eyes. Though they were safely seated outside of the closed arena, most people were terrified when they heard the lion roar, and everyone was sure that the skinny Jahdar was, in a matter of seconds, going to be torn to pieces. Then Al-Walid signaled for Jahdar to be escorted into the arena. Perfectly calm and with an air of confidence, Jahdar turned to Al-Walid and said, "May Allah honor the leader. This is the final hour, so will I gain your pardon if I am victorious?" Al-Walid answered, "If you are victorious, then you will have indeed gained my pardon."

Jahdar looked straight into the lion's eyes, showing not even an iota of fear; it almost seemed as if he were hunting a deer and not a lion. The lion roared, but of the two it was Jahdar who was the first to approach the other. He called out in a loud voice so that all could hear: "A lion and a lion, both in a narrow place, both strong and fierce."

Contrary to what most had expected from the skinny prisoner, Jahdar raced towards the lion after letting out a warrior-like cry. When he came near enough, the lion leapt towards him, but with a stealthy and lithe maneuver Jahdar was able to move out of the way just in time. By the time the lion was able to dig its paws into the ground and turn around for another attack, Jahdar was already upon it with his sword; he struck the lion with a strong but non-lethal blow. In pain, and angrier than ever, the lion bared its teeth and prepared for another attack, but Jahdar was too fast: he dealt a lethal blow to the lion's neck.

Despising the man earlier for his crimes, the crowd now jumped to their feet in amazement and admiration. They wished that his bravery and intelligence could be used for good, as they were once used for evil. As for Jahdar, he wiped off the sweat from his forehead and walked towards Al-Walid, showing neither pride nor boastfulness in his comportment. The two shook each other's hands and the ruler congratulated him for his bravery. Al-Walid made official his pardon of Jahdar, after which the latter made an oath to use his sword for good and not for evil. Once a major threat to the peace and stability of society, Jahdar now became its policeman and defender. He thereafter constantly strove to atone for his past sins, and other than his civic duties, he also became known for his worship and piety. Thus in deed and in heart did he strive to repent to Allah, the Most Merciful, for his past sins.

The Potent Effects of Supplication

Many centuries ago, a woman married a man named Isma'il, who, having studied under the tutelage of Imam Malik, became a venerable scholar in his own right. One of the fruits of their blessed marriage was the birth of a son, whom they named Muhammad. Shortly afterwards, however, Isma'il died, leaving behind a great deal of wealth for his wife and young son. The mother then took up the full responsibility of giving her son a good Islamic upbringing. She might have had ideas about her son becoming a noble scholar, but sadly, there was a barrier preventing that from happening - the boy was blind. These days, it is perhaps not so impossible for someone who is blind to pursue a higher education. Yet in those days, in order to become a scholar one had to travel from country to country and from *Shaikh* to *Shaikh*, something that was of course difficult for a blind person. Yet the mother did not lose hope: with sincerity and a good intention, she constantly invoked Allah ﷻ for help. Then one night, while she was sleeping, she saw the Prophet Ibrahim ﷺ in a dream. He said to her, "Indeed, because of your many supplications, Allah has returned your son's sight back to him." The woman woke up with a start, went to her son, and saw that the dream had come true. How perfect Allah is! Indeed, He is the One Who answers the supplications of those who are in need.

After Allah blessed her son, Muhammad bin Isma'il, with the ability to see again, the mother set him on a course of studying and learning. Later in his life, that boy grew up to compile a book that is the second most authentic book in the world – the most authentic being the Book of Allah. The name of that book is *Sahih Bukhari.* Yes, its author's full name is Muhammad bin Isma'il Al-Bukhari, whom Allah blessed with knowledge, a brilliant mind, and a retentive memory.

The First Step to Becoming Governor: Giving Away a Bunch of Grapes

> "Verily, he who fears Allah with obedience to Him (by abstaining from sins and evil deeds, and by performing righteous good deeds), and is patient, then surely, Allah makes not the reward of the Muhsinun (good doers) to be lost." (Qur'ân 12: 90)

To say that he became governor because of a bunch of grapes would be an unwarranted exaggeration; the grapes are merely representative of the path he chose in life – the path of generosity, truthfulness, and righteousness. His life both before and after becoming governor was characterized by hard work and sincerity.

I am referring to Yahyah bin Muhammad bin Habirah Ash-Shaibani. Born in the year 499 H in the town of Ad-Daur, which was not too far from Baghdad, Yahyah became governor during the rule of the 'Abbasi leaders, Al-Muqtafa Li-Amrillah and, his son, Al-Mustanjid Lillah.

Before becoming governor, Yahyah lived a life of poverty and humiliation, but he remained patient and content with his circumstances. And after he climbed the ladder of success and became governor, he did not exact retribution from those who had previously inflicted harm upon him. This alone proves the loftiness of his character, for the highest level of forgiveness is to forgive when one is able to exact revenge.

One day, the police brought before him a man who was accused of murder. Yahyah recognized him immediately, for they both grew up in the town of Ad-Daur. When everyone, both the accused and the family of the victim, were gathered before Governor Yahyah, Yahyah agreed to pay 600 dinars as blood money to the family of the victim. When they left, Yahyah gave 50 dinars to the accused and then ordered him to leave. He then turned to those that were seated beside him and said, "Do you know that I cannot see with my right eye?" They said, "No, we didn't know that." He said, "Indeed, I cannot see with my right eye, and the reason for that is the accused man on whose behalf I just paid blood money. Long ago, when I was once seated on one of the pathways of my hometown, I was reading a book on Islamic jurisprudence. Then the man you just saw came to me, holding in his hand a basket of fruits. He asked me to carry the basket for him, and I refused, telling him that that was not what I did for a living. He then struck me with his hand on my right eye, and from that time onwards I never again saw anything with my right eye. A few minutes ago, realizing that I could now exact revenge upon him, I decided to repay his evil with forgiveness and kindness."

On another occasion, a soldier entered into his presence. Yahyah instructed his guard to give the soldier 20 dinars and to never again allow him to return to his office. Of course, those that were present were somewhat bewildered by what had just occurred. He said to them, "When I was in my hometown, Ad-Daur, a killing took place, which quickly precipitated into a feud with outsiders. Soldiers were sent into our town, and every man was rounded up and taken away. I, along with many others, was under the charge of the soldier whom you just saw. He led us away from our hometown, and of course we could not escape, for our hands were tied behind our backs. As we were marching forward, my companions began to offer money and valuable possessions to the soldier, in order to ransom their freedom. One by one, he let them go, until I was the only one who remained. I was in a very tight situation, for I had nothing with which I could ransom my freedom. He continued to lead me away from my hometown, goading me forward with his whip, which he often used to strike me violently. I remained silent and did not complain, but when the time for *'Asr* prayer commenced, I asked him permission to allow me to stop and pray. But he refused my request." Yahyah had instructed his guard to give the soldier 20 dinars as a sign that he forgave him for his harsh treatment, but had made it clear that the soldier was no longer welcome in his office, a sign that he could not forgive him for not allowing him to properly perform a prescribed prayer.

Now let us take a look at the road Yahyah took, a road that led him from being poor to becoming a governor. In the town of Ad-Daur, Yahyah grew up in a poor family, all of the members of which were farmers who worked the fields. But Yahyah was not concerned about farming or planting; no, all of his energies were expended on the pursuit of knowledge - reading and studying under the tutelage of learned scholars. When he was old enough, he left his home and traveled to Baghdad, where he studied the Noble Qur'ân, the sciences of *Hadith,* Islamic jurisprudence, literature, and rhetoric. He soon became an accomplished scholar in all of those sciences, but particularly in Islamic jurisprudence, in the *Hanbali Madhab*. He also became a renowned poet.

Based on his accomplishments, Yahyah began to look for a job in Baghdad. He went to a place that was essentially an office for government jobs. Every single time he went there, he was told that there was no opening available at the time. He probably would have continued to return over and over again had it not been for the fact that he was running out of money and could ill afford to remain in the capital city. Furthermore, he was beginning to lose hope of finding a job in Baghdad; and so he decided to return to his hometown.

He left Baghdad after having spent his last dirham. Having no money with which he could rent a mount, he began what promised to be a long, arduous journey on foot. After he traveled only a short distance, the time for *'Asr* prayer commenced. Although he was in an uninhabited area, he noticed an old *Masjid* that was on the side of the road. Having entered it and having commenced his prayer, he heard a moaning sound coming from the corner of the *Masjid*. And so when he completed his prayer, he walked toward the sound of the noise, finding a sick man sleeping on the ground. Yahyah put his hand over the man and found that he had a high fever. He asked him how he felt, and the man told him that his entire body was in pain. He also told him that he was a stranger and had no one to look after him, which is why he took refuge in that particular *Masjid*, away from the city. Yahyah asked him if he wanted anything. The man said, "I have a strong craving for a bunch of grapes." Yahyah thought to himself: "Where am I to find grapes in this uninhabited area, especially considering the fact that I have no money." Strange though the request was, Yahyah decided that he was going to try and fulfill it, mostly out of compassion for a sick man who was now spending his last moments in this world, and facing the first moments of the next one. "Perhaps he will supplicate to Allah for me, which will result in Allah providing relief for me regarding my sad financial situation," thought Yahyah. Expecting no reward whatsoever from the sick man, Yahyah went out to search for grapes. As I alluded to earlier, this was the turning point of his life.

Yahyah did not walk but ran back to find a store on the outskirts of Baghdad. Finally, he reached a fruit store, and in it he found bunches of grapes. Taking a large bunch, Yahyah said to the owner of the store, "How much is this?" He said, "One-half of a dirham." Yahyah said, "I don't have any money right now, but I will leave my cloak with you as collateral, until I return with that amount." After the storeowner told him that he was satisfied with the arrangement, Yahyah took off his cloak and handed it over to him. Yahyah then took the grapes and ran back towards the *Masjid,* finally reaching it just before nightfall. He made ablution, performed *Maghrib* prayer, washed the grapes with water, and then proffered them to the sick man.

The sick man was extremely happy, and he ate all of the grapes, after which he said, "All praise is for Allah, Who has provided me with what I have desired for a long time now." He then went on to tell Yahyah his story:

I desired eating grapes for a long time now, but had not the money with which I could purchase any. You are indeed a mercy that Allah has sent to me. Now, my son, hear my story before I die, for I feel that I have only hours if not minutes left to live. My name is Ahmad, and I was a well-respected and successful businessman in Kharasan. I had a younger brother, Mahmûd, who was also a businessman. Approximately one year ago, we decided to join up with a caravan that was going to Baghdad. We intended to buy goods from Baghdad and then return to sell them in Kharasan. Before leaving, I purchased local goods, hoping to sell them in Baghdad and then, as planned, to purchase goods to bring back home from Baghdad. My brother didn't buy anything, instead choosing to use his 1000 dinars solely for the purpose of buying merchandise from Baghdad. Just before we departed for our journey, he gave me the money to hold for him as a trust, because I was older and was generally more responsible. We finally left, and everything was going well until we almost reached Baghdad. But then a group of highway robbers attacked our caravan, stole all of our merchandise, killed many among us, and injured others. I was among the injured ones, and as I lay on the ground, the robbers thought that I had died, and so they left me alone. I lay there, pretending to be dead, until they left. Then I got up and searched for my brother among the corpses and among the wounded, but I could not find him. I thought to myself that perhaps my brother was able to escape from the attackers and that he went to Baghdad, since it was so close, and since he didn't have any money with which to make the return journey. After first tending to the wounded, I nursed my own wounds and then set out for Baghdad. The robbers took all of my merchandise, leaving me with nothing; all that I had with me were the 1000 dinars that my brother had entrusted me with along with a few dinars of my own. To take care of my needs, I spent from my own money, until my funds were exhausted. I refused to use my brother's money, for he gave that money to me as a trust, and so when I wasn't busy searching for my brother, I was busy working in order to earn enough for my upkeep. This continued for an entire year, and still I could find no trace of my brother, and still I kept his money safe with me. Then I became sick and was no longer able to work; it is a little while now that I have been sick, and I have felt for a while now that my sickness is fatal. Having no one to take care me, I came to this forsaken place to die. When I die, I hope that you will wash my body and bury me. And I want you to take the money and find my brother, Mahmûd. If you find him, then give him the money; if you don't, then do with the money as you please.

During that night, as Yahyah was sleeping, he heard the sick man utter the Testimony of Faith and then make a croaking sound. Yahyah looked at him and knew that he had just died. As no one else was there, Yahyah, all by himself, went about the duties of washing his corpse, performing his funeral prayer, and burying him. Also, he took the bag that contained the money. He no longer had any reason to return to his hometown of Ad-Daur; after all, he did promise to search for the man's brother in Baghdad. Also, he had a new supply of funds that he could use, only when necessary of course, for his upkeep. And so he returned to Baghdad on the following morning, and on his way, he stopped at the fruit store to pay for the grapes and to reclaim his cloak. He then went to the shores of the Tigris (Dijlah River), where he found a boat that was taking people to the other side of Baghdad for a fee. After he boarded the boat, Yahyah found out that he would have to wait about half an hour before it would depart, and so he began to pass his time by engaging in a conversation with the boat's captain. Finding that the captain's accent was different from that of the inhabitants of Baghdad, Yahyah asked him where he was from. He said that he was from Kharasan. Yahyah then asked him why he came to Baghdad, but the captain refused to go into the details of his story, saying that it brought back painful memories and that it was no one's business but his own. But Yahyah persisted, insisting that he tell him his story. The man then began his story by explaining that he and his brother Ahmad were businessmen from Kharasan and that they had planned to come to Baghdad in order to buy merchandise. He then went on to give an account of their journey, telling it exactly, to the minutest detail, as the man who died in the *Masjid* had told it. When he got to the part of the highway robbers attacking the caravan, he said, "Just before we reached Baghdad, a group of highway robbers attacked us and stole all of the goods that were with us. They killed some and injured others. As for my part, I was able to flee from them before they reached me. On the following day, I returned to the scene of the attack, and though I searched hard and long among the corpses and the wounded, I could not find my brother. It seems as if he became over ambitious and wanted to keep the 1000 dinars for himself. I think that he took the money and ran away with it, leaving me to deal with the hardships of poverty. I then came to Baghdad and sat down to rest on the shores of this river. The owner of this boat saw the sad expression on my face and asked me if there was anything that was wrong. After I told him my story, he offered me a job on this boat, telling me that he had become old and weak and could no longer work on it by himself and that he had no son who could help him. I worked with him, and after a short while passed, he married his daughter to me and gave us a place to stay in his house. Then a few months ago he died – may Allah have mercy on him."

Yahyah then asked him to describe the bag that he had given to his brother; after the man gave a correct and precise description of the bag, Yahyah became certain that he had the right man. He took out the bag and gave it to the man, who practically fainted. Yahyah sprinkled water onto his face, and when the man came to, he exclaimed, "Where did you get this from!" After Yahyah told his story, he said, "Indeed, your brother did not run away with the money; rather, he was searching for you throughout Baghdad in order to return the money to you." The man said, "Allah's mercy is indeed vast." Yahyah then asked him to count the money, and when he saw that a little was missing, Yahyah told him that the missing money was used to buy grapes for his brother. The man forgave him for that amount and said, "And here are 10 more dinars for you."

Now that he was in Baghdad and had some money with him, Yahyah thought to himself, "As long as I am here, why don't I return to the job office and ask them if there is any employment available." When he arrived there, the clerk said, "Where have you been? We have been searching all over for you, for a position in the ministry has just opened up, and that position is yours." Based on his skills and knowledge, Yahyah was constantly being promoted in the ministry, until he became Treasurer for the ruler Al-Muqtafa Li-Amrillah. He also became an official scribe for the ruler. When Al-Muqtafa Li-Amrillah became certain of Yahyah's skill, trustworthiness, and sincerity, he appointed him as governor in the year 544 H. Yahyah continued to serve in that position throughout the rule of Al-Muqtafaa Li-Amrillah, and then on into the rule of his son, Al-Mustanjid Lillah. In fact, Yahyah remained governor until he died in the year 560 H. May Allah have mercy on him.

Virtue and Integrity

During the first part of the 'Abbasi rule, a man from the tribe of Shaiban had a very delicate government job. Every morning, it was his duty to patrol the streets of the marketplace until noon, to observe what people said and did, to write down the main doings of the day in a report, to stamp that report, and to then send it to his superior. His superior would gather all of these reports and present the most salient aspects of them to the ruler; this was supposedly done in order to ensure peace and stability in the country.

One particular morning, after he finished making his rounds in the marketplace, the man became preoccupied with some other business. And so after he stamped the report, he called his nephew, whose name was Ahmad, and said, "O Ahmad, do you know where my superior works, the place that I go to every day to submit my reports?" The young boy said, "Yes." His uncle said, "Then go with today's report and submit it on my behalf to my superior, and tell him that I became preoccupied with some important and sudden personal business."

After he took his uncle's report, the boy began to walk towards the heart of the city, where the office of his uncle's superior was located. Had he followed his uncle's instructions, nothing significant would have happened, and there would not have been any reason for history to remember this story. We only remember it today, 14 centuries later, because the young boy did something wonderful, something that indicated what he was going to be like when he grew up. On the way to the heart of the city, the boy had to pass a bridge that was located over a river. And as he crossed the bridge, he began to say to himself, "O Ahmad, you are indeed young; yet you know what your uncle does: he writes what he hears people say and what he sees people do in the marketplace. What he does is prohibited in Allah's religion, for what he does is a form of spying, and Allah says: {And spy not}. O Ahmad, you are therefore carrying a forbidden thing, and are thus an accomplice in a crime that is prohibited in the Qur'ân." Having come to the said conclusion in his mind, Ahmad immediately held up the report and threw it into the river, after which he returned to his home.

Because the report was not received on time at the security headquarters, men were sent to Ahmad's uncle. He told them that he had been busy and that he had sent his nephew to submit the report on his behalf. The boy was summoned, and when he was asked about the report, he straightforwardly said that he had thrown it into the river. The officers who had come were shocked, and they wondered why he would do such a thing. They asked him for his motives, and he said, "Because it (the report and all that it involves) is forbidden... it is a form of spying, and we have been prohibited from spying. And I don't want to implicate myself in that crime."

The officers quickly returned to their headquarters and told their superior everything that had happened and everything that the boy had spoken. When they were finished telling their story, their superior clapped his hands and said, "Such is the integrity of that young boy... but what about us!" From that day forward, people began to treat that young boy as if he were a prominent and well-respected man in society.

And do you know who that young boy was? He was Imam Ahmad bin Hanbal, one of the most distinguished scholars in *Hadith* and Islamic jurisprudence; he was later given the title, "The Imam of Virtue and Integrity." His virtue and integrity helped serve him later on in life, during the trials of Al-Ma'mûn's era. With courage and patience that are still remembered today, Imam Ahmad defended our Islamic creed and endured the frequent torture that was inflicted upon him. Yet throughout, he refused to abandon the beliefs he knew to be true from the Qur'ân and *Sunnah*. The people who tortured him were quickly forgotten, yet the name and deeds and integrity of Imam Ahmad are still remembered today. From his childhood onward, he refused to compromise his beliefs and actions, which were both based on the Qur'ân and the *Sunnah*. May Allah have mercy on him.

It Runs in the Family

The following story is related about a man who long ago became lost during a journey. In the middle of a wide area in the desert, he unexpectedly came across a house and decided to stop there for help, but mainly for nourishment. When he reached the house, a woman came out, greeted him and said, "Who are you?" He said, "A guest." She said, "Welcome indeed, our guest! Stay here and be comfortable." She did not lose much time before serving him food and drink, and while he was eating, the man of the house approached and asked, "Who is this?" His wife said, "He is a guest." He said, "Not welcome is he, for what do we have to do with a guest!"

Of course feeling insulted and unwelcome, the lost traveler had to leave, fearing that the miserly host would hold him accountable for the food that he had already eaten. On the following day, he saw another house in the open desert. Hungry and forlorn, he decided to test the hospitality of its inhabitants. Again a woman met him first, and she asked him, "Who are you?" He said, "A guest." She said, "Not welcome is a guest over here, for what do we have to do with a guest!" As she was speaking to him in that uncouth manner, the man of the house approached and asked, "Who is this?" His wife said, "He is a guest." He said, "Welcome indeed, our guest!" He then came out with delicious food and served it to his guest. While the traveler was eating and drinking, he mused over the events of the last two days and smiled. The host asked, "Why are you smiling?" The traveler told him about the husband and wife that he encountered the day before and expressed his amazement over how opposite the members of the two households were. The host said, "Do not be amazed, for the woman you met yesterday is my sister, and her husband is the brother of my wife. Each has been stamped by the predominant characteristics of his or her family."

A Confession

My story is plain enough, nothing strikingly poignant about it, but I tell it to you so that perhaps you can learn from my mistake. My marriage began as a very happy union between my husband and me. We weren't rich, but we were contented with what we had, and we had a daughter whom we both loved dearly. In the early stages of our marriage, we would put our daughter to sleep, and we would then pray, glorify Allah ﷻ, and recite the Qur'ân.

One day, we checked our savings and realized that we had saved a considerable sum of money, and so I suggested to my husband that we should buy interest-bearing shares, the proceeds of which we could definitely use to help our daughter later on in life. We invested all that we had, including the money I made from selling all of my jewelry. After only a short time passed, the prices of the shares plunged, we went bankrupt, and we were left with many debts. We came to learn the hard way that:

> "Allah will destroy Riba (usery) and will give increase for Sadaqat (deeds of charity, ominous, etc.)." (Qur'ân to: 276).

During one of the difficult nights that followed, I got into a huge argument with my husband and demanded that he divorce me. He then screamed out, "You are divorced from me... you are divorced from me!" Both my child and I cried, and through the many tears, it was this that was constantly going through my mind: We were joined together through obedience to Allah, and we then became separated through disobedience to Him.

'Let No One Issue an Islamic Ruling While Imam Malik Is in Madinah'

The phrase of the title above is one that we hear often when the biography of Imam Malik is being discussed; it indicates his high ranking among the Muslims and his profound knowledge. In the following story, we will see what occasioned the use of that phrase for the first time.

It is related that on one occasion, when a woman in Madinah died, another woman came to wash her body. The corpse was placed on a table, and the woman began to wash it, beginning by pouring water over the corpse and rubbing over it with her hand. When she reached the dead woman's private parts, she said, "Frequently have these private parts been engaged in illegal sexual intercourse." After she said that, her hand became stuck to the body of the deceased woman, and as hard as she tried, she could not separate her hand. She quickly closed the door of the room, so that no one could see what had happened. But outside, the family of the deceased was waiting for her to come out, so that they could then proceed with the funeral preparations. When they got tired of waiting, a woman among them entered and saw what was going on. They all tried to separate the woman's hand, which mysteriously became glued to the body of the deceased. They asked scholars about what should be done; many among them were bewildered as to what they should do, and others differed among themselves: should a part of the deceased's body be cut, so that the hand could be saved? Or should the woman's hand be cut and buried along with the corpse? Finally, everyone said, "Why should we differ among ourselves, when among us lives the scholar of Madinah, Imam Malik?" When they asked to meet with him, he came to them, and standing behind the door, he asked the afflicted woman, "What did you say about the deceased woman?" She immediately confessed the truth, admitting that she had accused the deceased of having fornicated. The Imam said, "This woman has accused another of fornication, and the punishment for such an accusation (when it is not supported by clear proofs) is 80 whippings." He gave the order, and the woman was then whipped 80 times. After the punishment was meted out, the woman's hand somehow unglued itself from the corpse of the deceased, and the problem became solved. From that time onward, people in Madinah would say, "Let no one issue a legal ruling while Malik is in Madinah."

The Sacrifice That Comes with Knowledge

He resorted to promises of reward and threats of punishment, but nothing Al-Mo'tasim said had any effect whatsoever on making Imam Ahmad rescind his views regarding the Noble Qur'ân. After all such verbal attempts failed, Al-Mo'tasim resorted to physically torturing the Imam. Al-Mo'tasim's lackeys beat the Imam until blood began to pour down from his back. Then the ruler, Al-Mo'tasim, said, "O Ahmad, say this one phrase, and I will free you, and I will bestow upon you many gifts and favors." Patient and steadfast as he was, the Imam said, "[Instead] give me one Verse or one *Hadith* [that supports your view]."

The ruthless ruler then ordered his guards to inflict more punishment upon Imam Ahmad, which resulted in more bruises and more wounds. A supposedly learned man who was with the ruler then said to Imam Ahmad, "Did not Allah say {And do not kill yourselves}?"

Imam Ahmad turned to him and said, "Go out and see what is beyond the door." The man went out and saw a huge crowd of people gathered outside of the castle, and many of them had papers and pens win them. The man who was deemed a scholar by the ruler called out to crowd, saying, "What are you all doing over here?" They answered, "We are waiting to hear what Imam Ahmad says, so that we can record his words." He returned inside and told Imam Ahmad what he saw and heard outside. Imam Ahmad said, "Shall I lead all of them into misguidance! Nay! I would rather kill myself (though of course it was they who were trying to kill him) than lead them into misguidance." Imam Ahmad chose torture and pain over misguiding others. May Allah have mercy on him.

A Difficult Predicament Indeed

One of our pious predecessors, Thabit bin Nu'man, was hungry and tired as he was passing through a garden that bordered a river. He was so hungry that he could hear his stomach growling, and so his eyes became fixated on the fruits he saw on the various trees of the garden. In a fit of desperation, he forgot himself and extended his hand to an apple that was within reach. He ate half of it and then drank water from the river. But then he became overcome by guilt, despite the fact that he had only eaten because of dire need. He said to himself, "Woe unto me! How can I eat someone else's fruits without his permission? I make it binding upon myself to not leave this place until I find the owner of this garden and ask him to forgive me for having eaten one of his apples." After a brief search, he found the owner's house. He knocked on the door, and the owner of the garden came out and asked him what he wanted.

Thabit bin Nu'man said, "I entered your garden that borders the river, and I took this apple and ate half of it. Then I remembered that it does not belong to me, and so I ask you now to excuse me for having eaten it and to forgive me for my mistake." The man said, "On one condition only will I forgive you for your mistake."

Thabit bin Nu'man asked, "And what is that condition?" He said, "That you marry my daughter." Thabit said, "I will marry her." The man said, "But heed you this: indeed my daughter is blind, she does not see; mute, she does not speak; deaf, she does not hear." Thabit began to ponder over his situation; a difficult predicament indeed did he find himself to be in now; what should he do? Not get out of it, thought Thabit, for he realized that to be tested by such a woman, to take care of her, and to serve her, are all better than to eat from the foul pus matter of the Hellfire as a reward for the apple that he ate. And after all, the days of this world are few and limited.

And so he accepted the condition to marry the girl, seeking his reward from Allah, Lord of all that exists. He was nonetheless somewhat anxious in the days prior to the marriage; he thought, "How can I have relations with a woman who neither speaks nor sees nor hears." So miserable did he become that he almost wished for the earth to swallow him up before the appointed date; yet despite such apprehensions, he placed his complete trust upon Allah, and he said, "There is neither might nor power except with Allah. Indeed to Allah do we belong, and to Him are we returning." On the day of his marriage, he entered upon her and saw her for the first time. She stood up before him and said, "Peace be upon you, and the mercy and blessings of Allah." When he saw her grace and beauty, he was reminded of what he would see when he would imagine the fair maidens of Paradise. After a brief pause, he said, "What is this? She indeed speaks, hears, and sees." He then told her what her father had said earlier.

She said, "My father has spoken the truth. He said I was a mute because I do not speak any forbidden word, and I have never spoken to a man who is not lawful to me. And I am indeed deaf in the sense that I have never sat in a gathering in which there is backbiting, slander, or false and vain speech. And I am blind in the sense that I have never looked upon a man who is not permissible for me."

Noble reader, reflect on and learn a lesson from the story of this pious man and this pious woman and of how Allah brought them together. The fruit of this noble marriage was the birth of a child who grew up to fill the earth with knowledge; yes, their son was Imam Abu Hanefah An-Nu'man may Allah have mercy on him.

When Judges and Rulers Are Fair Let Them Do Their Job, Justice Is Achieved

The third Caliph of the 'Abbasi rule, Al-Mahdi, was looking for a pious, knowledgeable Islamic jurist, whom he could appoint for the position of Chief Judge in the city of Kufa. He was told about a man who possessed all of the said qualifications, a man who feared none save Allah ﷻ. His name was Sharik bin 'Abdullah. The Caliph summoned him and then said to him when he came, "I indeed want to appoint you for the position of Chief Judge in Kufa." Sharik said, "I certainly do not want to become a judge ever." Deeming it his right to pursue the matter further, Al-Mahdi asked, "Why?" Sharik answered, "I fear that I will make a mistake in one of my judgments, for I am, after all, a mere man; and I fear that, as a result of that mistake, Allah will admit me into the Hellfire. I also fear that, if I issue a ruling against a leader or governor, my ruling will not be executed."

Al-Mahdi said, "[You know that] if you strive to judge by the truth but you then make a mistake, Allah will not hold you accountable for it; rather, He will only hold you accountable if you judge unjustly on purpose, or if you judge, again on purpose, by other than what Allah has revealed. As for the execution and application of your rulings, I promise you that all of your judgments will indeed be executed, even if one of them is against me. If ones such as you righteous Islamic jurists do not agree to become judges, then who will take upon themselves such responsibilities? Would you like for the ignorant ones, unjust ones, or deviant ones to become judges? The sin of that happening will be upon you, based on the fact that you will have, in that case, fled from applying the truth."

These arguments were too strong for Sharik to ignore them, and so he decided to accept the appointment of becoming Chief Judge of Kufa. The governor of Kufa at that time was Mûsa bin 'Īsa, the uncle of the Caliph, Al-Mahdi. Every morning, Sharik would go to the courthouse and judge between the litigants that came before him. True to the hopes of the Caliph, Sharik was a very competent and just judge, and in regards to his rulings, he feared none but Allah ﷻ.

Sharik remained untroubled until he had to deal with a special case, the details of which are as follows. Situated on the shores of the Euphrates River in Kufa was a beautiful garden. It was owned by a resident of Kufa; one day the governor of Kufa, Mûsa bin 'Īsa, decided that it would be nice to own that garden, especially since it was located right beside his castle. He made an offer for the property, but the owner refused to sell it. When the owner died, the garden then became the joint property of his children - a number of sons and one daughter. Having failed to secure the purchase of the property from its previous owner, Mûsa bin 'Īsa went to the new owners and gave a generous offer to buy the garden. All of the sons of the previous owner were willing to sell the garden, but the daughter refused, despite the fact that Mûsa bin 'Īsa offered a huge sum of money, an amount that was much more than what the property was actually worth. And in spite of the daughter's refusal, the sons sold their shares to the governor. To protect her share of the garden, the young woman built a fence around it. Not satisfied at all by having part of the garden and not all of it, Mûsa bin 'Īsa decided to take the young woman's share of the property by force. He gave some instructions to his guards, who then proceeded to destroy the fence that the young woman had built.

The young woman then went to the courthouse and presented her case before Sharik, who ordered that the governor should present himself in his courtroom, so that he could hear what both the plaintiff and the defendant had to say. As governor of Kufa, Mûsa bin 'Īsa felt insulted by the request, for why should he dispute a case with a mere common woman. Mûsa bin 'Īsa sent his chief guard to go in his place, ordering him to convey the following message to the judge: "How can you accept the claim of a woman when she has no witnesses with her." Sharik looked angrily at the governor's representative, and after hearing the message he came with, Sharik said, "Why are you here, when this matter has nothing to do with you. I requested the governor to come and not you; therefore, your punishment is temporary imprisonment." The judge gave instructions to his guards, who then proceeded to arrest the governor's representative and to put him into prison.

When the governor found out what had happened, he sent some of Kufa's leaders to the judge, in order to try to reason with him and appease his anger. After they introduced themselves to him in his courthouse, they said, "The governor must not be treated like a common man; rather, he must receive special treatment, treatment that is in keeping with his position and status." Sharik said, "Before the law, all people are equal. As for you, you have interfered with the law, and the punishment for that is temporary imprisonment." Again, Sharik gave instructions to his guards, who then arrested the men and put them into prison.

When Mûsa bin 'Īsa found out what had happened, he had finally had enough, and so he forthwith set out with some of his men; they went together to the prison and released all those who were imprisoned by the judge for interfering with the case. The prison guards, who really couldn't do anything to stop the governor, went to Sharik to tell him what had just occurred. He exclaimed, "I did not seek out to be a judge; instead, it was the Caliph who coerced me into taking the job, which I only accepted based on the condition that all of my rulings will be executed." He gathered his papers, his books, and his personal possessions, and then climbed his mount in order to head towards the capital city, Baghdad.

When the governor found out that the judge was leaving, he became very afraid. For he knew that if the Caliph were to find out what had happened, he would fire him from his post as governor, regardless of the fact that he was the Caliph's uncle. And that is why he rode out to catch up with the judge before he got too far; he caught up with him on the outskirts of Kufa, and when he reached him, he pleaded with him to return to Kufa, and he promised to fulfill all of his requests. Sharik said, "I will not return until all of the prisoners return to prison and until you present yourself in my courtroom, in order to plea your case against the woman who owns the garden." Having no other realistic option in the matter, the governor accepted all of the judge's terms: the prisoners returned to prison, and the governor present himself at the courthouse. When both the plaintiff and defendant were finished presenting their cases, Sharik ruled in favor of the woman, ordering the governor to rebuild her fence and to abstain from any future attempt at forcing her to sell her share of the property. The governor accepted his ruling and quickly complied with its terms. When all was said and done, Sharik ordered for the prisoners to be released from jail. Later on, in what perhaps seemed to be an awkward meeting for the governor, Sharik went to him and extended greetings of peace to him. Sharik then said, "Do you now order me to do anything?" Seeing the surprised expression on the governor's face, Sharik said,

"What happened before had to do with a right in the *Sharia,* and my coming to you now has to do with the rights of good manners."

True to His Word

History most often remembers only one aspect, albeit a dominant one, of an important person's personality. The first century ruler Al-Hajjaj is no exception: all of his qualities are overshadowed by the one characteristic that he is remembered for today: his tyranny, not necessarily against everyone, but at least against those who spoke out or rebelled against him.

One day, a group of rebels were captured and brought before Al-Hajjaj. After a perfunctory review of their cases, he ordered that each one of them, save one, should be executed. As for the one who remained, Al-Hajjaj was reviewing his case when the call for prayer was made, leaving no time for the man's case to be judged that day. And so Al-Hajjaj turned to Qatibah bin Muslim and said to him, "Keep this man in your custody, and bring him to me tomorrow morning." Qatibah left the ruler's court, taking the prisoner along with him. As they were walking in the streets of the city, the man turned to Qatibah and said, "Do you wish to do a good deed."

"And what is it?" asked Qatibah.

"I have valuable things that people have kept with me as a trust, and as you know, your ruler will soon have me killed. Release me now and allow me to return to my home, so that I can bid farewell to my family and return the things that were entrusted to me to their rightful owners; also, so that I can update my final will and testament. And Allah is the Guarantor for me to return to you tomorrow morning." Amazed at the man's words, Qatibah began to laugh. The man was not discouraged, however; instead, he repeated his request and gave extra stress to the words: "Allah is the Guarantor for me to return to you." On the spur of the moment, and without really knowing why, Qatibah said, "Go."

After the man had left and was out of sight, Qatibah felt as if he had just woken from a state of heedlessness, and he began to have many doubts about allowing the man to go. He then exclaimed, "What have I done!" He returned home to his family and endured a long, sleepless night, but no sooner was it morning than he heard a knocking at his door. When he opened the door, he was happy to see that his prisoner was true to his word and had actually returned. At first, he didn't believe his eyes, and so he exclaimed, "You have returned!"

The man said, "I made Allah my Guarantor, and you think that I should not then return?" They both went together towards Al-Hajjaj's court, and when Al-Hajjaj saw them and saw the tired yet strange look in Qatibah's eyes, he knew that something had happened. Upon Al-Hajjaj's request, Qatibah gave him an account of the events that took place the day before and that morning. Perhaps it was because Al-Hajjaj was impressed by the man's trustworthiness; perhaps it was because he was impressed by Qatibah's trust in Allah; or perhaps it was because he was moved by the action of both men;

whatever the reason, he turned to Qatibah and said, "Release your prisoner, for he is free to go."

When both Qatibah and the prisoner were standing outside of the ruler's court, the former said, "Go wherever you want." Almost as if he were ignoring Qatibah, the man raised his gaze towards the sky and said, "O Allah, all praise is for you." Without saying a single word of thanks to Qatibah, the man left. Having trusted the man when perhaps no one else would have done the same, Qatibah, to be sure, felt somewhat disappointed at their parting; after all, a simple gesture of gratitude would have been sufficient. But on the following day, the man returned to Qatibah and said, "May Allah reward you with the best of rewards for what you did for me. By Allah, while we were together yesterday, I was not unmindful of what you had done for me, yet I said nothing of that to you, for I indeed disliked that I should, with my praise, associate any partners with Allah."

Is Not Goodness the Reward of Goodness?

Imam, Al-Qadi, Abu Bakr Muhammad bin 'Abdul-Baqi Al-Ansari - may Allah have mercy on him - used to live in Makkah. Having gone without food for longer than was comfortable for him, he became extremely hungry, but had nothing with which he could fend off his hunger. As he was walking through the streets of Makkah, thinking about his predicament, he found a silk bag that was tied by a silk string. After he picked up the bag, Imam Abu Bakr took it to his house. There he opened the bag and found in it a pearl necklace, the likes of which – in terms of beauty and quality – he had never before seen in his entire life. But if he felt any joy at having found such a valuable thing, that joy was short-lived, for when he went out into the street, he came across an old man who was announcing that he had lost a silk bag that contained a valuable necklace. The old man said that there was a reward of 500 dinars for the person who returned the bag and necklace.

Many others who are put through a similar test fail, especially those who are poor and for whom the temptation of a valuable item is simply too much. But not so for Imam Abu Bakr, who instead of reflecting on his own situation, took the old man back with him to his house and asked him to describe the bag, the string, the pearls, and the string to which they were attached. The old man of course gave an accurate description of everything, after which Imam Abu Bakr took out the lost items and gave them to him. The old man immediately took out 500 dinars and tried to hand them over to Imam Abu Bakr, but he refused to take the reward, explaining that it was a religious duty upon him to return the lost items and that, therefore, it was not befitting for him to take a reward for having fulfilled that duty. The old man continued to insist for a while, but Imam Abu Bakr was adamant in that he was not going to take the money. The old man then took his leave and went on his way.

Shortly thereafter, Imam Abu Bakr, perhaps seeking out a

new life and a new means of gaining sustenance, left Makkah and became a passenger on a sea vessel. During his journey, the ship began to sink, and as a result, many people died, and their wealth went with them to the bottom of the sea. The ship was breaking into pieces, and with a great deal of difficulty, Imam Abu Bakr managed to hold on to one of those pieces and thus remain afloat. He continued to hold on to the broken piece for a long time, and when he finally reached an inhabited island, he could not tell how many days he had spent all alone in the sea.

As a newcomer to the island, he did not know anyone, and needing a place to rest and recuperate, he sat down in a *Masjid*. While he was seated in the *Masjid*, reading the Qur'ân, many people heard him and approached him, asking him to teach them the Qur'ân. He was all too happy to teach them, and as a reward for his services, they paid him a significant amount of money.

Later on, he found papers on which was written chapters of the Qur'ân. He finally found an opportunity to read directly from the Qur'ân instead of reciting from memory. Apparently, at least most people on the island were illiterate, for seeing that he could read, a throng of people approached him and asked him if he was able to write. He answered in the affirmative, and they said, "Teach us how to write." They then brought to him children of all ages, and he became their teacher. And again, in return for his services, he was paid a handsome sum of money.

Being pleased with both the character and knowledge of the newcomer, the leaders of the island approached him, saying, "Among us lives a young female orphan. She is rich, and we want you to marry her." At first Imam Abu Bakr refused, but they insisted until he finally gave in and agreed to marry her.

On the day of their marriage, the leaders of the island presented Imam Abu Bakr's new bride to him. With a look of utter amazement in his eyes, he began to stare at the necklace that she was wearing. So long did he stare at it, that the leaders of the island said, "You are breaking the heart of this young orphan, for instead of looking at her, you are looking at her necklace." Imam Abu Bakr then told them of his story with the old man in Makkah. Everyone present began to pronounce the Testimony of Faith and to extol Allah's greatness; they were so loud that their voices could be heard by all of the inhabitants of the island. Imam Abu Bakr asked, "What is the matter with you?" They said, "The old man who took the necklace from you is the father of this girl, and he used to say: 'I have never found [a true and sincere] Muslim in the world except for the man who returned this necklace to me.' And he used to supplicate, saying: 'O Allah, bring me and that man together, so that I can marry my daughter to him.' And now that has happened."

Imam Abu Bakr outlived his wife and the children she bore him. Inheriting the necklace and then selling it for 100,000 dinars, he remained a wealthy man to the end of his days.

Allah's Countless Favors

The following story is related by a woman who, centuries ago, endured a difficult, though ultimately faith-increasing, hardship:

I was once a passenger on a sea vessel, and traveling with me were many businessmen. While we were in the middle of the sea, the winds became tempestuous, and our ship began to sink. Every passenger and crew member of the ship drowned except for three: myself and my young child, for we both held on to a piece of wood that had broken off from the ship; and a black man, who was holding on to another part of the boat that had broken off. It was during the night that the ship began to sink, so it was near impossible to see anything, but in the morning, the other survivor saw us and began to swim towards us, holding on with one hand to a piece of wood and struggling with the other in the water in order to reach us. Meanwhile, while holding on to my son, I was able to climb the piece of wood that I was hanging on to.

After a long struggle in the water, the man finally reached us and climbed the piece of wood we were sitting on. I felt very much disconcerted when he then came and sat down beside me. When he then tried to seduce me, I said, "O slave of Allah, do you not fear Allah. We are in a difficult predicament, one from which we can little hope to escape, even if we are obedient to Allah; what do think you, then, our chances are if we disobey Him?" He said, "Don't make me here such words, for by Allah, this is something that I must have." My child was sleeping in my lap at the time, and I stealthily poked him, hoping that he would wake up. He did wake up, and with a loud cry. I turned to the man and said, "O slave of Allah, please give me a chance to put my child to sleep, and then after that we can see what Allah has decreed for us."

Instead of heeding my words, the man tore my son away from my lap and threw him into the sea. I raised my gaze towards the sky and said, "O One Who is most capable of coming between a person and his heart, make something, by Your Might and Power, come between me and this man. Indeed, You are upon all things capable." No sooner did I finish saying the last of those words than did a large sea creature rise above the surface of the water, open its mouth, and swallow the man who was about to try to rape me. It then plunged back into the sea, and Allah kept me protected from its jaws.

Although one problem was solved, I was still stranded in the middle of the sea. The waves continued to propel me from one direction to another until I finally washed ashore onto an island. I remained positive and thought to myself: "I will eat whatever I find here, and I will wait until Allah provides relief for me, for only He can bring help to me now."

Four days passed, and I was struggling as best as I could to survive. On the fifth day, as if out of nowhere, a ship appeared. I climbed a hill and waved my arms frantically, signaling to the passengers of the ship that I needed help. They saw me, and three of them climbed a small raft and came towards me. After they came and took me back to their ship, I looked around at the ship's passengers, and not believing my eyes, I saw my child sitting down with one of the men. I ran towards my child, embraced him, and kissed him between his eyes. I said, "This, by Allah, is my dear child." The people on the ship began to look at me as if I were a crazy woman, but I told them that I was perfectly sane, after which I gave them an account of my story, concentrating on the events that led to the separation between me and my child.

Each one of them, as he heard me tell my story, had a look of amazement in his eyes. One of them said, "You have told us an amazing story indeed, and we too have a story that will amaze you. While we were traveling in the calm waters of the sea, a large sea creature suddenly blocked our way, and on its back this child was seated. From we know not where, a caller called out, saying, 'If you do not take this child from its back, you will be destroyed.' One of us climbed the back of the sea creature, picked up the child, and then took him back to the safety of the ship. As soon as our man returned to the ship with the child safely tucked in his arms, the sea creature plunged back down into the sea. We are truly amazed at what happened to us and at your story. We indeed make a pledge to Allah that, after this day, He will not see us disobeying Him." Each one of the ship's crewmembers then repented for his past sins. How perfect Allah is indeed! He is indeed All-Knowing, All-Wise, Most-Merciful.

A Very Special Dream

History books contain the mention of an amazing incident that took place in the year 557. At the time, the 'Abbasi dynasty was experiencing a sharp decline. As the lands of the Muslims became plagued by weakness and even chaos, some Christians got together and plotted to remove the Prophet's body from his grave and to transport it back to their own lands, in what would obviously be a serious blow to the morale of the Muslims. For this diabolical plot, they sent two men to Madinah, both of whom disguised themselves in Moroccan garments and claimed to be travelers who came to visit the holy city.

The two men stayed in a well-known house that was adjacent to the Prophet's *Masjid*. In order to blend in with their milieu, they performed acts of worship in a conspicuous manner, always hoping to be seen by others in order to gain their trust. But on the inside, they were plotting to achieve the task for which they had been sent.

Having come up with a plan that, at least in their minds, was sure to work, they began to execute it. They secretly began to dig a tunnel from inside their house, and by continuing to dig, they hoped to eventually reach the Prophet's grave. Every day, they would dig a little bit, placing the extra dirt in bags. They of course did not want to be seen by anyone when they would dispose of the extra dirt, and so they would get rid of it while they would take their daily walk in Al-Baqi', the famous graveyard of Madinah. As they would walk through the graveyard, they would slowly pour out the dirt from underneath their cloaks. And all the while they would be giving others the impression that they were visiting the graveyard in order to remember death and the hereafter. At times, they would also spill the excess dirt into a well that was near their home. After many days of secret toil, the two men were finally near the grave of the Prophet ﷺ. Feeling sure now that they would succeed in their mission, they began to concentrate their thoughts on concocting a plan to actually transport the Prophet's body to their homeland. But they could plot and plan as much as they wanted, for Allah ﷻ had other plans for them, and what He wills, He does.

Far away from Madinah, the ruler during that era, Nurad-Din Muhammad bin Zanki, saw a troubling dream. In that dream, he saw the Prophet ﷺ pointing to two men of red complexion, and instructing Nurad-Din Muhammad to protect him from them. Nurad-Din Muhammad then woke up, both frightened and agitated. In order to calm his nerves, he stood up to pray, after which he went back to sleep. But during that night, he saw the same dream three times. When he woke up the third time, he summoned for one of his ministers to come to him. That minister was Jamal Ad-Din Al-Musili, a wise minister who was a practicing, righteous Muslim. When the ruler finished telling him about his dream, Jamal Ad-Din said, "This is concerning something that is happening in Madinah. Go now to the Prophet's city and keep secret what you have seen."

For the remainder of that night, Nurad-Din Muhammad made preparations to leave. 20 mounts were loaded, and 20 men, one of them being Jamal Ad-Din, made preparations to go with their leader. They made the journey from Ash-Sham (Syria and surrounding regions) to Madinah in 16 days. When they reached their destination, Nurad-Din Muhammad went to Ar-Rauda (a special place in the Prophet's *Masjid*) and prayed, but as of yet, he had no idea what he should do about his dream.

His minister, Jamal Ad-Din, asked him if he remembered what the two people he saw in his dream looked like. Nurad-Din Muhammad said that he remembered them clearly, and that if he were to see them now, he would certainly recognize them. Jamal Ad-Din had a plan to apprehend the two men, and he immediately put it into action. When the inhabitants of Madinah were gathered in the *Masjid*, Jamal Ad-Din made the following announcement: "Indeed, the ruler has brought with him a great deal of wealth that has been earmarked for charity. Have the poor ones among you register their names, and then bring them, so that each can take his fair share." While each person came to take a share of the handout, Nurad-Din Muhammad was standing right there, looking at each person, in the hope of seeing one or both of the men he saw in his dream. Many people came and went, but Nurad-Din Muhammad saw no one who resembled either of the two men.

He then asked, "Is there anyone left who still has not taken his share?" Someone said, "There remains two men from Morocco; they refuse to take their share, and indeed, they are both very righteous." "Bring them to me," were the immediate words that came out of Nurad-Din Muhammad's mouth. When the two men were brought before him, Nurad-Din Muhammad immediately recognized them: they were the two men that the Prophet ﷺ pointed to in his dream. Nurad-Din asked them, "Where are you from?" They said, "We are from the West, and we have come here in order to perform *Hajj*. After we arrived, we decided to stay here this year."

Perhaps their plot was not exactly clear to Nurad-Din at that moment, but he knew they were guilty of something, and so he continued to interrogate them, hoping that they would confess their crime, whatever it was. But they kept to their story, and with no proof against them, Nurad-Din couldn't justly take any steps against them. Nurad-Din then ordered for their home to be searched. After a thorough search, they found nothing peculiar save a large amount of money that the two men had stored in their home. As everyone began to file out of the two men's home, Allah guided Nurad-Din to look at the wooden floor. One of its boards was loose, and Nurad-Din stooped down to have a closer look. He realized that the board was not attached solidly to the floor, and so he picked it up. The people of Madinah were shocked to see the entrance of a tunnel and even more shocked to see where it led to, for they had been certain that the two men were righteous Muslims.

After being beaten by the irate ruler, the two men confessed that they weren't really from the West, but were instead two Christians who had been sent by their leaders with a great deal of wealth that was paid to them upfront for the job of removing the Prophet ﷺ from his grave and transporting the body back to their lands. Nurad-Din ordered for the two men to be executed and for the tunnel to be blocked up and filled with dirt. When these two orders were executed, he returned to Ash-Sham. And Allah ﷻ knows best.

"Even the Ministers of Fir'aun Are Better"

One day after he executed the noble Companion 'Abdullah bin Az-Zubair ﷺ, the infamous tyrant Al-Hajjaj bin Yusuf Ath-Thaqafi was sitting down in a gathering, when he turned to his guard and said, "Bring me the *Hururiyyah* woman." When she was brought before him, he said to her, "Yesterday, you were present at his death (i.e., at the death of 'Abdullah bin Az-Zubair ﷺ). And you were inciting people to kill me, to kill my men, and to take my wealth: is that true?"

"Yes, that is what happened," said the woman.

"What should I do with her?" Al-Hajjaj asked, addressing the question to his ministers.

"Make haste in executing her," they said. When they said that, the woman began to laugh out loud, and her voice echoed throughout the room. It was a laugh that angered Al-Hajjaj. He turned to her and asked, "What has made you laugh?"

"Even the ministers of Fir'aun are better than these ministers of yours," she exclaimed. Al-Hajjaj then turned to his ministers and saw the embarrassed expressions on their faces. He then asked the woman, "And why is that?"

"When Fir'aun consulted them about killing Musa ﷺ, they said that he should give Musa ﷺ respite until a later time," said the woman. "And these ones are asking you to make haste in killing me." The woman's witty remark penetrated the outer shell of Al-Hajjaj and made him laugh. He was so pleased by her words that he freed her after first ordering for gifts to be given to her.

"The woman is correct and 'Umar ﷺ is in error "

One day, 'Umar bin Al-Khattab ﷺ addressed the people, announcing that the dowry of no woman, regardless of how rich or high ranking she or her family may be, should exceed 40 *Uqiyyah* (a form of measurement). He then said that if the dowry of any woman exceeds that amount, then the excess was going to be seized and placed in the Muslim Treasury. A woman in the crowd called out, saying, "You have no right to do that!" He said, "And why is that?" She said, "Because Allah ﷻ said:

> "But if... you have given one of them a Qintar (of gold, i.e. a great amount) as Mahr (dowry), take not the least bit of it back" (Qur'ân 4:20)."

Before the entire crowd that was present that day, 'Umar ﷺ said, "The woman is correct and 'Umar is in error. O 'Umar, every single person has a better understanding of the religion than you."

"But the Lord of 'Umar Sees Us"

During 'Umar's caliphate, it was not unusual for him to be seen patrolling the streets during the night. It was in fact his routine to do so in order to make sure that everyone was safe. On one such night, he was patrolling the streets with his servant. Becoming tired after a while, both of them stopped to rest beside a house. They could clearly hear the voice of an old woman from inside the house; she was ordering her daughter to water down the milk they were going to sell the following day. But the daughter refused her request; instead, she said, "Indeed, the Leader of the Believers has sent someone to make the announcement that it is forbidden to mix milk with water (of course, referring to milk that is for sale and not for personal consumption)."

The mother was not necessarily angry with her daughter, but she insisted that her daughter comply with her request. She even tried to reason with her, saying, "Where is 'Umar now? Verily, he does not see us." Her believing, trustworthy daughter answered, "If 'Umar does not see us, then indeed, the Lord of 'Umar sees us." The Leader of the Believers was very impressed by what he heard from the young woman, impressed by her faith and by her trustworthiness. On the following morning, he asked about her and found out that her name was Umm 'Ammarah bint Sufyan bin 'Abdullah Ath-Thaqafi and that she was unmarried. He then married her to his son 'Aasim. Allah blessed their marriage, for one of their grandchildren turned out to be a just and pious Caliph: of course, I am referring to 'Umar bin 'Abdul-'Aziz.

"He Is Irreplaceable"

It is related that a woman once openly accused her husband, her son, and her brother of plotting to assassinate the ruler Al-Mustansir Billah. The three were then apprehended and sent to prison. After their cases were reviewed, the ruler judged that each of them should be executed.

When the woman learned of Al-Mustansir Billah's judgment, she went and stood at the door of his court. She was waiting for him to come, and when she finally saw him approaching, she threw herself at his feet, crying bitter tears and beseeching him to pardon her family or to at least have her killed along with them, stating that she had no desire to live if they were to die. At least somewhat moved by the woman's pathetic condition, Al-Mustansir Billah thought about the matter for a moment and then said, "Woman, I accept your intercession, but on behalf of only one of the three. And I leave it up to you to decide which of the three will be saved."

Loving all three of them, the woman was literally torn apart on the inside, not being able to decide between them. After thinking about the matter for little while, she said, "Another husband can be married; another son can be born to me; as for my brother, he is irreplaceable, for if he dies, I will never again have a brother. I therefore choose my brother." Impressed by the woman's logic and reasoning, Al-Mustansir Billah said, "Go, woman, for I will spare the lives of all three of them for you."

"Inform the Women You Left behind"

Asma bint Yazeed ﷺ once went to the Prophet ﷺ and said, "Be my mother and father held ransom for you, O Messenger of Allah: indeed, there is no woman in either the east or the west of our lands except that her opinion is similar to mine. Indeed, Allah ﷻ has sent you to both men and women. And we have believed in you and in your God, Who has sent you. As a group, we women are confined and limited; we take care of the affairs of your homes, we bear your children, we preserve your wealth, we are what you leave behind when you go on journeys, and we are your caregivers when you remain at home. And indeed, as a group, you men have been favored with...congregations (i.e., congregational prayer), with visiting the sick, with attending funerals, with *Hajj* and 'Umrah, and with better than all of that *Jihad* in the way of Allah. Indeed, when you go out to perform *Hajj*, to perform *Jihad*, to do business, or to simply travel, we preserve your wealth for you and we raise your children for you. Furthermore, we sew your garments for you, and we put food (i.e., meals) together for you. Then will we be partners to you in reward, O Messenger of Allah?"

The Prophet ﷺ said to his Companions ﷺ, "Have you ever heard any speech of a woman that is better than her speech, in terms of the good way in which she is asking about her religion?" He ﷺ then addressed her, saying, "Return, O woman, and inform the women you left behind that for one of you to be a good wife to her husband, to avoid making him angry, and to do that which pleases him are equivalent to all of that (i.e., are equivalent to the rewards for all of the deeds you mentioned)." As Asma ﷺ turned to leave, she expressed her joy by magnifying Allah (i.e., saying, "Allah is the greatest") and by pronouncing the Testimony of Faith.

The Woman Who Humiliated Al-Hajjaj

Few men could have claimed that they had gotten the better of Al-Hajjaj, a tyrant who would mercilessly kill his enemies. At least one person for certain could have truthfully made that claim, and that person wasn't even a man. Rather, that person was a woman who used all of her wit and female abilities to get the better of him and to humiliate him.

Her name was Hind bint An-Nu'man, one of the most beautiful of women that was alive at that time. When Al-Hajjaj heard of her superior beauty, he proposed to her, and to increase the chances of her accepting him, he offered her a great deal of money. They ended up marrying, and after a while, they left the land they were in and traveled to Iraq. Hind was an educated woman, well-versed in literature and poetry. One day, though she did not perceive his presence, Al-Hajjaj entered a room wherein she was standing and looking at herself in a mirror. As she was looking at herself, she read lines of poetry, in which she was praising her lineage and appearance and saying that, if she was going to have a good-looking child, then it would be to the credit of her lineage; but that, if her child ended up being not so good-looking, then that would be ascribed to Al-Hajjaj's lineage. During the short duration of their marriage, Hind got a close look at her husband's character, and she saw that he was a cold, ruthless man, and so it is not surprising that she felt revolted by him.

Al-Hajjaj left before she could see him. He was so angry that he sent someone to give her 200,000 dirhams and to inform her that he was divorcing her. The messenger then went to give her both the money and the news. Contrary to what he was probably expecting in terms of her reaction, she rejoiced and said that she felt no regrets and was happy to be freed from "the dog" of the Banu Thaqif clan.

At the time, Al-Hajjaj was only a governor. A report of what happened was sent to the then ruler, 'Abdul-Malik bin Mirwan. Not only did 'Abdul-Malik receive a report about what had happened, but he also received a description of Hind's exceptional beauty. 'Abdul-Malik then sent a message to Hind, asking her to marry him. She sent a letter back to him, in which she wrote, "Know, O Leader of the Believers, that a dog has licked the [inside of the] dish." Here, Hind, with a double meaning in mind, was alluding to a saying of the Prophet ﷺ. For her part, the dog represented Al-Hajjaj and the dish represented her, and the dog licking the bowl represented their brief marriage together. Immediately grasping her double meaning, he appreciated her sharp wit, and he even laughed at what she wrote. Not to be outdone by her, he wrote back with a solution to the problem, using the exact same *Hadith* that she mentioned. Quoting the *Hadith* in its entirety, he said, "When a dog licks a dish that belongs to one of you, then let him wash it seven times, and one of those seven washings should be with dirt." He then wrote, "So wash the dish, and it will become lawful to use again."

After Hind read his response, she wrote back, saying that she would only agree to marry him on one condition. She said that the condition was for Al-Hajjaj to steer her riding camel from her country to his; and throughout the journey, he should be walking barefoot. Upon reading her letter, 'Abdul-Malik began to laugh a great deal. He sent for his governor, Al-Hajjaj, and ordered him to comply with Hind's request. Al-Hajjaj of course had no choice but to execute his leader's command. And so 'Abdul-Malik sent another message to Hind, telling her to prepare her things for the journey.

A compartment was built over a wooden frame and it was placed on top of the camel that Hind was to ride upon during the journey. When the traveling party, which consisted of a number of servants, was ready, Al-Hajjaj took the camel's reins and began the long, arduous walk - barefooted of course - to the land of the Caliph. Throughout the journey, Hind lost no opportunity to laugh at and ridicule Al-Hajjaj. She continued to do so until they almost reached their destination. She then threw a dinar onto the ground, after which she called out to Al-Hajjaj, "I dropped a dirham, so pick it up and give it to me." A dinar was actually worth much more than a dirham. When Al-Hajjaj stooped down to the ground, he said, "It is a dinar." Again with a cruel double meaning in mind, she said, "I dropped a dirham, and Allah replaced it for me with a dinar." Since was she was about to become the wife of the ruler, Al-Hajjaj of course could not respond to her insult. After they reached their destination, Hind officially became 'Abdul-Malik's wife, and the wedding banquet took place. No mention is made in the story regarding whether Al-Hajjaj attended the wedding or not.

The Wife of Khusru and the Fishermen

It is related that the king Khusru bin Burwiz used to love eating fish. One day, he was sitting down with his wife Shirin, when a fisherman came with a huge fish, which he presented to the king as a gift. So impressed was the king by the size of the catch, that he gave a reward of 4000 dirhams to the fisherman.

When the fisherman had left, Shirin expressed her strong disapproval of her husband's action. When he asked her why she disapproved, she said, "If you give one of your close followers a similar amount - which is a considerable sum - he will complain and say, 'You have given me the same amount of money that you gave to a fisherman!'"

Khusru said, "What you have said is true, but it is not befitting for a king to take back a gift. Besides, it is too late now."

"I have a sensible plan to get back the money," said Shirin.

"What is it?" asked Khusru.

"First, call the fishermen back," said Shirin. "Then ask him whether the fish is male or female. If he says that it is a male fish, say to him that what you were really expecting was a female fish. And if he says that it is female, then say that you had really wanted a male fish." The fisherman was summoned, and when he returned, he knew that something was up. He was both intelligent and quick-witted, and he quickly perceived that they were going to somehow ask for the money back; he perhaps knew something about the nature of the king's wife, perhaps the fact that she was not as generous as the king was.

The king then asked him, "Regarding the fish you gave me, is it male or female?"

"Neither, it is bisexual," said the fisherman." The king laughed, realizing that the fisherman knew the purpose behind his question. Feeling that he deserved an extra reward for his quick wit, the king gave him 4000 more dirhams. As the fisherman was walking away with a bag full of 8000 dirhams, a single dirham fell from his bag and landed on the ground. Removing the heavy bag from his shoulders, he knelt down to the ground and picked up the dirham, and as he did so, the king and queen were staring at him.

Shirin said, "Did you see the baseness of that man! A single dirham fell from his bag, and in order to retrieve it, he put down his other 7999 dirhams and knelt to the ground in order to pick it up. Could he not have just left it there, so that one of your servants could pick it up and use it for his benefit."

"You have spoken the truth, O Shirin," said the king. He then summoned the fisherman back to him and said, "Have you no dignity! It is with difficulty that you placed the heavy bag of money down onto the ground, and you did so only so that you could pick up a single dirham. Could you not have left it in its place?"

"May Allah give you a long life, O king," said the fisherman, with a look of cunning that he hid very well. "I did not pick up this dirham because it was important to me; rather, I picked it up from the ground because on one side of it is your picture, and on the other side your name is written. And I feared that someone would come and inadvertently step on it, which would be tantamount to your name being debased. I feared that, if that were to happen, I would be the cause of the tragedy and crime." Again, the king was impressed by his words, and again he gave him another 4000 dirhams. The fisherman took his leave for the last time, taking with him 12,000 dirhams. And the king then made the following announcement to his people: No one should act based on the opinion of a woman, for if one does so, he will lose his dirhams.

Al-Hajjaj bin Yusuf, the ruthless tyrant, would crush all opposition and show no mercy to anyone who criticized him. One of his targets was the noble companion of the Prophet ﷺ, Anas bin Malik ؓ. He heard that Anas ؓ had spoken out against him, and so he sent his guards to search out for him; but they weren't able to locate him. Finally, Al-Hajjaj sent 'Abdullah bin Hibban Ath-Thaqafi ؓ to search out for him.

When 'Abdullah went out with his horse, he was under the impression that Anas ﷺ would be hiding from him; but much to his surprise, he found Anas ﷺ to be sitting in front of his home, relaxing with his legs extended. 'Abdullah said, "Answer the ruler's summons to appear before him."

"Which ruler," Anas asked.

"Abu Muhammad Al-Hajjaj," answered 'Abdullah.

"Allah has indeed lowered him, and I do not see why I should honor him (i.e., by answering his summons to appear before him)," said Anas, with perfect calmness and composure. "For indeed, the honorable one is he who is honored through the obedience of Allah; and the ignoble one is he who is lowered through the disobedience of Allah, and indeed your companion has tyrannized, oppressed, and transgressed; furthermore, he has opposed Allah's Book and the *Sunnah* [of the Prophet ﷺ]. Therefore, Allah will indeed exact retribution from him."

"Save your speech and answer the summons of the ruler," said 'Abdullah. The two, along with the company of armed guards, made their way to Al-Hajjaj's court. When they arrived there, Al-Hajjaj looked intently at Anas, trying to intimidate him with his look; he then said, "Are you the one who is supplicating against us and cursing us?"

"Yes," answered Anas.

"And why is that?"

"It is because you are disobedient to your Lord and because you act contrary to the *Sunnah* of your Prophet ﷺ. You honor Allah's enemies, and you debase His obedient slaves."

"Do you know what I want to do with you?" asked Al-Hajjaj.

"No."

"I want to inflict upon you a gruesome death," said Al-Hajjaj.

"Had I known that the choice to do that was in your hands, I would have worshiped you instead of worshipping Allah," said Anas. He then informed the tyrant that the Prophet ﷺ taught him to say a supplication every morning, a supplication that, by the permission of Allah, would protect him for the rest of the day from sudden harm; and he told Al-Hajjaj that he had made the said supplication on that very morning. The ruler asked him to teach it to him, but he refused, not wanting to give the tyrant the means to live longer and inflict harm on even more people. Everyone that was present in the ruler's court was expecting nothing other than an order for Anas's immediate execution. None of them was prepared for what Al-Hajjaj said next. "Let him go," said the tyrant, seeming to be somewhat distraught.

As soon as Anas رضي الله عنه left, unharmed and untouched, Al-Hajjaj's chief guard began to complain: "O leader, we have searched for him for so many days, and now that we finally have him, we are letting him go!"

Al-Hajjaj looked somewhat humbled by the experience, and he felt compelled to tell the truth. "I saw perched on his shoulders two huge lions with their mouths wide open," admitted the tyrant. Filled with terror by what he saw, he felt compelled to release the prisoner.

Regardless of whether this narration is authentic or not, the lesson it imparts is very important: by placing one's complete trust in Allah ﷻ, by fearing none save Allah, and by invoking none save Allah, one treads the path of safety and success. And in fact, there is a *Hadith* in which the Prophet ﷺ taught us a supplication, the effects of which are similar to those described in the above-mentioned narration. He ﷺ informed us that whoever says the following supplication every morning and every night, remains protected from harm: "In the name of Allah with Whose name nothing is harmed on earth nor in the heavens and He is the All-Seeing, the All-Knowing."

The Supplication Of The Wronged

Ibn 'Abbas ؓ related that the Prophet ﷺ said, "Beware of the supplication of the wronged one, for indeed between him and Allah there is no barrier." Therefore, when someone wrongs us, we need neither worry nor complain to any human being; rather, we should direct all of our energies to invoking Allah ﷻ for help.

Arwa bint Uwais, once went to Muhammad bin 'Amr bin Hazm and complained about Sa'id bin 'Amr bin Nufail ؓ, claiming that he wrongfully took some land from her. She said, "By Allah, if he does not return it to me, I will yell out [and expose him] in the *Masjid* of the Messenger of Allah ﷺ."

"Do not harm a companion of the Messenger of Allah,"

exclaimed Muhammad. "Sa'id would neither wrong you nor take away any of your rights." Not satisfied with what he said, she then went to 'Umarah and 'Abdullah bin Salamah; she made the same complaint and uttered the same threat: either Sa'id ﷺ return the land that she claimed to be hers, or she would cry out in the *Masjid* that he wrongfully took her land. 'Umarah and Abdullah then went out to meet with Sa'id, and when he saw them approaching his property, he asked, "What [business] has brought you here?"

"Arwa came to us earlier and claimed that you wrongfully built [something] on her land, and she swore by Allah that either you desist or she will expose you in the *Masjid* of the Messenger of Allah ﷺ. We came here, wanting to inform you about what she said."

Sa'id bin 'Amr said, "I heard the Messenger of Allah ﷺ say, ' whoever wrongfully takes land that is equivalent to the span of a hand, then (as punishment) he will be embraced by it (like one is embraced by a collar) on the Day of Resurrection in the seven earths.' Let her come and take [what she claims to be] her right. O' Allah, if she lied upon me, then do not make her die until You take away her sight and make that to be the cause of her death." Sa'id then turned to them and said, "Return to her and tell her what I said." When Arwa found out that she had gotten her way, she went about destroying what Sa'id had built, and she then built a house in its place.

We know that the supplication of the wronged one is answered, and we also know that Sa'id bin 'Amr was a noble and upright Muslim; therefore, most of us can rightly guess what happened next. Before much time elapsed, Arwa lost her sight; and because she was blind, she used to take her servant with her to be her guide when she needed water from the well or anything else during the night. One night, she decided to go out without waking her servant, and as a result she fell into her well and died.

Temptation

One certainly needs to be careful when one comes across Israelite narrations, for it is near impossible to ascertain whether such narrations are authentic or not. The following narration, which appears to be an Israelite narration, is a good example. But regardless of whether it is authentic or not, it does convey an important lesson: fear of Allah ﷻ saves one from complete destruction.

Two youths were seated together, when a beautiful woman came and sat beside them. In plain view of the three was a monastery of a monk who would spend his days and nights busy in worship. While they were talking, the woman noticed the monastery, and an idea came to her head. She said to her two companions, "What would you say if I told you that I was going to go and tempt the monk towards evil?"

"We would tell you that you will fail in the attempt," said the two youths.

"You are wrong, for I am able to do so." She then stood, applied perfume to her body, and wore her best and most enticing attire. Instead of going immediately, she waited until the night, for she knew that devils are most active during that time. When nighttime came, she went to the gates of the monastery and called out, "O slave of Allah, open the gate for me, for I am afraid and am in need of a safe shelter."

Having no reason to doubt the stranger and wanting to help her, the monk quickly opened the gates for her. When he let her in, he saw her beautiful figure and face and realized that it was not safe to be alone with her, and so he climbed the stairs of his monastery, instructing her to remain alone on the first floor. Upon reaching the second floor, he was surprised to see that she had followed him; he had nowhere to escape, and so he tried to keep a safe distance from her. She then removed all of her clothing and came near to him, offering her body for his pleasure.

He had dedicated all of his life to worshipping Allah, and now, in the middle of the night and hidden to all created beings, he had before him a temptation that was very difficult to resist. If he could have escaped, he probably would have tried, but the woman stood between him and the door that led to lower floor. He quickly put his smallest finger into the fire of the lamp that was beside him, and as his finger burned, he tried to think about the Hellfire. Thus he lost his smallest finger, but the woman still stood there, tempting him towards evil. Again, to remind himself about the fire of the hereafter, he placed his next finger into the fire of the lamp. When the light of morning appeared through the windows, the monk had not succumbed to evil, but he had no more fingers remaining on his hands. So overcome was the woman by the experience of the previous night, that she repented and changed her ways: she built a monastery alongside that of the monk, and she spent her remaining days worshipping alongside him.

The Supplication Of Dhan-Nun

Sa'd bin Abi Waqqas said, "I once passed by 'Uthman in the *Masjid* and extended greetings of peace to him, and though he was staring right at me, he did not respond to my greetings."

He then went to 'Umar and said, "O Leader of the Believers, has something new happened in Islam?"

"And why do you ask that?" asked 'Umar.

"A short while ago I passed by 'Uthman and extended greetings of peace, but he did not answer me." 'Umar sent for 'Uthman, and when he came, 'Umar said, "What prevented you from returning greetings of peace to your brother?"

"I did not do that," said 'Uthman.

"Indeed you did," interjected Sa'd. Each one of them swore that he was telling the truth, but then 'Uthman remembered what happened, and so he said, "Indeed, [what he said] is true. I indeed ask Allah to forgive me, and I repent to Him. Verily, you did pass by me a short while ago, but at the time I was thinking over in my mind words that I heard from the Messenger of Allah ﷺ. By Allah, whenever I remember them, I feel a blur coming over my sight and heart."

Now understanding why 'Uthman ﷺ was so mentally occupied that he did not answer him, Sa'ad ﷺ said, "Then I will inform you of what [you were thinking about]. Indeed, the Messenger of Allah ﷺ told us about the first supplication, [but before he could mention it] a Bedouin came and kept him busy. Then the Messenger of Allah ﷺ stood up and left. I followed him, but when I realized that he would reach his home before I could catch up to him, I struck my feet on the ground. He turned towards me... and said, 'Abu Ishaq?' I said, ' Yes, O Messenger of Allah.' ' What is it?' he asked. I said, ' By Allah, nothing other than the fact that you told us about the first supplication, but then [before you could mention it to us] a Bedouin came.' He said, ' Yes, it is the supplication of Dhan-Nun: "None has the right to be worshiped but You (O Allah), Glorified (and Exalted) be You [above all that (evil) they associate with You]. Truly, I have been of the wrongdoers.". Indeed, whenever a Muslim invokes his Lord about something with it (i.e., with that supplication), He answers [it] for him.'"

Sincerity

We have hitherto discussed how sincerity plays an important role in gaining sustenance or in having our hardships removed. One of the offshoots of sincerity is to do good deeds secretly to make a concerted effort to do good deeds when and where no other human being is there to witness them being performed.

Once Ibn Mukandir went out to pray during a dry spell. As he was supplicating near the pulpit of the Messenger of Allah ﷺ in Madinah, he noticed a man whose head was lowered, and he heard him say, "My Lord, the dry spell has become very difficult for Your slaves, and I swear by You, my Lord, that you will indeed provide rain for them." Within an hour, clouds began to approach, and shortly thereafter it began to rain.

Now, Ibn Mukandir made it a point to acquaint himself with every scholar and righteous man in Madinah, but here was a man whom he did not know and who appeared to be righteous, for his supplication was quickly answered. He made haste and followed the man to his home, and shortly after the man entered, he knocked on the door. Upon being admitted inside, Ibn Mukandir saw very few material possessions and realized that the man was poor. He also discerned, based on the man's [rough] hands and on the materials he saw scattered about, that the man had been busy crushing wheat, a task that only poor people occupied themselves with, since they could not afford to buy bread. "How are you doing?" asked Ibn Mukandir. The man answered politely, yet he seemed to be taken aback by the openness of the stranger. Noticing the man's nervousness, Ibn Mukandir quickly explained the reason for his visit: "A short while ago, I heard the oath that you made by Allah... do you not have enough money to free yourself of the burden of the task that you were occupied with, so that you can concentrate on performing deeds for the Hereafter."

Here, the man realized that he had been found out, and he knew that if the stranger went out and spoke to others about him, he would soon become famous, and people would take him to be a pious man. And so he said, "Do not mention me to anyone, and do not mention what happened until I die. Anddo not return to my home, for if you do, you will make me known to others." Even though Ibn Mukandir promised not to tell anyone about him or about how his supplication was quickly answered, the man was not satisfied, and he feared that, even if others knew nothing about him, Ibn Mukandir would still, when he saw him, think him to be a righteous man. He moved from his home and traveled to another city; no one from Madinah ever saw him again, and no one knew where he went. Much later, when people learned of his story, his neighbors grieved for having lost a righteous man and his supplications. They actually blamed Ibn Mukandir, saying that he was the reason why the man left Madinah.

What concerns us in this story is that the pious man did good deeds not for people or for fame, but for Allah ﷻ; in fact, he hated for others to see the good deeds that he performed. When it came to performing good deeds, he would keep matters between him and Allah ﷻ. It is exactly that sincerity which our pious predecessors were known for and which we should strive to achieve, for it is because of their sincerity that their supplications were not rejected. When we invoke Allah ﷻ for help, we may even refer to past good deeds that we had performed sincerely for Allah, thus increasing the likelihood of our supplications being answered. This point is clearly illustrated in the following narration, which is related in *Sahih Bukhari*.

As three men were walking together, it began to rain, and

so they sought refuge in a cave. But after they entered it, its entrance became blocked, and they all feared that they would remain stuck in the cave and die as a result. They then said to one another, "By Allah, nothing will save you except for sincerity (and truthfulness), so let each man among you supplicate with what he knew himself to be sincere about." One of them said, "O Allah... I had an employee who would work for a measurement of rice. But then he left without taking it (i.e., without taking his wages). I betook myself to that measurement [of rice], and I planted it. From the proceeds [of what grew from that], I purchased cows. He later returned to demand his wages, and I said to him, 'Go to those cows and steer them away (i.e., they are yours). He said, 'All that you own me is a measurement of rice.' I said, 'Go to those cows, for they are indeed from [the proceeds of] that measurement [of rice].' He then steered them away. [O Allah] if You know that I indeed did that from fear of You, then provide relief for us." The boulder that blocked the entrance of the cave then moved, making an opening, but not one large enough for them to leave through it. The second man among them said, "O Allah... I had two very aged parents, and I used to go to them every night with the milk of a sheep that I owned. One night, I was slow to go to them, and by the time I reached them, they had already fallen asleep. Meanwhile, my wife and my dependents were crying from hunger, but I would never give them drink before first giving drink to my parents. I disliked the idea of waking them up, and I [equally] disliked leaving them because they might not be able to see the drinks [when they were going to wake up]. So I continued to wait until the break of dawn. [O Allah], if You know that that was from fear of You, then provide relief for us." The boulder then moved, making an even wider opening, but one that was still not wide enough for them to pass through to safety; it was wide enough, however, for them to be able to see the sky through the hole, and they were instilled with a greater sense of hope. Then the last one among them spoke: "O Allah... I had a female cousin who was among the most beloved of people to me; I tried to seduce her, but she refused, saying that she would only have me if I came to her with 100 dinars. I searched out for that amount, until I was able to get it. I then went to her with it and gave it to her. She allowed me to come to her, and when I was seated between her legs, she said, 'Fear Allah, and do not break the seal without having the right to do so (i.e., do not make me lose my virginity in this unlawful manner).' I stood up and left, leaving the 100 dinars [with her]. [O Allah] if You know that I did that from fear of You, then provide relief for us." Allah ﷻ then provided relief for them: the boulder moved, making a sufficient gap for them to go out to safety. Thus it was through the sincerity they had in performing those deeds that Allah ﷻ provided a way out for them from a very difficult situation.

Humbleness And A Sound Outlook

We often look around us and see two matters that are confusing to some: the pious person whose supplications seemingly go unanswered, and the wicked person or the disbeliever whose supplications are answered.

First, let us consider the situation of the righteous believer who constantly supplicates, though his supplications go unanswered. Such a person must realize that he is being tested and that he must be patient. He must remember the saying of the Prophet ﷺ, "The slave [of Allah] continues to remain upon a good situation as long as he does not hurry - by saying, 'I supplicated, but I have not been answered.'' Next, he must reflect on his situation: Are his food, drink, and clothing lawful and lawfully derived? Is there a sin from which he did not repent? Or is his heart in a state of heedlessness when he invokes Allah? If he arrives at a negative answer to any one of these questions, then he must rectify his situation. In this regard, we have the example of Ibrahim bin Al-Khawwas, may Allah have mercy on him. He once went out to stop others from perpetrating evil deeds, but when he left his door, he couldn't go any further, for there was a menacing dog standing in his way, barking and showing him his teeth. Ibrahim quickly retreated inside; he performed two units of prayer, and then he went out again for a second time. This time, the dog looked docile; it was wagging its tail, as if it were pleased with Ibrahim. He was later asked about what had happened, and he said, "I myself had committed an evil deed. After the dog prevented me from leaving, I returned and repented for my sin. And you saw what happened after that."

Even if one comes up with positive answers to the above-mentioned questions, he must take a number of matters into consideration. First, life is a test; and to pass the test that one is going through, one must be both patient and thankful. The Prophet ﷺ said, "Wonderful is the affair of the believer: indeed, his affair in its entirety is good, and that is for no one save the believer. If goodness befalls him, he is thankful, and that is good for him. And if harm afflicts him, he is patient, and that is good for him."

Second, one might supplicate for something that he ardently desires, but by achieving that thing, he might end up sinning or losing out on something he may otherwise have gained. For example, it is related that one of our pious predecessors would ask Allah ﷻ the ability to go out for battle, but then he heard a caller call out, "If you were to go out for battle, you would be taken prisoner, and you would then have converted to Christianity." And how often is it that we long for things that are bad for us, and through His Mercy and Wisdom, Allah prevents us from achieving those things.

> "And it may be that you dislike a thing which is good for you and that you like a thing which is bad for you. Allow knows but you do not know." (Qur'ân 2: 216)

Third, when a believer is in need, he turns to Allah, asking Him for help; now, whether he is answered immediately or not, he is, by supplicating to Allah, performing an act of worship, for which he will be rewarded. It is often the case that one who is leading an easy life forgets Allah ﷻ and the Hereafter. Such a person might need a hardship to wake him up and to make him remember his purpose in life. It is related that Yahyah ﵇ once cried a great deal, and then when he fell asleep, he spoke to his Lord during a dream. He said, "O my Lord, how much indeed I have invoked You, yet You do not answer me?" He said, "O Yahyah, indeed I love to hear your voice [when you invoke Me for help]."

Fourth, one must remember the following saying of the Messenger of Allah ﷺ: "No Muslim prays with a supplication that involves neither sin nor the breaking off of family ties, except that Allah gives him for it one of three things: either, He hastens [the answer to] his supplication (i.e., He answers it in this world), or He saves it for him for the Hereafter, or He wards off from him evil that is equivalent (i.e., equivalent in degree to the good that he asked for)."

Now let us consider the opposite situation, that of the disbeliever whose supplications are answered. When we look around us, we will find no shortage of examples of people who, despite being wicked and evil, are materially well off. We must realize that such people are taking their paltry share in this life, saving nothing for the Hereafter. When a disbeliever refuses to change his ways and rejects the message of Islam, then as a reward for his haughtiness, cockiness Allah ﷻ might give him much in terms of material possessions and worldly comfort, thus leading him further and further away from the straight path. That is why one should never feel a false sense of security when he is successful in life, for Allah ﷻ gives both to the righteous and to the wicked, and when He gives to the wicked, He does so in order to lead them away from the straight path. Therefore, even when things are going well for a believer, he should not become self-complacent; rather, he should hope for Allah's Mercy, yet at the same time he should fear Allah's punishment. Driven by fear and hope, the believer constantly strives to better himself and to reach safety in the Hereafter.

Refusing All Help, Except Help From Allah

In times of need, we tend to turn to people for help, knocking on the doors of our friends, neighbors, relatives, and anyone else that we expect help from. But we should turn to none of these or to any other created being for help; rather, we should turn to Allah alone for help. When Ibrahim ﷺ was about to be thrown into the fire, the angel Jibrail came to him and asked if he needed anything. He answered, "From you, no; but from Allah, yes." And this is a supplication that each one of us should make: "O Allah, suffice me with what is lawful, so I have no need for what is unlawful, and free me from having to depend on anyone other than You."

Gathered around Al-Hasan bin Sufyan were a number of students who had traveled from distant lands in order to learn from him. For the most part, they were affluent students who had the means to journey to various lands without the fear of poverty. Al-Hasan wanted to remind them that seeking knowledge is not an easy task and that to become a scholar one has to endure many hardships along the way. With his students paying close attention to him, he said, "Let me tell you about some of the hardships that I endured. Leaving my homeland, I made my way to

Egypt, in the company of 7 fellow students. We would all go to the study circle of the most knowledgeable and eminent scholar that was alive at that time. Every night, he would dictate notes to us. But as time went on, we began to run out of money, until finally, we had to sell the little furniture we had. Then when our situation reached its nadir, we ran out of money, food, and drink. We then spent three long hungry days. So malnourished and weak did we become that it became difficult for us to get up and walk about. The obvious thing to do was to go out and beg, but we were certain that we did not want to ask any human being for help. Our situation then worsened, and so at least one of us had to go out and beg for money. To choose who it was that had to go, we drew straws. Having drawn the shortest straw, I was the one who had to go. Instead of leaving right away, I first prayed two units of prayer and invoked Allah for help. No sooner did I finish my supplications than a young man entered and said, 'Who among you is Al-Hasan bin Sufyan?' 'Me,' I answered. He said, ' The ruler, Tulun, extends greetings of peace to you, and he apologizes for having been heedless and not coming earlier to check up on your well-being. Not being able to visit you until tomorrow, he sent me with this.' He then gave each one of us 100 dinars. We of course did not personally know the ruler, and considering ourselves to be of little importance, we had no idea why he would give us money. We asked him to inform us about the story behind him being sent to us. He said, ' As was my custom, I entered the chambers of the ruler this morning to ask him if he needed anything. The first thing I noticed when I entered was that he had his hands on his sides, and from his expression it was clear that he was in a great deal of pain. He then asked me if I knew Al-Hasan bin Sufyan. After I said no, he told me to come here and give each one of you 100 dinars. And then in the following words he explained to me why he wanted to help you: Upon falling asleep last night, I saw a rider in the sky with a spear in his hand. He descended to the door of this house and he then poked me in my waist with the bottom of his spear. He told me to go to Al-Hasan bin Sufyan and his companions, informing me that they had been hungry for three days. I asked him who he was; he told me that he was Ridwan, caretaker of Paradise. From the time he poked me with a spear, I have continued to feel a great deal of pain in my waist. Go quickly and give them this money, for until it reaches them, I fear that I will continue to feel this pain."

"Amazed by what had happened, we praised and thanked Allah," Al-Hasan said to his students. "On that very night, we left Egypt, fearing that if we were to stay, news of our story would spread and we would then become famous. By the blessings and grace of Allah, each one of us ended up becoming a pre-eminent scholar in his own right." Here was a group of students who had all of the necessary ingredients for their supplications to be answered: they were sincere, they refused to procure sustenance through unlawful means, and they turned only to Allah ﷻ for help. Thus His help came to them in the most unexpected of ways.

"And whosoever fears Allah and keeps his duty to Him, He will make a way for him to get out (from every difficulty).

And He will provide him from (sources) he could never imagine. And whosoever puts his trust in Allah, then He will suffice him." (Qur'ân 65: 2, 3)

"And whosoever fears Allah and keeps his duty to Him, He will make his matter easy for him" (Qur'ân 65: 4)

How Perfect Allah Is!

A ruler from centuries ago, Sultan Suqailah, was an easy sleeper, but one night, he couldn't fall asleep. As the minutes passed by during that night, he tossed and turned, trying as hard as he could to fall asleep. Finally, frustrated after numerous failed attempts, he decided that, since he was awake anyways, he would get up and take care of some of his country's business. He summoned for the general of his small naval fleet to come to him, and when he came, Suqailah said, "Send one of our ships to Africa, and tell the captain of the ship to bring back news of what is happening there."

Still not being able to fall asleep, Suqailah made his way to the docks later on that night. Much to his chagrin, he saw that all of his ships were still docked at the harbor. He angrily went to his general and said, "Why didn't you carry out the orders I gave you?"

"In fact, I did carry out you orders," said the general. "I sent a ship and it set sail, but one hour after it had departed, it returned. But let us go to the captain of the ship, so that he can give you a firsthand account of what happened."

When they reached the captain, he began to give an

account of what had taken place. "We set sail, and though we couldn't see anything because of the darkness of the night, we heard a man's voice calling out, 'O Allah, O Allah, O One Who helps those who call out to You for help.' We changed course and followed the sound of his voice, and as we drew nearer, we yelled out, ' We are coming to you.' Finally, when we reached him, we were able to see that he was drowning. We then quickly pulled him up to safety. He later told us that his ship had sunk and that for more than a day he was calling out for help, until we finally came and saved him."

How perfect is Allah, Who made the Sultan go sleepless in his castle, so that a man could be saved from 3 kinds of darkness: the darkness of the night, the darkness of the sea, and the darkness of loneliness. How perfect Allah is indeed! And none has the right to be worshiped but Allah.

Ease After Hardship

While in Baghdad, Aba Dhar would spend much of his time learning from his *Shaikh*, 'Umar bin Ahmad. The former was once reading *Hadith* narrations back to the latter, while both were seated in a perfume store, when a man who appeared to be an itinerant perfume salesman passed by. Not having a store of their own, such salesmen would buy perfume from the owner of the store that the *Shaikh* and student were seated in, and then walk around the marketplace, trying to sell what they bought for profit. Unlike other itinerant salesmen, who were strong and hardy, this man was middle-aged and weak. He proffered 10 dirhams to the owner of the store and said, "Give me such and such amount of such and such perfume." When the transaction was completed, he walked away with a tray full of perfume bottles. But he only took a few steps before he stumbled and all of the bottles fell to the ground, with most of them breaking. He then began to cry, and thus drew the attention of Shaikh 'Umar bin Ahmad and his student, Aba Dhar, both of whom had been busily occupied, studying together at the back of the store.

Seeing what had taken place, the *Shaikh* felt sorry for the man. Turning to the owner of the store, he said, "Perhaps you can help him out a little." The owner of the store had a great deal of respect for the *Shaikh*, and so he stepped down into the street, helped pick up the bottles that were still intact, and then paid for the ones that had broken. Wanting to comfort the salesman, the *Shaikh* went to him and said, "Do not lose your nerves, for worldly things are not deserving of your grief."

"*Shaikh*, simply losing these things is not what brought about my grief," said the man. "Allah indeed knows that I was with such and such caravan and that during our voyage, I lost a bag, which contained 4000 dirhams and some precious stones, which were equivalent in value to the money. Shortly thereafter, my wife gave birth to a baby boy, and she needed money for her upkeep and for the upkeep of our child. All the money I had left was 10 dirhams, and I feared that, if I gave her my remaining money, I would have no more capital with which I could do business. And I have become an old man, who cannot easily find work. Thus the idea came to me that I should buy some perfume with my remaining money and then try to sell it for profit, so that with the proceeds, I could give my family what they needed and still have money left over with which I could do business. That is how I wound up at this store. When the bottles broke, I feared that I would have to run away from my family, whom I could no longer support. And that is what caused me grief."

As all of this was taking place, a soldier was seated nearby, and he heard what everyone had said. After hearing the old man's story, the soldier turned to the *Shaikh* and said, "Noble *Shaikh,* I impress upon you the need of bringing this man with you to my home." Everyone there thought that he either didn't trust the old man and wanted to punish him, or felt sorry for him and wanted to help him out. He spoke in a respectful yet authoritative tone, and so instead of questioning his motives, they all simply followed him to his home. After they entered, the soldier turned to the old man and said, "Were you really with such and such caravan?" The old man said, "Yes, traveling with it were such and such people." Still not fully satisfied, the soldier asked, "Describe the bag that you were carrying? And where did it fall?"

After the old man gave a minute and detailed description of the bag, the soldier asked, "And if you see it, will you recognize it?"

"Of course," said the old man. The soldier then took out a bag and placed it before the old man, who, immediately upon see it, yelled out joyfully, "Indeed this is my bag." And to leave no room for doubt as to his veracity, he then proceeded to give a detailed description of the precious stones that were inside the bag. Now certain that he was being truthful, the soldier said, "Take your money and stones, may allow bless you with them." The old man said, "Leave me the money and take the precious stones for yourself, for indeed they are equivalent in value to the money. Please don't refuse, for I give it to you with an open heart and without any resentment." The soldier answered, "I cannot comply, for it is not befitting for me to take money in return for having fulfilled a duty that was incumbent upon me to fulfill." He gave everything to the old man, who then departed, leaving rich after having entered poor. How perfect indeed Allah is, Who provides relief for those in need.

"So verily, with the hardship, there is relief. Verily, with the hardship, there is relief (i.e., there is one hardship with two reliefs, so one hardship cannot overcome two reliefs)".

"Whatever Hardship You Are Afflicted With Is A Result Of What Your Own Hands Have Reaped"

Many people, and not just non-Muslims, become resentful when they or someone they love is afflicted with a calamity. To be sure, many people around the world are afflicted with difficult hardships and trials. Upon contemplating the situation of many among them, I asked myself, "How perfect Allah is!

Indeed, He is the most generous of all, and generosity necessitates forgiveness. Then why is it that so many people are being punished?" It did not take long for me to find the answer to that question, for I came to the realization that most people lead worthless lives: they do not contemplate the numerous signs that point to the oneness of Allah; they care not about Allah' commands and prohibitions; instead, they live as beasts do, caring for nothing except for food, drink, pleasure, and sleep. And here I am not referring only to non-Muslims, for there are many Muslims who apply the teachings of Islam only when doing so is easy or in agreement with their desires; otherwise, they blindly follow their lusts, caring not about how they earned their wealth – whether it is from lawful or unlawful sources. If it is easy for them to pray, they will pray; otherwise, they will often forsake compulsory prayers. Others among them perpetrate grave sins, without afterwards feeling any remorse or guilt. Thus I came to know that, for many people, the punishments, trials, and afflictions that befall them – however great they may be – are less severe than the severity of their sins. Upon suffering a calamity, one might call out, "Why did this happen to me?" Yet he forgets the many sins he perpetrated throughout his life. And in his old age, a man might suffer a great deal of humiliation, to the degree that, by just looking at him, people pity him; yet perhaps they do not know that he is being punished for not having fulfilled Allah's rights during his youth. So whenever you see one who is being punished, know that it is because of his sins.

"(What is the matter what you?) When a single disaster

smites you, although you smote (your enemies) with one twice as great, you say: "From where does this come to us?" Say (to them), "It is from yourselves (because of your evil deeds)." And Allah has power over all things." (Qur'ân 3:165)

And this brings us to the point:

The Good Life Is Achieved Through The Performance Of Good Deeds

Whoever wants the good life - sufficient provision, peace of mind, health, etc. - should strive to do good deeds, performing them only for Allah. Allah ﷻ said:

"If they (non-Muslims) had believed in Allah, and went on the Right Way (i.e., Islam) We should surely have bestowed on them water (rain) in abundance." (Qur'ân 72: 16)

In a *Qudsi Hadith,* the Prophet ﷺ related that Allah said, "Had my slaves obeyed me, I would have provided them with rain during the night, caused the sun to rise upon them during the day, and I would not have made them listen to the sound of thunder."

Abu Sulaiman Ad-Darani, one of the most eminent of scholars during his time, said, "Whoever makes pure [his intentions and deeds], then his life is made pure [and good] for him. Whoever does the opposite, then his life is made bitter and spoiled for him. Whoever does good deeds in the night is provided for during the day. And whoever does good deeds during the day, is provided for during the night." It is related about a *Shaikh* that he would go from one gathering to another, stopping at each gathering only to make this announcement: "Whomsoever it pleases to remain in a state of safety, health, and prosperity, then let him fear Allah." Al-Fudail bin 'Iyadh, a well-known scholar of the first century, said, "Whenever I disobey Allah, I perceive the effects of that [sin] in the treatment I receive from my riding animal and my female servant." Whenever you are going through a difficult situation in life, try to remember some blessing for which you were not thankful, or some sin from which you have not repented. Allah ﷻ said:

"Verily! Allah will not change the good condition of a people as long as they do not change their state of goodness themselves (by committing sins and by being ungrateful and disobedient to Allah)." (Qur'ân 13:11)

"None has the right to be worshiped but You (O Allah), Glorified (and Exalted) be You [above all that (evil) they associate with You]. Truly, I have been of the wrongdoers." (Qur'ân 21: 87)

"So We answered his call, and delivered him from the distress. And thus We do deliver the believers (who believe in the Oneness of Allah, abstain from evil and work righteousness)." (Qur'ân 21: 88)

"And they said: "Allah (Alone) is Sufficient for us, and He is the Best Disposer of affairs (for us)." (Qur'ân 3:173)

"So they returned with Grace and Bounty from Allah. No harm touched them." (Qur'ân 3:174)

"And my affair I leave it to Allah." (Qur'ân 40:44)

"So Allah saved him from the evils that they plotted (against him)" (Qur'ân 40:44)

"That which Allah wills (will come to pass)! There is no power but with Allah." (Qur'ân 18:39)

"It was better for you to say, when you entered your garden: "That which Allah wills (will come to pass)! There is no power but with Allah." (Qur'ân 18:39)

The Answer To Your Supplications Is Delayed For A Reason

There is an interesting situation that confuses many: the believer who is afflicted with a calamity, and who then invokes Allah constantly, yet sees no signs of an answer to his prayers. Then when he comes near to the point of hopelessness, the true worth of his heart is found out. If he is pleased with what Allah ﷻ decreed for him, without losing hope of Allah's Favor, then in most situations it is at that point that such a person's supplications are answered, answered because his test is over: his faith has shined through and the Devil has been defeated. So it is at the time of near hopelessness that the worth of man is judged. This meaning is alluded to in the saying of Allah:

"Or think you that you will enter Paradise without such (trials) as came to those who passed away before you? They were afflicted with severe poverty and ailments and were so shaken that even the Messenger and those who *believed along with him said, "When (will come) the Help of Allah?" Yes! Certainly, the Help of Allah is near!" (Qur'ân 2: 214)*

After Ya'qub ﷺ lost his son, much time elapsed, yet he never lost hope of relief. Instead of relief, another of his sons was then taken away, and even then he did not lose hope of Allah's Favor and Mercy:

"So patience is most fitting (for me). It may be that Allah will bring them all (back) to me. Truly He! Only He is All-Knowing, All-Wise." (Qur'ân 12: 83)

And similar were the words and sentiments of (Zachariya) Zakariyyah ﷺ:

"And I have never been unblest in my invocation to You, O my Lord!" (Qur'ân 19:4)

Never, therefore, should one feel that too much time has passed by without his supplications being answered. One should realize that, whenever one is tested with hardship, one's mettle and faith are being tested. To pass such a test, one must drive away the whispers of the Devil and then turn for help to the Most-Merciful, the Most-Generous, the Most-Wise.

References

◆ Tafsir Ibn Kathir	
◆ Tafsir Al-Qurtubi	
◆ Al Bidayah wan-Nihayah	
◆ Fath Al-Bâri	Ibn Hajar
◆ Musnad Al-Imam Ahmad	
◆ Sahih Al-Bukhari	
◆ Al-Bayan wat-Tabyin	Al-Jahiz
◆ Rare Stories in History	Salih Az-Zuman
◆ A Hundred Stories and One	
◆ Firasatul-Mu'min	Ibrahim Al-Hazimi
◆ Atta'ibun ila Allah	Ibrahim Al-Hazimi
◆ Al-Faraj B'ad Ash-Shiddah	Ibrahim Al-Hazimi
◆ Very Smart Women	Gasim Ashur
◆ Mu'jam Al-'Udaba'	Yâqut Al-Hamawy
◆ Al-'Isabah	Ibn Hajar
◆ Al-Isti'âb	Al-Qurtubi
◆ Tabaqat Ibn Sa'd	
◆ History of Baghdad	Al-Khatib Al-Baghdadi
◆ Distinguished Women	Mohammad Rida
◆ Tahdhib Al-Kamal	Imam Mizi
◆ 'Uyun Al-Akhbar	Ibn Al-Qayyim
◆ Al-Mustatraf	Al-Aysheihy

References